Drugs in Britain

Drugs in Britain

Supply, Consumption and Control

Edited by

Mark Simpson, Tracy Shildrick
and
Robert MacDonald

First published 2007 by
PALGRAVE MACMILLAN
Houndmills, Basingstoke, Hampshire RG21 6XS and
175 Fifth Avenue, New York, N.Y. 10010
Companies and representatives throughout the world

PALGRAVE MACMILLAN is the global academic imprint of the Palgrave
Macmillan division of St. Martin's Press, LLC and of Palgrave Macmillan Ltd.
Macmillan® is a registered trademark in the United States, United Kingdom
and other countries. Palgrave is a registered trademark in the European
Union and other countries.

ISBN-13: 978–1–4039–3697–4   hardback
ISBN-10: 1–4039–3697–8   hardback
ISBN-13: 978–1–4039–3695–0   paperback
ISBN-10: 1–4039–3695–1   paperback

This book is printed on paper suitable for recycling and made from fully
managed and sustained forest sources.

A catalogue record for this book is available from the British Library.

Library of Congress Cataloging-in-Publication Data

Drugs in Britain: supply, consumption, and control/edited by Mark Simpson, Tracy
   Shildrick, and Robert MacDonald.
      p.cm.
   Includes bibliographical references and index.
   ISBN-13: 978–1–4039–3697–4 (cloth)
   ISBN-10: 1–4039–3697–8 (cloth)
   ISBN-13: 978–1–4039–3695–0 (pbk.)
   ISBN-10: 1–4039–3695–1 (pbk.)
      1. Drug abuse—Great Britain. 2. Drug control—Great Britain. 3. Drug abuse and crime—
Great Britain. 4. Drug traffic—Great Britain. I. Simpson, Mark, 1973-II.
shildrick, Tracy, 1966-III. MacDonald, Robert, 1962-

HV5840.G7D53 2007
363.450941—dc22

2006050824

10   9   8   7   6   5   4   3   2   1
16   15   14   13   12   11   10   09   08   07

Printed in Great Britain by Creative Print & Design (Wales), Ebbw Vale

Contents

List of Tables

Notes on Contributors

Amanda Barrett is Project Manager – Dual Diagnosis. The post entails leading on the development and implementation of the Dual Diagnosis Strategy for County Durham and Darlington. She is a member of the National CISP/NIMHE Steering Group to develop Dual Diagnosis staff capabilities.

Shane Blackman is Reader in Cultural Studies and Sociology, Canterbury Christ Church University. He is the author of *Chilling Out: The cultural politics of substance consumption, youth and drug policy and Youth: Positions and oppositions.*

Chris Crowther-Dowey is Senior Lecturer in Criminology at Nottingham Trent University. His research and teaching interests include the police and policing, the modernisation of criminal justice, social divisions and crime.

Mike Hough is Director of the Institute for Criminal Policy Research, King's College, London. He has published widely on topics including sentencing and attitudes to punishment, policing, drugs and anti-social behaviour.

Robert MacDonald is Professor of Sociology at the University of Teesside. He is the co-author of Disconnected Youth? Growing up in Britain's Poor Neighbourhoods (Palgrave) and has researched, written and taught about young people and social and economic change for many years.

Alison McInnes is the Programme Leader for the MSc Contemporary Issues in Drug Use, University of Teesside. She has published widely in the field of drugs and alcohol and is a qualified social worker.

Tim McSweeney is Research Fellow at the Institute for Criminal Policy Research at King's College, London. His research interests include substance misuse, treatment and criminal justice interventions. He has been involved in a number of research studies.

Russell Newcombe is Senior Researcher, Lifeline, Manchester. He is the author of *Potology* and *Tripology* and the co-author of *Living with*

Heroin, and the co-editor of *The Reduction of Drug-related Harm*. He has worked on dozens of different projects as an action researcher on drugs issues.

Geoffrey Pearson is Professor of Criminology at Goldsmiths College, University of London. From 1998 to 2006 he was Editor-in-Chief of *The British Journal of Criminology*. His published work includes The Deviant Imagination, Working Class Youth Culture and Middle Market Drug Distribution.

Toby Seddon is Senior Research Fellow in the School of Law at the University of Manchester. He is currently engaged in research on the government and regulation of drug problems, particularly in criminal justice settings.

Tracy Shildrick is Senior Lecturer in Sociology and Youth Studies at the University of Teesside. She has published widely in areas including young people, youth culture, illicity drugs, social classs and inequality.

Mark Simpson is Principal Lecturer in Criminology at the University of Teesside. He has published extensively in the areas of drug use and youth criminology. His research interests lie in illicit drug use, drug use and crime, and youth crime and youth justice.

Paul J. Turnbull is the Deputy Director of the Institute for Criminal Policy Research at King's College, London. He has published widely on a range of drug related topics including drugs and HIV, harm reduction, drug users in the criminal justice system and prisons.

Colin Webster is Reader in Criminology at Leeds Metropolitan University. He is the co-author of *Poor Transitions: Social exclusion and young adults* and the author of *Race, Youth Crime and Justice*.

1

Introduction

Tracy Shildrick, Mark Simpson and Robert MacDonald

Concern about illicit drugs ranks high on the list of issues that consistently excite public, political and academic debate. When considering illicit drug use, there are many questions and few straightforward answers. As this books shows, contradictions and controversies abound. To take one recent example, prior to being elected as the leader of the Conservative Party in 2005, David Cameron's alleged drug use while he was a university student came under intense media scrutiny. The issue emerged as Cameron was fighting his campaign for the leadership, and when he was questioned about it in an interview, Cameron responded that he had had a 'normal university experience' (Branigan and Glover, 2005). When pressed he admitted that he did things as a student that he did not find 'appropriate to talk about as a politician' (ibid.). This further fuelled media speculation. For some, such an admission and Cameron's unwillingness to deny the accusation was taken as certain evidence of his guilt and, further, his unsuitability for high political office. For others, Cameron was a refreshing example of someone in the media and political spotlight who was willing to tell the truth about behaviour which many now perceive as a perfectly normal aspect of growing up. As media stories piled up, it emerged that the drug alluded to may, in fact, have been cocaine rather than cannabis. Cameron also admitted that he had a relative who was recovering from heroin addiction. Some predicted a radical decline in support for David Cameron (Cusick, 2005), seeing his apparent admission of illegal substance use as a clear blight on his credibility and authority and the death knell of his political career. For others, however, it served to illustrate his 'normality' and apparent 'ordinariness', adding that minor demeanours of the past should have little bearing on Cameron's political career aspirations. As ever, where drugs are concerned, viewpoints became polarised. What is perhaps most interesting about this story is that it seems to provide a very clear example of the increasing cultural toleration of illicit drug use in British society. It is hard to imagine that, until very recently, a prospective leader of a British political party, especially the Conservatives, could enter into a discussion of personal drug use with such little ill-effect. In fact, one might say that his leadership campaign benefited from the story and the position he took. His declaration, on the BBC's *Question Time* programme (3rd November 2005), that the general public would not be happy if all 'politicians were robots' was met with rapturous applause from the audience. Cameron went on to become the elected leader of the Conservative Party.

Drugs in Britain attempts to unravel some of the contradictions and controversies that surround illegal drugs. It presents a careful reading of many of the key issues and debates which characterise drug use in Britain. Such a book can never be all encompassing and will always be selective. The field is wide-ranging, diverse and fast-changing, and no one text can claim to cover all of the ground with any authority. Notwithstanding these caveats, we hope that this book will provide students, researchers, drugs professionals and academics with a useful, stimulating and precise understanding of the drugs field.

The format of the chapters has been designed with undergraduate students in mind and, to this end, each chapter (bar this introduction and the conclusion) contains suggestions for further readings and study questions to aid learning. The book is primarily about drug use in Britain, but it also necessarily involves some reference to broader, geographic contexts and examples from other national societies as well (see Chapters 2 and 8, in particular). The book's main concern is with illegal drugs (and the illicit use of legal ones), with only occasional reference, for instance, to alcohol and tobacco use (Plant and Plant, 1992; Bennet and Holloway, 2005; Dingwall, 2005; Berridge, 2005). In the final, concluding chapter we identify some other themes and topics that have not been explored in any detail and give some brief commentary.

The Chapters

Part 1 of the book is concerned with the *Distribution and Consumption of Illicit Drugs*. It commences with Russell Newcombe's discussion of *Trends in the prevalence of Illicit Drug Use in Britain*. The second chapter does exactly what its title suggests, but it also usefully contextualises the discussion with evidence of international trends. Although Newcombe argues that we may be seeing a levelling off in the rates of consumption in Britain, there can be little doubt that illicit drugs are now more widely available and consumed than at any time since proper surveying began (Ramsay and Partridge, 1999). Newcombe's suggestion that we are currently in a 'plateau stage' of drugs consumption is supported by the recently published 2004/05 *British Crime Survey* (2005) which shows that there has been no significant, overall increase in drug use over the last two years.

Newcombe's trawl through the prevalence data reminds us that the generalisations that sometimes characterise the field tend to hide a more complicated reality. Hence, while rates of overall drug use may be relatively stable, closer examination of trends in relation to particular drugs reveals a much more complex picture. Cocaine use provides one example. While Class A drug use overall remains relatively small and reasonably stable, the use of cocaine has found new popularity in the dance club scene. Although it shares the same Class A categorisation as heroin (and therefore is scientifically assessed as presenting a similar level of potential harm), it shares much less of the social stigma of heroin use, perhaps in part due to its strong association with glamorous media, fashion and pop-culture personalities.

It is hard for research to keep pace with the fast-changing nature of patterns of drug use. While not perfect, surveys and other methods can provide increasingly accurate snapshots of, and trends in, overall drugs consumption (as Chapter 2 shows). The aggregated statistics that make up national trend statistics can, however, mask local geographic variation (see Chapters 4, 9 and 10) and particularised trends in respect of some forms of drugs consumption. For example, we know that clubbers and those involved in the dance scene are the most prolific users of ecstasy (Parker, Aldridge and Measham, 1998b). Measham (2004) has, however, drawn attention to the popularity of *powdered* ecstasy, a development that is not revealed in national measurements of the use of ecstasy *per se*.

The question of drug 'normalisation' referred to by Newcombe towards the end of his chapter is picked up by Shane Blackman in Chapter 3: '*See Emily Play*': *Youth Culture, Recreational Drug Use and Normalisation*. Blackman's methodological and theoretical approach is quite different to the sort of social epidemiology set out in Chapter 2. Rather, he presents an account firmly rooted in social history and cultural theory. It begins by documenting the ways that illegal drugs have featured in popular culture – in films, music and novels. Blackman's cultural perspective nicely demonstrates the early history of prohibitionist drugs messages in these media; messages that typically point to the social/ physical degeneracy and moral corruption of young drug users. His chapter also usefully describes the less well-known, early tradition of more sympathetic and pro-drug stances in popular culture (such as in the 1920s and 1930s US jazz scene), before charting the close attachment between, for instance, popular music, youth (sub)culture and drug use in the latter half of the twentieth century.

It is this relationship between youth culture and drug use – and cultural development more generally – that Blackman identifies as having provided the impetus and forum for, and the best indication of, the normalisation of drug use (Muncie, 2004). On the basis of his cultural history, he argues that normalisation should not, however, be understood as a very recent, end-of-the-century turn of events. Rather, progress towards normalisation can be traced back through the twentieth century. The dance culture of the 1990s has been firmly associated with widespread drug use (of ecstasy, most symbolically), but it had precursors in the 1970s (Punk and amphetamine), in the 1960s (Hippies and LSD) and in the 1950s (Beat and heroin).

The thesis of drug normalisation is most clearly described by Howard Parker and colleagues in their book *Illegal Leisure* (1998b). One of the alleged consequences of the widespread popularity of the club dance scene is that drug use has moved from the subcultural margins towards the social mainstream:

> The concept of normalization has been used in many contexts but essentially it is concerned with how a 'deviant', often subcultural population or their deviant behavior is able to be accommodated into a larger grouping or society ... Normalization in the context of recreational drug use cannot be reduced to the intuitive phrase 'it is normal for young people to take drugs'; that is both to over-simplify and overstate the case. We are concerned only with the spread of deviant activity and associated attitudes from the margins *towards* the centre of youth culture, where it joins many other accommodated 'deviant' activities such as excessive drinking, casual sexual encounters and daily cigarette smoking (Parker, Aldridge and Measham,1998b:152).

Parker *et al.* (1998b, 2002) have identified several, specific dimensions to drug normalisation, including the increasing rates of availability and accessibility of drugs; drug trying; knowledge about drugs (i.e. being 'drug wise'); regular drug use; social acceptance (e.g. by non-users) of recreational drug use; and non-users accepting that they *may* use drugs in the future. Parker (2005:213) recently identified a further dimension of the normalisation thesis evident in changing government and state responses to the processes of normalisation. Here he points to a 'welcome, fundamental shift' in official responses to 'non-problem drug use', with views moving away from the perception that all drugs are dangerous and health threatening, to one which implicitly acknowledges 'that most drug use is not seriously problematic' (ibid.).

In short, the normalisation thesis describes the processes and changes which have resulted in a situation where young people perceive the use of drugs to be an integral aspect of their leisure and cultural landscapes. It refers not only to the increasing propensity of young people to *use* illicit drugs, but also to the fact that young people are simply more 'drug-wise' (Parker *et al.*, 1998b). They know more about drugs and their effects and find themselves in situations where they are offered drugs more frequently, where others use drugs and where others' use is viewed with tolerance. As such, drugs are no longer deemed to be part of an unknown, unorthodox world that is alien to the majority of 'ordinary' young people. They have become a common aspect of the cultural worlds they inhabit. Hammersley (2005:2) suggests that drug use is normal in the 'sense that it is integrated into user's lives and to some extent, accommodated, tolerated or ignored by society'. Parker (2005) argues that even though his studies point to very high rates of consumption – 76 per cent of respondents to this study had done so by the age 22 – drug normalisation is at least as strongly evidenced by the social accommodation of illicit drugs among those who abstain. Taylor, on the other hand, stresses the proliferation of cultural representations of drugs as the key to proving the normalisation thesis (2000; see Blackman, Chapter 3). He too concludes that 'young people increasingly see the use of illegal drugs as a lifestyle choice' leading to a situation where 'the use of drugs in a recreational context is regarded by young people as a normal feature of everyday life, regardless of whether they approve of it or not' (2000:333).

The normalisation thesis is not without its critics. Most significantly, Shiner and Newburn say that claims about the 'extent and normative context of youthful drug use are exaggerated and inaccurate' (1999:142). They argue that it presents a picture of drug use which emphasises the normality of drugs consumption when, in reality, the majority of young people refrain from using drugs. Ramsay and Partridge (1999:57), too, are sceptical of the 'full blown normalisation thesis'. Wibberley and Price (2000:161) conclude that available consumption prevalence evidence can be used to both support or refute the normalisation thesis and that 'there is insufficient evidence one way or the other' in respect of the alleged social toleration of drug use by young people.

Normalisation theory rests upon a distinction between 'recreational' drug use and more chaotic or 'problematic' consumption of opiates (Parker, Aldridge and Measham, 1998b); although Parker now acknowledges that this clear, binary division may (now) not be wholly accurate. Most recently he argues that some recreational drug users are now crossing the boundary into more problematic drug-using behaviours (Parker, 2005). In Chapter 10 we provide further discussion of drug careers and transitions, but note here that our own studies also question the sharpness of the divide that is often drawn between categories of drug-using behaviour (see Shildrick, 2002; Simpson, 2003; MacDonald and Marsh, 2002). Qualitative studies like these are better suited than large-scale, quantitatively-oriented social surveys at delving into the social and cultural meanings of drugs for users. Drug use that, on the face of it, may appear to fit with descriptions of recreational consumption may have problematic consequences for some users (Simpson, 2003). Some can use allegedly harmful 'hard' drugs with few or none of the problematic consequences typically associated with them (Warburton, Turnbull and Hough, 2005). Longitudinally or biographically-oriented methods can also help reveal how the 'drug careers' of some young adults can span from recreational to more dependent, problematic drug use (see Chapter 10). Thus, we argue that a 'differentiated' understanding of normalisation may help to reveal the complexity of young people's use of drugs and move us beyond static and over-generalised accounts which sometimes characterise the debate (Shildrick, 2002).

Chapter 4, *The Hardest Drug? Trends in Heroin Use in Britain* by Toby Seddon, details the changing experience of heroin use in Britain, starting from the relatively liberal use of heroin in the nineteenth and early twentieth centuries, through to the 1980s and 1990s 'heroin epidemics', ending with some observations on the potential future of this drug. Of all drugs, heroin is perhaps the most demonised and mythologised, with discussions plagued by inconsistencies and contradictions. For some, heroin is very dangerous, while for others, it is relatively harmless (Carnwath and Smith, 2002), and attention is drawn to the 'relatively safe' administration of heroin within modern medicine. Empirical research on the less-harmful, but illegal, consumption of heroin is scant and more research is needed (Hammersley, 2005), but one such study by Shewan and Dalgarno (2005) managed to explore heroin use in this relatively 'hidden population'. They focussed on 126 long-term heroin users who had never been in treatment and found that, for their sample, heroin could be taken with few or none of the long-term negative social and health outcomes usually associated with long-term use. Their participants were mostly well educated and in employment, usually at the higher end of the occupational spectrum. They concluded that while 'some drug related negative health and social outcomes had occurred over a life-time basis, ongoing problems were rare and heroin use was not a predictor in either context' (2005:33). They argue, thus, that the social and health problems commonly associated with heroin use are a result of the nature and context of much heroin use, rather than the drug itself. As Seddon's chapter illustrates, many of the recent outbreaks of heroin have been in some of Britain's deprived neighbourhoods and contextualised within the deprivation of Britain's most de-industrialised communities. When the ready availability of heroin collides with poverty, economic marginalisation and a lack of legitimate opportunities, the individual, health and wider social consequences are rarely less than disastrous for all concerned (see Johnston *et al.*, 2000; Webster *et al.*, 2004; MacDonald and Marsh, 2005). Given these apparent paradoxes and ambiguities, it is perhaps of little surprise that Seddon concludes that heroin use remains one of the hardest challenges for public policy of our times.

In the final chapter in this first part of the book, Geoffrey Pearson discusses *Drug Markets and Dealing: From 'Street Dealer to 'Mr. Big'*. Pearson details the position of drug dealers at different levels of the market, starting with the 'retail level' dealers who supply drugs to consumers. He usefully draws attention to the blurring of the distinction between consumer and dealer, which has become more apparent with the popularity of the dance drugs scenes (Parker, Aldridge and Measham, 1998b, 2001). Drug dealers often figure as modern 'folk devils' in public and political debate, but as Pearson's chapter illustrates, some drug dealing has now become very much part of the mainstream, night-time economy. Moreover, as Pearson points out, there is actually very little research evidence on the workings of drugs markets, with most research focussing on consumption. Consequently, it becomes easier to paint inaccurate portraits of drug dealing and drugs markets and much harder to understand properly how they operate. For example, relatively little is known about the positive impact that drug dealing can have for both the dealers and their wider communities. While not wanting to downplay the social damage that drug dealing can cause, May *et al.* (2005) argue that drug dealing can also benefit communities. For instance, people living in poverty can welcome the increased market for stolen, cheaply sold goods. They argue that to assume that the consequences of drug dealing and drugs markets are always negative oversimplifies a more complex story.

Pearson's chapter draws attention to some of the inaccuracies that blight understanding of drugs markets through a detailed exploration of different levels of drugs markets and dealing. The expansion of the night-time economy and the apparent normalisation of some drug taking within it has allowed for the expansion of drugs markets. Saunders (2005), for example, conducted research while working as a bouncer in a London club. He uncovered a 'lively drug culture and a prosperous drug economy' (ibid.:252–54) among the door staff. He argues some door staff perceived that they were doing 'nothing wrong' in selling drugs to customers and furthermore that this 'service' was actually something that they '*should*' in fact be doing. Dealing in drugs not only provided a 'valued commodity' requested by clubbers, but also helped to sustain the overall longevity of the club by providing a 'self-contained, self-policed and self-sufficient' environment where clubbers could obtain and take drugs with little threat of sanction.

Finally, Pearson reminds us of the lucrative nature of drugs markets, with heroin-dealing operations, for example, generating potentially huge profit margins. Furthermore, these operations are often based upon carefully maintained market fragmentation so that the 'small-fry retail dealers' know little about the market structures above them. Given these two factors, effectively policing, stopping or containing these markets is very difficult, if not impossible. As street-level dealers are taken out, others move in to reap the benefits associated with this activity. Even when high-level interception operations are successful, Pearson and Hobbs (2001) argue that the associated costs are absorbed and the market continues as before (see Chapter 10).

The second part of the book focuses on *Policing, Control and Care*. It starts with Chapter 6 by Tim McSweeney, Mike Hough and Paul Turnbull: *Drugs and Crime:Exploring the Links*. The authors immediately dismiss any simplistic, unidirectional hypothesis about the relationship between drug use and crime. As Bennett and Holloway (2005) have pointed out, it is important to delve into the complexities of this relationship if criminal justice policy is to be targeted appropriately. The possible relationships between drugs and crime are many and various, even when we narrow down to particular drugs and particular crimes (e.g. between alcohol and violence or heroin and burglary). McSweeney *et al.* describe the most likely, general relationships between drugs and crime: firstly, illicit drug use may lead to other forms of crime; secondly, crime may lead to drug use; thirdly, drug use *prompts* other forms of crime or crime *facilitates* drugs use; or, lastly, there may be an association rooted in other common factors but no direct, causal link between the two phenomena. Gossop (2005) suggests that whatever the detail 'there are powerful interactions between the two' and it is the nature of this interaction which occupies much of this chapter.

McSweeney *et al.* remind us that for the majority of drug users in Britain there is *no* relationship between drug use and other forms of offending. For recreational users, for instance, there is no persuasive evidence of any causal linkage between offending and drug use. However, as noted by Pearson (Chapter 5), *some* of these users do become involved in drug dealing and become user/dealers and further research is needed in this area. A small proportion of drug users become 'problematic' users who finance their use through crime (largely through shoplifting, burglary and selling drugs) and become extensively involved in the criminal justice system. This chapter points out the links between problematic drug use and the social, legal and health risks that often come together in the lives of socially excluded, problematic drug users. Chapter 10 returns to these themes and considers the difficulties facing effective policies to control the supply and consumption of harmful drugs.

In Chapter 7, Chris Crowther-Dowey's considers *The Police and Drugs*, highlighting the difficulties faced by the former in respect of the latter. Crowther-Dowey notes, for instance, how the policing of drug laws can exacerbate the problems caused by drugs. He examines drug prohibition in the context of 'the Brixton/Lambeth cannabis experiment'. This provides for an interesting case study of the changing, contemporary relationship between communities, policing and illicit drugs in this country. Policing drugs in accordance with the letter of the law, as Crowther-Dowey shows, can have the effect of alienating already disadvantaged sections of British society (socially excluded Black young men in this case) and stimulating serious social unrest. The Brixton/Lambeth example also highlights the growth of multi-agency and partnership work in responding to drugs. Crowther-Dowey extends this discussion with reference to recent criminal justice policy interventions (such as the Drug Arrest Referral Scheme) that combine criminal justice and treatment agencies. What is interesting about these partnerships is that they aim to bring together agencies with often conflicting aims: control/punishment on the one hand, care/treatment on the other. Although such approaches can receive positive comment (Edmunds *et al.*, 1998; Sondhi, O'Shea and Williams, 2002), Webster (in Chapter 9) also reminds us that these inherently competing philosophies are not easily combined in contemporary drug policy.

Drugs Education in schools and for young people is the focus of Chapter 8 by McInnes and Barrett. School-based drugs education has expanded rapidly since the late 1990s, when the government introduced strategies to ensure that all school-age pupils had access to good-quality drugs education. Recent OFSTED reports suggest that 'marked improvements' (2005) have been made with the quality of drugs education in schools, although there was still room for further work, particularly in relation to understanding pupils' needs (ibid.). There has been a long-standing tension between education strategies that aim to minimise the harm that might come to young people if they do use drugs and those that aim to educate young people to avoid drug use *per se* (i.e. prohibition). As the authors point out, these points of view sit uneasily together. The enforcement of zero-tolerance, anti-drug policies in schools (with greater, closer surveillance of pupils and the potential exclusion of drug users) can undermine attempts of drugs educators to provide neutral, objective advice and help to children and young people so as to reduce the harm that can come from drugs. As the chapter makes clear, while drugs education has expanded there are few simple answers about how best to proceed, and there is still little evidence that conclusively demonstrates its effectiveness (whatever the particular, philosophical aim of the approach). Rather, many studies point to the limited success of drugs education, particularly of approaches designed to warn or scare children and young people away from drug use.

Webster's penultimate chapter, *Drug Treatment*, reviews contemporary thinking about and approaches to drugs treatment (chiefly in relation to heroin). The chapter considers what might be thought of as quite specific policy questions, for instance, the debate about whether the treatment of heroin users should be voluntary or coerced and which strategy might be the most effective. Webster couches this discussion, however, in an account of the changing political, ideological and international contexts of drugs treatment, making this a chapter of great relevance for the book as a whole. Drawing upon the work of key writers in the field and with the aim of understanding the UK situation better, Webster compares US and Australian approaches to drugs treatment, contrasting the punitive, social control-focussed starting point of the former with the harm-reduction and social-inclusion agenda of the latter. Webster argues that the UK follows neither approach exactly and he reveals the complex, shifting and ideological nature of national policy and practice in respect of drugs treatment. At the core of Webster's discussion is a debate about how society treats 'problem-atic' drug users: *as* problems (dangerous, immoral 'addicts' requiring pun-ishment, incarceration and forced treatment) or as people *with* problems (that may need help through health and social care interventions).

In Chapter 10 we conclude the book by highlighting this and the other key questions and controversies identified by the earlier chapters. This is not, however, simply a summary chapter, and we attempt to illustrate and further discuss some of the arguments and conclusions of the book via a case-study approach. Drawn from our own research, we present the story of one young man and his particular experiences of drug use, drug-related crime, policing, drugs education and drugs treatment. We use this cameo to reflect on what it tells us about – and the connections between – the topics that have been discussed separately in preceding, thematically organised chapters. As we show, it is a story that raises serious doubts about the di-rection and effectiveness of current British policy and practice in respect of drugs consumption, supply and control.

Part One

Distribution and Consumption of Illicit Drugs

2

Trends in the Prevalence of Illicit Drug Use in Britain

Russell Newcombe

Introduction

Research into trends in the prevalence of drug use and drugs consumption is important for various reasons, but particularly to assess whether our current drug strategies achieve their aims and objectives. For instance, since 2003, the first of the UK's eight key targets for national drug strategy is reducing the use of Class A drugs and frequent use of all drugs by under-25s by 2008 (Home Office, 2002). This chapter presents a critical overview of evidence about the trends in the prevalence of illicit drug use in the UK, particularly over the last two decades. Unfortunately, a full review of research into trends in drugs consumption – frequency of use, amounts used, routes of use, etc. – is outside the scope of this chapter.

The focus of this chapter is on the most commonly used illicit drugs, and no attempt is made to cover legal recreational drugs (alcohol, tobacco, caffeine) or uncontrolled medical drugs (eg. anti-depressants). This chapter is also concerned mainly with overall national trends. The UK comprises England, Wales, Scotland, and Northern Ireland – but one or both of the latter two countries are often excluded by relevant surveys, and so 'national' typically means mainland Britain, or England and Wales only, or even just England. Unfortunately, space constraints rule out a systematic assessment of trends in each UK country, region and locality.

Due to the range of statistics generated by prevalence studies, assessment of trends in the profile of drug users will be restricted to the core demographic variables of sex, age and ethnicity. Assessment of the relationship between drug use and the psycho-social characteristics of drug users (eg. social class, personality, lifestyle), though important issues, are also outside the scope of this chapter. Following a brief introduction to the concepts and methods of drug prevalence estimation in the next section, two types of research are reviewed. Section 3 assesses evidence from sample surveys of the prevalence of illicit drug use; and section 4 reviews agency-based counts of 'known' problem drug users (PDUs), including official statistics and 'drug indicator' studies. The concluding section presents an overview of the main trends in the prevalence of drug use, followed by a critique of the methodology of relevant research, and an assessment of the key issues for researchers and policy-makers.

The Methodology of Prevalence Estimation

The three main sources of national prevalence estimates on drug use are sample surveys of general and specific populations; agency-based statistics on PDUs (including multi-agency surveys and routine monitoring systems) and statistical methods of estimation (drug indicators). Two main groups of data-collection methods are used to count and/or identify cases of drug use:

(1) self-report (interviews and questionnaires) – used by almost all population surveys of drug use and
(2) official documentation (notably drug agency clients and drug offenders) – typically used by multi-agency surveys and routine monitoring systems.

Physiological measures such as testing body fluids (notably saliva and urine) provide a third potential method of identifying and counting drug users. However, they are generally restricted to monitoring systems in the criminal justice system (police, probation, prisons, etc.), and are rarely employed in surveys of illicit drug use (except as checks on self report data).

Repeat surveys employing standardised methods, along with routine monitoring systems, provide the best available evidence of national trends in drug use. With the aid of epidemiological models and theories, repeated estimates of annual numbers can provide a basis for extrapolating underlying trends (endemic, epidemic) and thus predicting future levels of drug use – though such research is very rare in the UK (see Hunt and Chambers, 1967, for a classic US study).

Whatever approaches and methods are used to count drug users, all prevalence estimates must clearly define four parameters to be meaningful:

(1) inclusion/exclusion rules are needed to define the cases being counted,   notably the type of drug (e.g. legal, controlled, quasi-legal), and the type of user (e.g. current/ex-user, regular/occasional);
(2) population: this includes (a) geographical population (e.g. England/ UK), (b) demographic population (notably adults, young adults or

secondary schoolchildren) and (c) other sub-populations based on specific characteristics such as occupation or leisure ('special groups');
(3) time period: the standard periods used to frame estimates of the prevalence of drug use are (a) lifetime (ever used), (b) past-year (use in last 12 months) and (c) past-month (use in last four weeks) – though some studies have also examined past-week use and/or use in the past 24 hours; and
(4) type of estimate: this covers (a) the distinction between prevalence (all users) and incidence (new users); (b) the descriptive statistics used to present the estimate, namely single sample figures and extrapolated population intervals (ranges) and (c) the form of the estimate, i.e. raw numbers and/or rates (sample percentages, rates per million population, etc.).

Researchers have also developed methods to improve and assess the validity and reliability of information about drug use. Such methods include dummy drug items and repeat questions in questionnaires; physiological checks on self-report data (e.g. saliva tests); cross-referencing of official statistical indicators; and double-counting (duplicate elimination) in multi-agency surveys. A critical evaluation of methodological issues in drug prevalence research is presented in the concluding section.

Population Surveys of Illicit Drug Use

A major difference between prevalence surveys – whether international, national or local – is the type of population sampled. The key distinction involves age-band – some surveys sample all adults (typically 16–59 year olds), most focus on young adults (16/18–24/34 year olds), and some focus on secondary schoolchildren (11–15/16 year olds). Population sub-groups are also based on occupation (e.g. students, doctors), leisure (e.g. night clubbers) or other social groupings (e.g. offenders, gays, homeless) – but these 'special group' surveys cannot be properly covered here.

National surveys of adults and young adults typically employ random sampling methods to ensure representativeness of the population. The findings of surveys based on convenience (opportunity) samples are not generalisable, though some studies approximate representativeness through quota sampling or multi-site sampling. Adults and young adults are generally investigated through household surveys (direct or postal), while under-16s are typically surveyed in school settings. Most population surveys of drug use employ self-report questionnaires, though some employ the interview method – notably telephone surveys. Also, researchers are increasingly making use of computer-assisted personal interviewing

(CAPI), in which respondents read the questions off a computer screen, and respond via the keyboard or other input device (e.g. the British Crime Survey (BCS)).

Before turning to an assessment of the main relevant national surveys of drug use, it will be useful to place the UK situation in its broader international context – firstly by examining evidence of global prevalence rates, and then by considering the nature and extent of drug use across Europe.

International Surveys and Comparisons

The United Nations Drug Control Programme (UNDCP) estimated in 1997 that the annual turnover for the international market in illicit drugs was $400 billion (United Nations International Drug Control Programme, 1998). This constituted 8 per cent of all world trade – the only other markets worth more were oil and weapons. In 1998, the UK government estimated that the illicit drugs market in Britain was worth between £4.3 and £9.9 billion (2.1 per cent of annual consumer spending) – far higher than other criminal markets such as prostitution, stolen goods and gambling (Office of National Statistics, 1998). Bramley-Harker's (2001) sophisticated analysis of research findings on the extent of use and consumption of the UK's six most popular drugs (heroin, crack, cannabis, cocaine, ecstasy and amphetamines) concluded that their total annual value was about £6.6 billion in 1998.

According to the latest UN figures (United Nations office on Drugs and Crime, 2004), 185 million people had used illicit drugs by 2002. When UN global rates are compared with those for England and Wales it can be seen that prevalence in England and Wales was over twice as high for cannabis use, and several times higher for use of cocaine and ecstasy. Overall, about 2 per cent of the world's past-year illicit drug users resided in the UK.

Two of the largest comparable western nations outside of Europe are the USA and Australia. When the findings of national prevalence surveys in these two countries are compared with the levels of drug use in the UK, British rates are generally somewhat lower (Table 2.1) – though figures are not directly comparable because samples in the US and Australian surveys include over-60s and some under-16s.

According to annual reports on 'the state of the drugs problem in the European Union', Britain has regularly topped the European league tables on rates of many types of drugs over the last decade. For instance, in the 2003 annual report (before the EU expanded), the 14 EU member states and Norway were compared on 16 indicators: lifetime and past-year use of cannabis, cocaine, amphetamine and ecstasy – for all adults and young adults (as reported by national surveys mainly conducted in 2000 and 2001). Britain had the highest or joint highest rates on 9 of the 16 indicators – higher rates of use for adults and young adults were reported only in Denmark

Table 2.1

Prevalence of drug use in the UK compared with the USA and Australia

	Age	Lifetime	Past-year	Past-month
Australia	14+	38	17	–
USA	12+	46	15	8
UK	16–59	34	12	8

Notes: Lifetime: 2001 for Australia, 2002 for USA, and 2000 for UK; past-year and past-month: 2001 in Australia and USA, and 2001/02 in UK.

Sources: US Department of Health and Human Services (2003); Australian Institute of Health and Welfare (2002); Ramsay *et al.*, 2001 (BCS).

for lifetime cannabis use (31 per cent and 45 per cent), Spain for past-year cocaine use (3 per cent and 5 per cent), and Ireland for past-year amphetamine use (3 per cent and 5 per cent).

Several other surveys have consistently found levels of drug use in the UK to be among the highest in Europe, particularly rates of use of cannabis, stimulants and hallucinogens (EMCDDA, 2003). For instance, a review of available survey evidence about lifetime prevalence of synthetic drug use among the adult population of nine EU states between 1994 and 1996 reported that the UK clearly had the highest rates of amphetamine use (9 per cent, compared with a range of 0.7–4 per cent in the other eight countries) and ecstasy use (3 per cent, compared with 0–1.6 per cent) (Griffiths *et al.*, 1997). Most recently, the World Health Organisation conducted a survey of Health Behaviour in School-Aged Children (HBSC), covering 162,000 young people aged 11, 13 and 15 years in 35 countries in Europe and North America in 2001/02, which included questions about cannabis use (Currie *et al.*, 2004). Rates of cannabis use were found to be much higher in the UK, particularly in England and Scotland. The only countries with rates of youthful cannabis use higher than those found in England were Canada, USA, Switzerland and Greenland.

National Population Surveys of Drug Prevalence Among Adults and Young Adults

An exhaustive review of about 40 national and 80 local prevalence surveys in Britain in the three decades between 1964 and 1994 found that the vast majority were focused on schoolchildren (11–15s) or 'young adults' (16–35 year olds, typically 16–24s) (Newcombe, 1995). Among young adults, the lifetime prevalence of self-reported drug use climbed steadily from less than 5 per cent in the 1960s, to around 10 per cent (5–15 per cent) in the 1970s, 15–20 per cent in the 1980s, and 25–35 per cent in the early 1990s (see also ISDD, 1996; DrugScope, 2000, 2002). Regular surveys of the prevalence of drug use among British adults began in 1992, with the BCS.

British Crime Survey

The BCS of drug use is based on interviews with representative samples of adults living in private households in England and Wales, plus a booster sample of 16–24 year olds. Following an initial survey of cannabis use in 1982, five two-yearly surveys of drug use were conducted between 1992 to 2000. The research programme was then upgraded to yearly surveys based on financial years, the first four of which covered 2001/02 to 2004/05. Since 1994, respondents have been questioned using Computer Assisted Personal Interviewing (CAPI), where they directly key their answers into a laptop computer. The BCS focuses on three measures of prevalence – lifetime, past-year and past-month – and now covers 14 key drugs/drug groups, which have become standard items for drug prevalence surveys. These include six Class A drugs (heroin, methadone, cocaine, crack, ecstasy, LSD), one Class B drug (amphetamine), three Class C drugs (cannabis, tranquillisers, steroids), three quasi-legal drugs (solvents, poppers, magic mushrooms), and an 'other drugs' category. A dummy drug item has also been included.

Before moving on to examine the BCS findings, it is important to note some of the potential limitations of this approach. Firstly, as noted by Barton (2003:31) 'the BCS only provides data on adults and thus fails to provide data on younger children'. Secondly, the BCS is a household based survey and authors of the reports have stated that the figures are likely to be underestimates – because of false denials, non-response, and exclusion of high-risk groups such as prisoners and the homeless. Drugs with the highest 'taboo' (social disapproval) level are likely to receive the highest rate of false denials, such as heroin and crack. Even so, less than 1 per cent of respondents have reported using the dummy drug Semeron, indicating high internal validity on false denials – though there are no measures of false admissions, external validity (e.g. saliva tests) or reliability (e.g. repeat questions). Finally, individuals may provide inaccurate information because they simply cannot remember, don't know or have trouble locating incidents within the timeframe. Cannabis use, for example, may be underestimated because up to 4 per cent of adults (7 per cent of young adults) reported having an 'unknown smoke'; similarly, use of ecstasy or other tablet-based drugs may be underestimated because 1–2 per cent of adults

(2–3 per cent of young adults) report using 'unknown pills'. However, only 1 per cent or fewer reported using unknown smokes or pills in the past year.

BCS figures support the picture painted by annual official statistics on offenders and addicts in Britain (see next section) – namely that the steepest rise in prevalence of drug use occurred between the early 1990s and the early 2000s. Between 2000 and 2004/05, drug use reached record levels: over a third of adults and around half of young adults admitted having used one or more drugs – though there were signs of a plateau stage for most drugs from 2001/02 (table 2.2 and 2.3).

Regarding lifetime use, cannabis clearly remains the most popular drug – rates increased sixfold in two decades, climbing from 5 per cent in 1982 to 30 per cent in 2000, and hovering around 30 per cent until 2004/05. The next two most commonly tried drugs were stimulant amphetamines (speed) and alkyl nitrites (poppers) respectively; followed by MDMA-type drugs (ecstasy), magic mushrooms (typically psilocin-based), cocaine hydrochloride and LSD.

Table 2.2

Self-reported use of illicit drugs in England and Wales, 1992–2005 (BCS): Lifetime prevalence–all adults

	92	94	96	98	00	01/02	02/03	03/04	04/05
Cannabis	14	21	24	27	30	29	31	31	30
Amphet amines	4	8	9	11	12	12	12	12	11
Poppers	–	5	7	8	8	8	8	9	8
Magic mushrooms	3	5	5	6	7	6	7	7	7
Ecstasy	2	2	4	4	5	6	7	7	7
Cocaine	2	2	3	4	6	5	6	7	6
LSD	3	4	5	6	6	5	6	6	5
Tranquillisers	1	3	3	3	4	3	3	3	3
Solvents	1	2	2	3	3	2	2	2	2
Crack	*	*	1	1	1	1	1	1	1
Heroin	*	*	1	1	1	1	1	1	1
Steroids	–	1	1	1	1	1	1	1	1
Methadone	*	*	*	1	1	*	*	*	*
Any drug	17	28	31	34	36	34	36	36	35

Notes : *, less than 0.5% ; -, not available.
Source : Ramsey *et al.* (2001), Aust *et al.* (2002), Condon and Smith (2003), Chivite-Matthews *et al.* (2005), Roe 2005.

Table 2.3

Lifetime prevalence – young adults

	92	94	96	98	00	01/02	02/03	03/04	04/05
Cannabis	24	34	40	45	46	44	43	41	41
Amphetamines	9	14	19	22	21	16	14	12	11
Poppers	–	13	16	18	15	15	13	13	12
Magic mushrooms	6	10	10	11	10	6	6	7	7
Ecstasy	4	6	12	11	12	12	12	11	11
Cocaine	3	3	4	7	10	8	9	9	9
LSD	6	9	13	12	11	7	6	4	3
Tranquillisers	1	3	4	3	5	3	3	3	2
Solvents	3	6	6	6	7	6	5	3	4
Crack	1	*	2	2	2	1	1	2	1
Heroin	*	1	1	1	2	1	1	1	1
Steroids	–	1	2	1	1	1	1	1	1
Methadone	1	1	*	1	1	1	*	1	*
Any drug	28	43	49	54	52	49	47	47	46

Notes : *, less than 0.5% ; -, not available.
Source : Ramsey *et al.* (2001), Aust *et al.* (2002), Condon and Smith (2003), Chivite-Matthews *et al.* (2005), Roe 2005.

Over the period 1992 to 2005, prevalence of use of most of these popular drugs increased steadily at first, then levelled out after 2000. The only two drugs to show a clear decline in use after 2000, on all three prevalence indicators, were amphetamine and LSD (see Table 2.3).

Compared with the top seven drugs, prevalence of use of the two most problematic drugs, heroin and crack, was far lower. That is, rates of use were typically less than 0.5 per cent for past-year and past-month use of each drug, and usually around 1 per cent for lifetime use – though this indicator rose to a record 2 per cent for both drugs among young adults in 2000.

Estimates based on BCS figures suggest that 10.9 million people had tried drugs in England and Wales by 2004/05, including 3.5 million in the past year, and 2.1 million in the past month. In the 2004/05 BCS, the past-year figure of 3.5 million included about 3.0 million cannabis users, 0.6 million cocaine users, 0.6 million ecstasy users, and 0.4 million amphetamine users. Among 16–24 year olds, about 2.8 million had tried drugs in 2004/05, including 1.6 million in the past year and about one million in the past month. But, as in previous years, the BCS estimates of the number of heroin users in 2004/05 seem particularly low: 38,000 in the past year and 21,000 in the past month (the respective figures for crack use also seem rather low: 32,000 and 16,000). Indeed, other sources suggest far higher annual numbers for heroin and crack users, and often steadily rising trends as well (see 'drug indicators' section). For instance, Bramley-Harker's (2001) efforts to establish the size of the UK drugs market produced estimates of 299,000 heroin users (about 1 per cent of adults), 475,000 cocaine users, and 210,000 crack users.

In short, distilling the BCS findings, five illicit drugs can be classified as the most 'popular drugs' in Britain. These are, first and foremost, cannabis, followed by cocaine and ecstasy, then amphetamines and poppers. Britain's rising levels of drug use are based mainly on the first three drugs. Whether or not use of these drugs has become 'normalised' is discussed in the concluding section (also see Chapters 1 and 3).

These statistics can also be examined in relation to age, gender and ethnic group. In terms of age, as already stated above, the main finding is far higher levels of use among young adults (16–24s) compared with older adults. The 2000 survey reported breakdowns by 5-year age-bands, revealing that all three types of prevalence peaked among 20–24s (58 per cent, 30 per cent and 20 per cent). The next highest rates of lifetime use were among 25–29s (50 per cent) followed by 30–34s (43 per cent); while the next highest rates of past-year and past-month use were among 16–19s (27 per cent, 16 per cent) followed by 25–29s (20 per cent, 12 per cent). Prevalence rates were notably lower for 35–59s (27 per cent, 6 per cent, 3 per cent).

Subsequent surveys gave less detailed breakdowns on age, but those reported reflected previous surveys. For instance, the 2002/03 survey reported past-year and past-month use rates of 28 per cent and 18 per cent for 16–24s, and 17 per cent and 11 per cent for 25–34s, with prevalence rates again being substantially lower for 35–59s (5 per cent and 3 per cent).

In terms of gender, despite claims made in the mass media and elsewhere, significant gender differences continue to be reported by the BCS. For instance, in the 2000 survey, about 1.5 as many men as women reported that they had tried drugs, ever and in the past year, while twice as many stated that they had used drugs in the past month. Regarding lifetime use, 1.5 times as many men as women had used cannabis and amphetamines; and twice as many men as women had used magic mushrooms, LSD, poppers, cocaine and ecstasy. Regarding past-year use, two to three times as many men as women had used the same seven drugs. Regarding past-month use, twice as many men as women had used cannabis (figures for other drugs were generally too small for proper comparison).

Though reporting of prevalence rates by ethnic group in BCS reports is patchy, a detailed ethnic breakdown was provided for the 2001/02 survey, from which it is possible to identify consistent trends and patterns (Aust and Smith, 2003). For instance, rates of lifetime drug use among White and Asian adults appear fairly level, while Black adults exhibit rising rates – 23 per cent in 1996, 28 per cent in 2000 and 34 per cent in 2001/02 (compared with 30 per cent, 34 per cent and 31 per cent for Whites, and 13 per cent, 13 per cent and 15 per cent for Asians). By contrast, young adults exhibit steadily rising levels of drug use in each ethnic group, though these trends were least pronounced for Blacks – for instance, between 1992 and 2000, lifetime use almost doubled for young Whites (from 29 per cent to 52 per cent) and Asians (from 10 per cent to 19 per cent), while increasing only by about a quarter for young Blacks (from 30 per cent to 37 per cent). There are no clear ethnic trends in past-year use, other than a moderate increase among Whites, particularly young adults (from 24 per cent in 1994 and 25 per cent in 1996 to 32 per cent in 2000/01 – compared with 18 per cent, 19 per cent and 18 per cent for Blacks and 8 per cent, 10 per cent and 9 per cent for Asians).

However, the 2000 BCS introduced a fourth ethnicity category – 'Mixed-race'. Breakdowns of prevalence rates by ethnic group since 2000 have shown that the general pattern is for Asians (including Chinese) to report the lowest levels of drug use, for Whites and Blacks to report intermediate levels, and for 'Mixed-race' people to report significantly higher levels of drug use than any other group – particularly White/Black 'Mixed-race' people (rather than White/Asian or other ethnic mixes). White rates are usually, but not always, slightly higher than Black rates. For instance, 2001/02 levels of lifetime drug use were 34 per cent among Blacks and 31 per cent among Whites, compared with 15 per cent among Asians and 45 per cent among 'Mixed-race' people. In summary, 'Mixed-race' people clearly report the highest rates of drug use – including recent use of cocaine and ecstasy – while Asians clearly report the lowest.

Other Official Surveys of Adults/Young Adults

There have also been a small number of other 'official' surveys of the prevalence of drug use in the UK, some of which are repeated periodically, and most of which are focused on young adults. The findings of these surveys are generally consistent with those of the BCS, providing evidence of external validity. For instance, a survey of 4,314 English adults aged 16–74 years was carried out by the Social Survey Division of the Office of National Statistics for the Health Education Authority (HEA) in 1997. It reported a past-year drug-taking prevalence of 27 per cent among 16–29s, compared with 25 per cent among 16–29s in the 1998 BCS (Bridgwood *et al.*, 1998). Another HEA survey of 4,647 English 11–35 year olds in 1996 (Drug Realities Survey) found that 23 per cent reported past-year drug use, and 12 per cent reported past-month drug use, though the survey used mixed sampling methods, and had a low response rate (Tasker *et al.*, 1999). Prevalence rates among 16–29s in the 1996 BCS were fairly similar – 24 per cent for past-year use, and 15 per cent for past-month use.

The British Psychological Morbidity Survey (BPMS) provides a more recent check on the reliability of the BCS figures. First conducted in 1993, it was repeated in 2000, and covered self-reported mental disorders, drug dependence, and – in 2000 only – past-year drug use (Meltzer *et al.*, 1995; ONS, 2001). The 2000 BPMS was based on interviews with 8900 adults aged 16–74 years from a random sample of British households, with findings adjusted for non-response and selection bias, and presented within 95 per cent confidence intervals. The survey used the same 13 drug types as the BCS, and differed mainly in the inclusion of Scotland and 65–74 year olds. The rounded-up prevalence figures for each of the 13 drugs and 'any drug' showed an almost identical profile to those for the 2000 BCS – overall, and for men and women.

Several market research polls of the national prevalence of drug use have also been conducted over the last decade (Newcombe, 1995; Drug-Scope, 2002). However, unlike official surveys, about half of these polls have reported notably lower rates of drug use than those indicated by BCS reports for the same or closest year (though about half have generally reported similar rates). It is possible that methodological shortcomings in some of these surveys (e.g. poor assurances of confidentiality, 'cold' telephone contacting) led to a reduction in honest reporting of drug use.

Agency-Based Surveys and Statistics on Problem Drug Use

A PDU is defined here as an illicit drug user whose drug-related problems have led to them becoming known to generic or specialist drug services, either voluntarily or involuntarily. There are two main sources of estimates about the prevalence of problem drug use:

(1) official statistics – quarterly to annual routine statistics, including direct indicators (number of drug users known to official agencies), and indirect indicators (such as the purity, price and availability of drug products) and
(2) multi-agency enumeration surveys – typically one-off snapshots of a geographical area (district/city/county, etc.) during a half-year or one-year period.

Official statistics on PDUs, whether based on single or multiple agency sources, cannot provide an accurate estimate of the true community prevalence of drug use without a 'multiplier' (see next section). Even so, because they provide a regular, systematic count of PDUs, they are often used as rough and ready indicators of 'underlying trends' in prevalence. Indeed, the trends and differences identified by sample surveys are generally confirmed by official statistics – though the latter are clearly influenced by other factors, notably changes in the policies of relevant agencies, and changes in recording and reporting procedures. Accurate interpretation of official statistics also requires proper attention to definitions and footnotes. The main official indicators of the prevalence of problem drug use come from two sources, and cover several decades:

(1) law enforcement statistics from police forces and Customs and Excise – notably people searched and arrested for drugs (1986–2003), and drug offenders (1921–2002) – for which the majority of cases involve cannabis and
(2) health statistics on PDUs from government agencies – particularly notified drug addicts (Home Office, 1935–1996), new PDUs Department of Health's (DOH) Drug Misuse Database, 1993–2001), and drug treatment cases (National Treatment Agency, 2000–2003) – for which the majority of cases involve heroin.

Law Enforcement Statistics

Annual statistics are available on the drug using clients/cases of all criminal justice agencies – police, customs, law courts, probation, prisons, etc. – though the main figures used as general indicators of wider trends in drug use are drug offences (convictions and cautions); searches and arrests; and seizure statistics (including purity and price – not covered here).

Drug possession and trafficking were first prohibited under the *Dangerous Drugs Act* 1920, which listed opium, morphine, heroin and cocaine; cannabis was added in 1928. In 1964 and 1966 the *Drugs (Prevention of Misuse) Acts* prohibited amphetamine and LSD respectively, while the 1971 *Misuse of Drugs Act* introduced controls on most of the other presently banned drugs, with a few exceptions (e.g. MDMA was not prohibited until 1977). Following initial annual UK numbers of 200–300 drug offences from 1921 to 1923, numbers remained fairly low, between about 50 and 100 per year, until World War II – when annual numbers returned to about 200–300 per year. From 1946 to 1959 annual numbers generally fluctuated between 150 and 250, but then rose steadily from 278 in 1960 to 659 in 1964 – before climbing steeply to almost 15,000 in 1973. From 1973 to 1979 there was a plateau stage, with the annual number of drug offences hovering between about 12,000 and 15,000. There was then another steady rise in drug offences, to 23,905 in 1986, followed by a very steep climb in numbers to a peak of 131,230 in 1998. Numbers then declined to nearer 100,000, before rising slightly to 110,920 in 2002.

For the first three decades of prohibition, the drug attracting the highest number of convictions was opium (followed by morphine). Then, in 1949, the most common drug offence became cannabis possession – and so it has remained for over 50 years (with cannabis now comprising over 80 per cent of all drug offences). Heroin became the second most common drug involved in offences from 1961, but was overtaken by amphetamines and LSD (respectively) from 1965, with cocaine occupying the fifth position. These rankings remained until 1977, when LSD slipped into fifth position. LSD then slipped into sixth position in the 1980s (after methadone), and to seventh position in the 1990s (after crack). From the mid-1990s ecstasy appeared, and swapped third and fourth position with amphetamine. The next most notable change occurred from 1999, with heroin offenders again reaching the second highest number after cannabis offenders – 11,790 in 2002, compared with 82,550 for cannabis. By 2002, the third to fifth ranks were closely occupied by ecstasy (6560), cocaine (5990), and amphetamine (5280); while the number of offences involving LSD (120) ranked lower than those for crack (1800), steroids (640) and methadone (470) (Home Office, 2004). In short, annual trends in the number of drug offenders consistently reflect the prevalence trends indicated by research, particularly over the last decade – notably, the substantial rises in the levels of use of cannabis, ecstasy, cocaine and heroin, and the notable drops in the use of LSD and amphetamines.

The number of persons/vehicles stopped and searched by the police on suspicion of drug offences in England and Wales climbed consistently from 32,500 in 1986 to 362,100 in 1998/99, before falling steadily to 236,900 in 2000/01. But it then rose again to 363,100 in 2002/03 – the highest number ever recorded – before falling slightly to 345,300 in 2004/05. The arrest (positive search) rate fell from 20 per cent to 9 per cent over the same 18-year period.

As expected, figures on the annual number and amounts of drugs seized in the UK mirror trends in the number of drug offenders – but also closely reflect trends in drug use identified by surveys. For instance, the amount of cocaine seized peaked in 2000 (almost 4000 kg), while 2001 witnessed record seizures of ecstasy (over eight million doses), heroin (3930 kg) and crack (60 kg). By contrast, in 2002 the amount of amphetamines seized dropped to an 8-year low of 1410 kg, while the amounts of LSD seized dropped to a record low of 20,000 doses (Home Office, 2004).

Health Service Statistics

Three related sets of official statistics on drug users known to health services in Britain provide further confirmation of key trends identified by research: notified drug addicts (new and renotified), PDUs (new only) and drug treatment cases (new and returning). The main type of drug user monitored by all three systems is the heroin/opiate user – simply because they comprise the majority of drug treatment and other drug service clients. Together these monitoring systems indicate that the UK has witnessed three increasingly large heroin 'epidemics' (sudden outbreaks and rises in use, followed by drops or plateau stages): the first across the late 1960s and early 1970s; the second across the early to mid-1980s; and the third from the late 1980s until the present.

Notified drug addicts (sometimes called 'registered addicts') were users of heroin, 13 other opiates and/or cocaine who were suspected or known by their GP or other doctor to be addicted to one or more of these drugs – and were thus notified to the Home Office, as required by law from the late 1960s until 1996. Prior to the 1960s, the vast majority of opiate and cocaine 'addicts' notified to the Home Office were either (a) 'therapeutic'/iatrogenic cases, i.e. patients who became addicted to their opiate medicines (over half) or (b) 'professional classes', i.e. 'occupational hazard' cases, notably doctors and pharmacists (up to a quarter prior to World War II). For instance, 80 per cent were 'therapeutic' addicts in 1958. The first year in which the proportion of therapeutic addicts dropped below half was 1964 (Bean, 1974) – meaning that most notified addicts were users of illicit drugs from this time. Up to the early 1960s, there were also typically more female than male addicts, though from the mid-1960s the annual ratio moved closer to three males to every female (as in 1996). Prior to 1963, most notified addicts were aged 50 years or older, but within a decade the majority were in the 20–34-year-old age band. For instance, in 1959, 61 per cent of 454 notified addicts were aged 50 years or more, 11 per cent were aged 20–34 years, and none were aged under 20. By 1970, only 10 per cent of 2661 addicts were aged 50 or older, while 68 per cent were aged 20–34 years and 15 per cent were aged under 20 years (Bean, 1974). Later bulletins reported mean age, which in 1996 remained similar to the mean age a decade earlier – around 26 years for new addicts and 30 years for renotified addicts (about 29 years overall).

Statistics for notified drug addicts go back to 1935, and show that, for the first two decades, numbers dropped fairly steadily – from about 700 in 1935 to 290 in 1953. Annual numbers then began rising slowly again, up to 927 in 1965, before rising more sharply to 2881 in 1969, and then falling again, down to 1406 in 1973 – this was the first UK 'heroin epidemic'. After a plateau stage of around 1400 addicts per year up to 1975, numbers then began rising steadily again, reaching 2441 in 1980, and then increased sharply to a plateau of around 8–9000 in the mid-1980s (the second outbreak of heroin use). Following this brief plateau, the number of notified addicts climbed more dramatically than ever before to a peak of 43,372 in 1996 (the third UK 'heroin epidemic'). Other evidence suggests that the number of opiate addicts has continued to grow into the 2000s (see below).

The majority of notified drug addicts were originally morphine addicts, though the proportion gradually fell from 90 per cent in 1935 to 64 per cent in 1952, and then to 30 per cent in 1962. Pethidine was the second most common drug of addiction until 1961. Then, in 1962, heroin became the main drug of addiction (33 per cent of all addicts) – which it remained, except for a brief period in the early 1970s when methadone was the main drug of addiction. Annual numbers of notified heroin addicts followed a similar trend to all drug addicts, rising from 54 in 1955 to 2240 in 1968, then dropping down to 812 in 1975, before rising steadily again to 30,573 in 1996. However, because of the long duration of heroin addiction (about ten years on average), prevalence often continues to rise when the number of new heroin addicts is waning – because incidence remains higher than the 'ex-user' (coming off) rate. The number of new heroin addicts is therefore regarded as a more useful indicator of the course of a 'heroin epidemic'. The number of new heroin addicts rose steadily from 508 in 1973 to 1151 in 1980, before climbing more steeply up to 5930 in 1985, then dropping below 5000 until 1990, when the number reached 5819. A further steep and steady rise then brought incidence up to a record 15,271 in 1996.

The number of drug addicts notified as addicted to methadone also increased over the same period, though this trend is much more likely to reflect prescribing practices than the increase in heroin addicts. Methadone became available in Britain after World War II – the first reports in 1949 listed two methadone addicts. Numbers then climbed gradually to 72 in 1965; and, following the launch of the new drug dependency clinics, rose steeply to 1820 in 1970. Figures for 1971–75 are not available, though those for 1976 –80 show a lower plateau stage of 600–700 methadone addicts per year. The second and largest surge of methadone addicts in Britain emerged from the early 1980s, particularly after mass methadone prescribing was sanctioned in 1988 because of the threat of HIV posed by injecting drug users. At first, the number of notified methadone addicts climbed slowly from 865 in 1981 to 2389 in 1988; but then rose steeply to 18,617 in 1996. By 2003, the estimated number of heroin addicts prescribed methadone had risen to over 80,000 (see below). The proportion of drug addicts notified for methadone in 1996 was 43 per cent, compared with 70 per cent for heroin, and 8 per cent for cocaine.

PDUs are 'new' clients of drug services (defined as first-time or returning after at least six months absence). Though the Drug Misuse Database (DMD) excluded continuing clients, it improved on the Addicts Index in two ways: (a) it covered users of all illicit drugs (not just opiates and cocaine); and (b) it incorporated information on PDUs known to all agencies, not just medical services. Information about each client's drug use (main drug, all drugs, consumption, etc.), demographic features, and planned service usage was recorded on special forms, and was compiled first by regional DMDs for each health region (eight in England), before national six-monthly statistics were produced by the DOH – mostly for England, with some statistics for Britain. One of the main shortcomings of the DMD was that agency participation and reporting varied widely from region to region, making regional comparisons somewhat unreliable. Another major limitation – the focus on new PDUs only – was overcome in 2001 by extending the DMD into the National Drug Treatment Monitoring System (see below).

The number of new PDUs in Britain climbed fairly steadily from 20,343 in the half-year ending September 1993, to 40,181 in the half-year ending March 2001 (the last period for which figures are available). The number whose main drug was heroin climbed from 9066 (47 per cent of all PDUs) to 26,424 (66 per cent) over the same period. The next largest numbers for main drugs involved methadone (from 3059 (15 per cent) to 3702 (9 per cent)), cannabis (from 1414 (7 per cent) to 3489 (9 per cent)), and cocaine (from 503 (2 per cent) to 2439 (6 per cent)). The two drug groups with both the lowest and most rapidly dwindling number of problematic users over this 8-year period were amphetamines (from 2310 (11 per cent) to 1092 (3 per cent)), hallucinogens (from 252 to 36), and solvents (from 261 to 141). Trends for all (main or secondary) drug use in Britain were fairly similar, though numbers were generally somewhat higher than for main drug alone – for instance, in the half-year ending March 2001, there were 29,137 heroin users (73 per cent of all PDUs), 10,828 cannabis users (27 per cent), 8327 cocaine users (21 per cent), 8039 benzodiazepine users (20 per cent) and 6942 methadone users (17 per cent). About three-quarters of PDUs were usually male, and about half were aged 20–29 years. In the half-year ending March 2001, 25 per cent of British PDUs were aged 20–24 years, 25 per cent were aged 25–29 years, 19 per cent were aged 30–34 years, 13 per cent were aged 15–19 years, and 10 per cent were aged 35–39 years. Only 7 per cent were aged 40 years or more, and just 1 per cent were aged under 15 years.

Rises in the number of PDUs have also been reported in Scotland and Northern Ireland (DrugScope, 2002). In Scotland, the number of drug misusers presenting to services climbed from 7694 in 1995/96 to 11,123 in 1999/2000 – with the proportion of cases reporting heroin as their main drug rising from 36 per cent to 54 per cent over the same period (Information and Statistics Division, 2000). In Northern Ireland, the number of registered drug addicts climbed from 60 in 1992 to 260 in 1998 (Northern Ireland Office, 1999).

Treatment cases are defined as including all PDUs attending Tier 3 (structured treatment) drug services. In England and Wales, they have been monitored by the National Drug Treatment Monitoring System (NDTMS) since 2001. As noted, the NDTMS was developed from the DMD, and so cases have a similar profile - for instance, about 85 per cent are primary users of opioids or cocaine (with most of the rest reporting cannabis or amphetamines as their primary drug). However, the NDTMS includes continuing as well as new treatment clients – and thus provides a full count of all 'known' PDUs. Numbers almost doubled from 85,000 cases in 1998/99 to 160,500 cases in 2004/05 (NTA, 2005). Between 2001/02 and 2004/05, the number successfully completing treatment dropped from 18,100 to 15,800; while the number retained in treatment climbed from 57,400 to 104,900. In a typical year, about three-quarters were male, about two-thirds were aged 25 years or older, almost three-quarters were primary heroin users, over four in ten were self-referred, and almost nine in ten were attending a drug dependency unit or community drug team. In short, the number of 'treatment cases' has risen dramatically, the typical case being a male heroin user in his late 20s. However, it should be noted that a news item in Druglink in December 2004 reported the claim of a former government consultant that DOH and National Treatment Agency (NTA) officials had 'adjusted' the 2003/04 treatment figures in order to appear to be reaching official targets.

Drug Indicator Studies

From the mid-1980s to the late 1990s, the total prevalence of opioid addicts was often estimated from the number of notified opioid addicts by employing a multiplier of five (see Hartnoll *et al.*, 1985, for the London-based study which originally suggested this multiplier). For instance, applying this 'rough and ready' multiplier to the final count of notified drug addicts in Britain in 1996 (43,372) produced an estimated total prevalence of about 216,000 drug addicts – including about 200,000 addicts of heroin and/or methadone (similar to official 'guestimates' at that time). Indeed, up to the late 1990s, the 'case multiplier' method and the related technique of 'capture-recapture' were the two main statistical methods of drug prevalence estimation to have been employed in studies of local communities. However, for various reasons, they have not been used to make estimates of national prevalence.

More recently, more sophisticated statistical techniques for estimating prevalence have emerged. In 1999, European Monitoring Centre for Drugs and Drug Addiction (EMCDDA) produced methodological guidelines for national drug prevalence estimation based largely on these drug indicator methods (Kraus *et al.*, 1999). The two methods share the common logic of estimating the total number of drug users (e.g. drug injectors) from the number of known drug users (clients of drug agencies). They vary in how many agencies they require to provide information on known drug users (one, two, multiple), and also in what additional information is required by their respective statistical formulae (the ratio of known to hidden users, the overlap between agencies, attendance rates, etc.). Their shortcomings include the methodologically restricted focus upon those kinds of PDU who are well represented among the clients of official agencies (notably opioid use and injecting drug use), and various assumptions about the populations of known and 'hidden' drug users.

Using such sophisticated techniques Kraus *et al.* (1999) and Frischer *et al.* (2001) have demonstrated that such methods can be used to estimate the prevalence of various types of problem drug use in Britain and other European countries. Estimates of the overall prevalence of problem opiate use in Britain were generated by various multipliers (notably treatment cases); the prevalence of injecting drug use was generated by a HIV/injecting drug users (IDU) case multiplier; and the prevalence of potential fatal overdose (OD) cases was generated by a mortality multiplier. The largest estimate was 268,000 for PDUs overall in 1996 – 4.9 per 1000 of the British population, or seven per 1000 in 15–64 year olds. This included about 225,400 in England, 30,200 in Scotland and 12,600 in Wales. About 202,000 of these PDUs (75 per cent) were problem opiate users (6.3 per 1000), around 165,000 (60 per cent) were injecting drug users (4.2 per 1000) and just over 160,000 were classified as potential fatal overdose cases. About a quarter of British IDUs were estimated to be resident in London (almost 40,000), compared with about 92,000 in the rest of England and Wales, and almost 30,000 in Scotland. Taking into account rises in the prevalence of heroin use and in the number of IDUs on the DMD since the mid-1990s, it seems likely that the prevalence of past-year injecting in 2005 had risen to nearer 200,000 – compared with 165,000 in 1996, and 100,000 in 1990.

Estimates of the overall prevalence of problem drug use were available for two other countries only (higher in Italy and lower in France). However, though the year of different national estimates varied between 1995 and 2000, Britain ranked third (after Italy and France) out of five countries on number of IDUs, second (after Germany) out of 10 countries on number of potentially fatal OD cases, and second (after Italy) out of seven countries on number of problem opiate users. But a fairer comparison is based on rates of problem drug use per 1000 citizens aged 15–64 years. On standardised population prevalence rates, Britain ranked second (after Portugal) out of five countries for overall problem drug use; fourth out of eight countries for problem opiate use and fourth out of ten countries for injecting drug use.

Summary of Prevalence Findings

Since the first surveys were conducted about four decades ago, the prevalence of illicit drug use in the UK has risen fairly consistently. In the 1960s, about 1 per cent of adults (16–59s) and less than 5 per cent of young adults (16–29s) had used drugs – compared with about a third of adults and around half of young adults in the early 2000s. In England and Wales, regular national surveys, official statistics and other evidence support the general conclusion that levels of both lifetime use and past-year use doubled between 1992 and 2004, among both adults and young adults, while past-month use rates climbed by about a quarter. By the early 2000s, surveys indicated that almost three in ten young adults were past-year drug users, and almost two in ten indicated past-month use – though the overall rate of drug use may be levelling out. Similar trends have been reported among secondary schoolchildren (11–15s) in Britain – regular annual rises in rates of drug use from the 1980s, reaching a peak around 2000, and fairly stable rates of overall use up to 2004. Alternatively, the evidence is also broadly consistent with the interpretation of the recent plateau in drug use as another step in an underlying stair-like prevalence trend characterising the last three decades – that is, prevalence repeatedly rising, levelling out, rising, and so on, presumably until some 'ceiling' is eventually reached. Whether that final 'ceiling' has been reached in the early 2000s remains to be seen.

By 2004 about ten million of the 12–59-year-old population of the UK had used drugs, over four million had done so in the past year, and about 2.5 million in the past month. These figures are generally believed to be underestimates (rather than over-estimates) of the true number of British drug users – by at least 10 per cent, though a precise reckoning of the underestimation factor is not possible given the current 'state of the art' (see below). Most surveys also rank England and Scotland above Wales and Northern Ireland on population rates of drug use, though there is puzzling variation in the evidence. Britain has slightly lower rates of drug use compared with the world 'leaders', the USA and Australia, but still ranks among those countries with the highest levels of both illicit drug use and problem drug use in Europe, along with such countries as Ireland, France, Spain and the Czech Republic.

There are also consistent demographic differences in levels of drug use. British men remain up to twice as likely as women to have used most popular or problematic drugs, though these differences have diminished among teenagers. As regards age, 20–24 year olds continue to exhibit the highest rates of drug use, closely followed by the 5-year age bands on either side, though there are no notable drops in prevalence of use until after 35 years. Ethnic differences are particularly salient: Asians have been found to have a significantly lower rate of drug use compared with Whites and Blacks, while recent research suggest that 'Mixed-race' people may have highest rates of all – an issue which requires far more research.

Although figures for 'overall prevalence' – use of one or more drugs – gloss over trends in the use of individual drugs, closer examination reveals that most drugs do follow the overall trend – with three notable exceptions.

But cannabis remains the most popular illicit drug in Britain, with rates of use just below those for overall use, while amphetamine and LSD have generally been the next most popular illegal drugs – closely followed by (or sometimes following) the two quasi-legal drugs, poppers and magic mushrooms. However, over the last decade, rates of recent (past-year and past-month) use of ecstasy and cocaine have gradually overtaken those of LSD and magic mushrooms, and to a lesser extent, amphetamines – particularly among young adults. The trend in ecstasy use is especially remarkable given that prior to the mid-1980s its use in Britain was practically unknown. Indeed, in the decade ending 2004, past-year use of cannabis and ecstasy by young adults doubled, though the most significant rise involved past-year cocaine use – a fivefold increase between 1994 and 2004. However, as noted, the latest survey evidence also supports the hypothesis that we have reached a plateau stage for many types of 'recent drug use', and there is also consistent evidence that some drugs – notably amphetamine and LSD – exhibit declining levels of use. By contrast, recent use of heroin and crack has remained at around 1 per cent or below in most population surveys since 1992, though recent surveys have reported rates of 2 per cent among young urban adults. However, estimates based on drug indicator techniques suggest that the rounded '1 per cent' or '>1 per cent' figure which population surveys almost invariably report for heroin and crack users has masked a steady rise in their numbers over the past two decades. This rise started from a near-zero prevalence prior to the mid-1980s in the case of crack. As regards our best estimates of trends in heroin use in the UK over the last half century, past-year prevalence was likely to have been between a quarter million and 300,000 in 2005, compared with around 150,000 in 1995, 50,000 in 1985, 10,000 in 1975, 5000 in 1965 and about a 1000 in 1955.

One method for extracting generalisations from the various drug prevalence statistics without resorting to the somewhat arbitrary classifications of British law – or to even more unscientific distinctions such as 'hard/soft' drugs – is the 'group model' (Newcombe 1990, 1995, 1997). Based on evidence from local and national research, this model proposes that there are four overlapping groups of illicit drug users in modern Britain, distinguished mainly by (a) the types of drugs they typically use, (b) their demographic characteristics and (c) the nature and extent of their involvement with drug agencies and professionals. Briefly, these are: opioid users and injecting drug users (Group A), stimulant and hallucinogen users (Group B), cannabis users (Group C) and solvents users (Group D). When represented as four overlapping circles inside a square, the space outside the circles represents non-users. The size of the circles and their overlap zones can be adjusted to represent the changing situation. The main 'overlap zone' at present involves cocaine, crack and amphetamine users in Groups A and B.

Implications for Theory, Research and Policy

Although the technology of drug prevalence estimation has undoubtedly improved over the last decade (Stimson *et al.*, 1997; Frischer *et al.*, 2001), many problems remain with the current approach to examining trends in levels and patterns of drug use. One clear conclusion to emerge from the present review is that research in this field needs to become more sophisticated and systematic (cf. Stimson *et al.*, 1997; Kraus *et al.*, 1999). In addition to agreeing upon standardised definitions and conceptual frameworks, there is a need to go beyond the established concepts of lifetime, past-year and past-month prevalence of individual drugs, to examine the prevalence and incidence of different patterns of drugs consumption as they occur in 'real life'.

For instance, prevalence surveys typically collect and/or present information about drugs in a 'singular' fashion – that is, statistics are reported on each individual drug, when in reality people often use more than one drug. Some surveys, such as the BCS, have reported the mean number of drugs used in particular time-periods, and/or the percentages using each number of drugs. However, it is very rare to find a study which makes any conceptual distinction between poly-use (drugs used by an individual across months/years) and multi-use (drugs used simultaneously or in same session) – or which attempts to identify common patterns of combined drug use. When the use of mixtures of drugs is examined, the focus is almost invariably on poly-use – yet multi-use is arguably a higher risk activity which requires as much if not more research attention. In short, although estimating the prevalence of use of each type of drug should continue to be a key aim of prevalence researchers, they also need to devise questions and response formats which permit estimates of the extent of the most common patterns of multi-use (e.g. heroin, methadone and crack) and poly-use (e.g. ecstasy, cocaine and cannabis). As regards data collection, the focus should be on the type and sequence of drugs involved in multi-drug use, since poly-drug use patterns can be inferred from these data.

Another key issue is the use of commonsense notions and everyday terms as theoretical concepts and research variables. Although this is a common practice, ordinary language terms are typically laden with value judgements and subjective connotations, and so adopting them for scientific usage requires that they be given a standardised operational definition, ideally within a broader conceptual framework. For instance, in the early days of drug prevalence research, it was common for surveys to produce estimates of the number/rates of 'recent' or 'current' drug users, without any clear definitions of these terms. Since then, most researchers have adopted the convention of measuring lifetime, past-year and past-month prevalence, which have clear and unambiguous definitions. However, other terms used by prevalence researchers remain problematic. Two key examples will be briefly described here.

First, the use of the terms 'regular' and 'occasional' to describe two broad classes of drug-taking frequency is common in prevalence research, though these terms are subjective and vague when employed without standardised definitions. Regular users have been variously defined in surveys as any cases which use between 'at least three times a year' (e.g. WHO) and 'at least once a week' – with 'at least once a month' probably being the nearest we have to a standard. An added difficulty is that commonsense definitions of regular use are likely to vary for different types of drug (e.g. consider tobacco, cannabis and LSD). Similarly, describing people as daily, weekly, and/or monthly users can be an equally 'messy' way of categorising the actual frequency of use – that is, over a four-week period, daily users are literally those respondents who used on 28 days, weekly users are those who used on between 4 and 27 days, and monthly users are those who used on one to three days. In short, weekly use masks a broad range of frequencies of use compared with the far narrower categories of daily use and monthly use. In addition, prevalence estimates are also undermined by the lack of standardisation of methods for calculating frequency of drug use – for instance, methods vary in whether they focus on the frequency of doses (e.g. spliffs, injections), drug-taking sessions or use-days.

Second, some researchers have focused on the prevalence of 'dependent' drug use (or 'addiction'), as contrasted with 'recreational' and/or 'experimental' use. Unfortunately, there has been a tendency by some researchers to neglect case definitions, and thus to conceptualise and present the latter groups as relatively healthy, law-abiding and sensible; while dependent users ('addicts') are more often construed as 'problematic' in respect of health, criminal involvements, social attitudes, etc. Indeed, some reports employ 'dependent user', 'problem user' and even 'known user' as if they were synonymous – yet experimental use may be just as problematic as dependent use (albeit for different reasons). Furthermore, it is not always clear to which of these three categories some common patterns of drug use should belong. For example, 'binge use' (intermittent episodes of heavy consumption) does not fit neatly into either dependent, recreational or experimental drug use – though, again, a proper assessment would require the adoption of standard definitions for these terms. In short, drug researchers need to be more careful in their use of labels like 'dependent' and 'problematic' in scientific research, if their interpretations and conclusions are to remain free of the 'commonsense' value judgments (biases) found in everyday discourse.

In addition to design and data-collection problems, the methodology of drug prevalence research also suffers from shortcomings in its sampling and data analysis procedures. For instance, although prevalence researchers generally employ probability sampling to obtain representative samples, there is also an urgent need for studies employing cohorts of drug users (see Parker *et al.*, 1998b, for a 5-year follow-up study of a cohort of teenagers in north-west England). Cohort studies permit an assessment of individual behaviour change, while repeat surveys with different samples are limited to measuring changes in group behaviour only (though self-report information about drug careers can illuminate individual differences) (see Chapter 10). For instance, consider a 5-year repeat survey of injecting among separate samples of 100 heroin users, which reports that 50 per cent inject and 50 per cent smoke heroin at both stages. Although it appears that there has been no change in methods of use, it is theoretically possible that the 50 injectors at stage-1 had all switched to smoking by stage-2, while the 50 smokers at stage-1 had all progressed to injecting heroin by stage-2. Although this is an extreme example, and in reality there would be far fewer heroin users switching from injecting to smoking, it should make it clear that a cohort study would be necessary to accurately identify prevalence trends in two sub-groups of users, which are often masked by general trends inferred from the findings of repeat surveys.

Standard procedures for calculating estimation errors also need to be developed by prevalence researchers – very few studies do more than identify whether their prevalence figures are likely to be overestimates or underestimates (typically the latter). Among other variables, the formulae for fine-tuning initial prevalence estimates should include adjustments for (a) excluded population sub-groups (e.g. prisoners), non-response and false admissions/denials in questionnaire surveys; and (b) double-counts and missing cases in multi-agency enumeration and drug indicator studies. For instance, as regards internal validity, though dummy drug items are increasingly used in population surveys to check false admissions, many studies do not report the rate of false admissions, nor explain how such cases were dealt with. In addition, more effort needs to be made to assess false denials. Many surveys do not even employ a general honesty question such as 'did you answer all of the questions honestly?' More use could be made of the standard question for assessing false denials developed by WHO for use in school drug surveys. This question is 'sign-posted' to respondents who state that they have not used drugs, and can be paraphrased as: 'do you think that you would have admitted it in this questionnaire if you had used drugs?' Similarly, as appropriate technologies become cheaper and accessible, physiological measures of drug use should be more frequently employed to assess the external validity of self-reported drug use, at least among a sub-sample. For instance, saliva swabs and skin swipes are generally more acceptable (e.g. less intrusive and easier to administer) than urine or blood tests, while hair tests can provide information about drugs used over several months (rather than days as with the other tests).

Lastly, it is also recommended that interval estimation should become a standard technique for representing and reporting prevalence statistics in population surveys. In addition to permitting generalisation from the sample to the population, confidence intervals can be applied to numbers, proportions (rates, percentages) and means. They also provide a stronger and more accurate foundation than a single figure for estimating the possible numerical range of drug users, and planning services accordingly.

While empirical evidence about the prevalence of drug use in Britain has much increased over the last decade, the quality of our scientific explanations has not kept pace. Hypothesis-testing studies of trends in drug use are very rare, mainly because few prevalence researchers operate within conceptual models which are sophisticated enough to generate testable predictions about future levels of drug use. Reflecting the complex, multidimensional nature of drug use, the best starting points for developing a conceptual model of prevalence trends are probably in three very different disciplines and approaches, namely: epidemiological models of the spread of drug use between individuals and groups (e.g. Hunt and Chambers, 1967); economic models of supply and demand factors in drugs markets (e.g. Bramley-Harker, 2001); and ethnographic accounts of the experiential world and social context of drug users (e.g. Preble and Casey, 1969).

One theoretical idea that has emerged from researchers' interpretations of trends in the prevalence of drug use is the 'normalisation hypothesis' – the claim that drug use has become normalised among young adults in Britain (e.g. Measham, Newcombe and Parker, 1994; Parker, Aldridge and Measham, 1998b, Parker, 2001). However, there is some debate about the validity of this conclusion – for instance, Shiner and Newburn argue that 'the notion of normalization exaggerates levels of youthful drug use' (1999:156). However, two types of normalisation need to be assessed: statistical normalisation means that more than 50 per cent indicate the behaviour; while cultural normalisation means that the behaviour is increasingly perceived and responded to as morally acceptable (or tolerable) behaviour. The question of cultural normalisation of drug use may not be decided by empirical evidence alone, since it is based on complex claims about the growing use of drug-related ideas and images in the mass media and consumer world, and the increasing use of drug-related concepts and terms in everyday language and life (South, 1999) (see Chapters 1 and 3).

But research evidence is clearly relevant to the issue of statistical normalisation, though only one indicator clearly and directly supports the hypothesis, namely: lifetime use of any drug among young adults, which was reported by over half in some recent BCS reports. This is largely attributable to the growth of cannabis use, and, allowing for underestimation in surveys, lifetime cannabis use is probably also statistically normalised among young adults. However, past-year and past-month drug use are not statistically normalised in the general youth population, nor is the prevalence of lifetime use of any drugs other than cannabis (Shiner and Newburn, 1997). Even so, there is evidence that past-year use of cannabis and other drugs may be statistically normalised in some population sub-groups, such as students and offenders. More relevantly, normalisation of drug use in the broadest sense applies not just to levels of prevalence, but also to drugs consumption and related mental states – notably, knowledge of drugs, exposure to drug-taking, acquaintanceship with drug users, access to drugs, and attitudes to drugs and drug policies. For instance, various evidence shows that over the past two or three decades, the propor-tions of young adults who report having been offered drugs, being able to get drugs easily, knowing drug users, and having pro-drug attitudes have gradually changed from a minority to a majority in each case (Newcombe, 1999; Parker, Aldridge and Measham, 1998b; Balding, 2000; Wright and Pearl, 2000). This broader statistical normalisation of drug involvements is increasingly evident among young adults for five illicit drugs: after canna-bis, these include cocaine, ecstasy, amphetamines and poppers.

Although the debate on normalisation is likely to continue, there can be little argument that rates of illicit drug use in the UK have risen fairly con-sistently for four decades, though a plateau stage may have been reached. This fact strongly supports the conclusion that prohibition is ineffective and should be replaced with an alternative drug policy, though supporters of the status quo have interpreted it as justifying continued prohibition – based on the assumption that the 'war on drugs' has just not yet been applied for long or hard enough. Though failure to meet policy targets has been partly tackled by revamping the national policy, it has also resulted in the targets being revised – or, more precisely in the case of some targets, downgraded (see Chapters 8, 9 and 10). As noted in the introduction, the UK's current set of about two dozen targets, which employ a 2002 baseline, are heav-ily based on two sets of performance indicators which generally measure (a) the contact rates and service delivery of organisations and agencies working with drug users, or (b) reductions in drug-related harms such as crime and death. Only a single target is directly aimed at changing behav-iour, though this key target actually breaks down into two targets, both focused on under-25s, namely: reducing the prevalence of Class A drug use, and reducing frequent drug use. Unfortunately, this two-part target does not distinguish the type of prevalence to be changed (lifetime, past-year, past-month), it specifies only the direction and not the level of change, and, like the other targets, it is not drug-specific (i.e. it concerns either Class A drugs or all drugs).

In conclusion, if policy-makers are serious about setting and assessing targets as the best scientific method for evaluating the effectiveness of drug strategy, then as well as designing more complete targets, they need to recognise the critical role that drug prevalence and consumption research should play in this evaluation. This is because they constitute primary measures of the two core principles from which all drug policy aims and objectives are generated: abstinence (reducing the number of people who use drugs) and risk/harm reduction (reducing risky consumption behaviour and consequent harms) (Newcombe, 2005). Each type of drug use is associated with particular risks and harms, and, alongside general responses (e.g. drugs education) most types of drug use attract particular responses or interventions (e.g. the National Crack Plan, cannabis reclassification). Thus, it seems reasonable that we should establish explicit prevalence and consumption targets for each type of drug or drug use if we are to properly implement and evaluate our national strategy.

Further Reading

Bennett, T., and Holloway, K. (2005). *Understanding Drugs, Alcohol and Crime*, Milton Keynes: Open University Press.
Bramley-Harker, E. (2001). *Sizing the UK Drugs Market*. London: Home Office.
Parker, H., Aldridge, J., and Egginton, R. (eds) (2001). *UK Drugs Unlimited: New Research and Policy Lessons on Illicit Drugs*. Basingstoke: Palgrave.

Study Questions

1. Briefly outline trends in the prevalence of the consumption of *different* drugs in Britain over the past 20 years.
2. Compare and contrast the strengths and weaknesses of different ways of measuring drug prevalence.
3. In what ways can research on – and the measurement of – drug prevalence be improved?

3

'See Emily Play': Youth Culture, Recreational Drug Use and Normalisation

Shane Blackman

Introduction

In recent years 'drug normalisation' has become a fashionable term to describe young people's consumption of recreational drugs. The chapter will be divided into two parts and will look at the connections between popular culture and drugs. The first section will examine the relationship between youth culture and recreational drug use through a series of representations including film, pulp fiction literature and popular music. The idea is to selectively map out the images and ideas of recreational drug consumption in terms of their potential influence on young people. I shall argue that youth culture and recreational drug consumption have been a constant commercial strategy used by capitalism to attract income generation. The second section of the chapter will critically address the dimensions of the drug 'normalisation' thesis, looking at the origins of the term, its specific definition by Howard Parker. Then I shall assess the challenge of the drug normalisation theory to drug prevention and consider in detail some of its criticisms. But I shall start the chapter with a short personal encounter with drugs.

Biographical Subcultural Encounter

On a winter Saturday morning, when I was 12 years old, I went on a bus journey to the seaside port of Folkestone. The trip was about 15 miles from my home and it was one of my first long excursions by myself. I was excited, it was a windy day, my long hair was whipping against my face as I moved from record shop to clothes shop in my long warm coat. At school my friends had spoken about so-called 'youth subcultures' that 'lived' in the town. Making my way to the bus garage to go home to my village, I was a little disappointed because I had failed to see any of these 'youth cultures'. Naively, I must have imagined that they would be visible somewhat like mannequins in a shop-front window. With 20 minutes to wait for the bus I strolled around the back of the bus station, where I saw a group of seven young people dressed differently, who stood out from the crowd. They were older teenagers having fun. One tall young man walked over, stood close, leant over me and whispered in my ear, 'Have you got any stuff?' I thought for a second, breathed in, stood straight, trying to suggest I was knowledgeable and cool, and said slowly, 'No, not at the moment', shaking my head to appear disappointed. He said, 'OK, man.' The bus arrived. I showed my ticket and sat at the back, thinking, 'Stuff'. What is 'stuff'? As the bus moved along with stops and starts I looked out of the window at the sea. I began to daydream and drift, thinking that I had come into contact with a subculture, but what was this stuff that they wanted?

Popular Culture: Youth and Drugs – a Commercial Strategy of the Culture Industry

For nearly a century youth and drugs has been an attractive theme in mass popular culture to encourage consumption. Comics, film, popular music and pulp fiction novels are mediums that have manipulated and promoted representations of young drug fiends as exciting and dangerous. The anxiety created by these cultural images quickly became a means to encourage further commercial exploitation via the theme of 'youth out of control'. These twentieth-century culture industries built on the Victorian moral panic focused on 'penny gaffs' and 'penny dreadfuls', where entrepreneurs crafted a product to meet the market demand for thrilling entertainment (Springhall, 1998). Mass-produced urban youth culture, initially on stage[1] and then in film, became a commercial success targeted at not only young people but also a wider adult audience. The new mass product appeared to present youth in their natural setting but these representations were a vehicle for increased political control of young people (Pearson, 1984). The artificial construction of deviant youth became the means whereby cultural products were advertised as sensational entertainment (Roberts, 1971). Youth became a fantasised attraction for adults and society, where fear and pleasure combined restlessly to promote attention and increase revenue through consumption.

The two films that set the modern standard for identifying young people as victims of drug and sex cravings were *Assassin of Youth* (1935) and *Reefer Madness* (1936). The narrative of both films imposes a reading on the audience to see the power of intoxication destroying the innocence of youth through drug seduction, which results in immorality, madness and murder. Exploitation movies were produced during the early days of the film industry, for example *The White Slave Trade* (1911).[2] The early exploitation cinema dealt with forbidden subjects such as sex and drugs, which were difficult for Hollywood to cover as a result of its moral disgrace in the early 1920s (Anger, 1975; Starks, 1982). The introduction of the Motion Picture Production Code in 1934 affirmed the position of drugs and youth corruption as one of the most attractive features of exploitation films, which toured different states in America. Exploitation movies traded under any banner: for example, 'adult entertainment', 'bare bold facts never told before', 'not recommended for children', 'dope-created ecstasy avalanching into frightful perversions', 'see what happens to thousands of high school girls yearly – when smoke gets in their eyes at reefer parties', 'it daringly exposes the moral decay of this younger generation' (Stevenson, 2000).

The post-1945 world of drugs and youth corruption flourished in pulp fiction literature, with lurid titles and sexually provocative covers explicitly promoting the links between intoxication, drug crime and the moral corruption of the young within a context of youth culture. Examples include David Dodge's *It Ain't Hay* (1946), Thurston Scott's *I'll Get Mine* (1951), C. R. Cooper's *Teen-age Vice* (1952), Luke Roberts's *Reefer Club* (1953), Leroy Street's *I Was a Drug Addict* (1953), Wenzell Brown's *Gang Girl* (1954), Jane Manning's *Reefer Girl* (1956), Ernie Weatherall's *Rock 'n Roll Gal* (1957), Jack Gerstine's *Play it Cool* (1959), Morton Cooper's *Anything for Kicks* (1959) and Valerie Jordan's *I Am a Teen Age Dope Addict* (1959). These novels were not authentic and bore little relation to empirical social research undertaken on young people (Brake, 1980). This literature represented a fantasised construction of youth and drugs sold to an adult audience who succumbed to easy voyeuristic pleasures. Popular fiction of the 1950s in America and Britain was heavily influenced by the anti-drug propaganda of Harry Anslinger at the Federal Bureau of Narcotics. He used the mediums of print, radio, film and television to deliver anti-drug propaganda based on his construction of psychotic youth under the influence of narcotics (McWilliams, 1990; Melechi, 1997).

Social realism within the context of literature focusing on young people and drugs emerged when Nelson Algren wrote *The Man with the Golden Arm* in 1949 and William Burroughs published *Junky*[3] in 1953. These modern novels revitalised the narcotic literary tradition established by Thomas De Quincey and then Aldous Huxley, but it was left to Jack Kerouac in *On the Road* (1957) and Colin MacInnes in *Absolute Beginners* (1959) to weave together young people in the context of drug culture. In both novels the dominant visual image of young people is coolness, while at the same time individuals are restless. They are searching for authenticity and pleasurable experience, but encounter hostility and deception and feel alienated. Drug consumption is identified as part of their cultural practice, shown as a routine activity. Recreational drug use was part of their scene, but it was not the scene itself; this error of misinterpretation is commonly found within drug prevention analysis.

More recently there have been five major films which build on the narrative of social realism, portraying the positive and negative impact of drug consumption among young people: *Easy Rider* (1969), *Saturday Night Fever* (1978), *Quadrophenia* (1979), *Trainspotting* (1995) and *Human Traffic* (1999). These films not only received awards but are also critically recognised as landmarks within this genre and are referential to youth cultural backdrops including rocker, mod, disco and rave (Blackman, 2004). With each film the soundtrack is intimately related to the social relations and context of drug normalisation. The films contain songs which have drug reference points as part of their recreational practices. Each of these films has been accused of encouraging drug consumption, through making intoxication a glamorous activity, but such an interpretation demonstrates a superficial reading (Shapiro, 2003). While in each film we see young people experiencing pleasure as a result of their drug consumption, yet we also see a conventional love story, personal struggle, sorrow and death. Drugs are clearly an intimate feature in the portrayal of these young people's actions, but we see them encounter danger and also show a willingness to suspend their drug consumption. These youth culture films celebrate the beautiful messiness of young people's lives, their fears, hopes and forms of estrangement. The success of these films relates to their personal and human biographical narrative. The characters create opportunities for empathy and the audience responds with agency. It is no paradox to argue that these films contain anti-drug messages for the audience to decode and critically assess, whereas the earlier films about drugs and young people conformed to the classic film theory where the cinema and its spectators are seen as conforming to a mechanistic reproduction of reality. The early drug exploitation films imposed one single message that drug consumption was a negative experience (Stevenson, 2000). Drug prohibition defined youth culture as a 'nest' for drug fiends and sought to achieve abstinence through negative representations of intoxication: this is the origin of death-led drug education (Blackman, 1996). This prevention strategy has subsequently been inverted and now films such as *Reefer Madness* and *High School Confidential* are recognised comedy classics (Shapiro, 2003).

Popular Music and Drugs

For over a century popular music has played a central part in the common culture of young people (Bailey, 1978; Thompson, 1991). Dick Hebdige in

Subculture: The Meaning of Style (1979) argued that modern popular music exercises a major determining influence over the development of youth subcultural style. In this sense music and youth culture can be seen as a symbolic meeting ground for young people. A fellow contributor to *Resistance through Rituals*, Iain Chambers (1981:38), suggested that music is put to use in youth subcultures through multiple narratives and practices as a series of critical interventions both intentional and reflective. Applying Claude Lévi-Strauss's idea, Chambers argues that pop music is 'good to think with'. Such a claim would appear to be at odds with Simon Frith's (1983) understanding of the work of cultural theorist Theodor Adorno. Frith identifies Adorno's analysis of popular music as a searing challenge to anyone who can see value in it. In popular-music studies Adorno is cast as the 'bad guy' who relentlessly harps on about popular music as a 'culture of degeneration' which encourages conformity through consumption of standardised products. While this position is perfectly clear, another reading is possible where Adorno (1999:12) argues: 'The criterion of the social truth of music today is the extent to which it enters into opposition to society from which it springs and in which it has its being – in short, the extent to which it becomes critical, however indirectly.' I want to argue that one way in which we can identify popular music as being critical is through the coverage of drugs within songs by popular-music artists. Popular music has a critical and subversive potential to deliver a range of messages about drugs themselves, drug experience and drug consumption through lyrics and related visual imagery.

Harry Shapiro in *Waiting for the Man* (1988) argues that the relationship between drugs and popular music has been historical and intimate. Even before Anslinger managed to usher in the *Marijuana Tax Act* (1937), black jazz musicians tended to use phrases in songs which restricted drug meaning through the use of argot. Charlie Hore (1993:93) argues that during the 1920s and 1930s drug consumption by black jazz musicians and their audience was closely related to their space and location in subcultural settings. This began to change with the introduction of the Hollywood film industry to drug songs such as 'Reefer Man', 'Minnie the Moocher', 'Kick the Gong Around' and 'Sweet Marijuana' by artists such as Cab Calloway and Gertrude Michael, and then through the publication of Mezz Mezzrow's book *Really the Blues* in 1946 with its heady biographical drug narrative of jazz musicians of the period.

By the 1950s black jazz musicians including Charlie Parker, John Coltrane, Billie Holiday and Miles Davis had troubling drug problems and suffered under Anslinger's 'star bust' drug policy. Drug consumption for these artists was experienced as another reality in their creative effort to challenge and escape white cultural hegemony (Townsend, 2000). Within black musical forms, songs about drugs were focused on everyday life, fun and danger, and drugs themselves could be part of a musical experimentation with sound. The primary reality for blacks in American society was racism, and drugs were simply another means whereby they were discriminated against (Neal, 1999).

In the early years of rock 'n' roll, drugs such as amphetamine were part of the infrastructure of maintaining television performances or constant tours, as shown by the Beatles in their Hamburg days in the film *Backbeat* (1993). In the new white modern pop boom of the 1960s drug reference points became more diverse but still sought to escape censorship and challenge state drug controls. During the 1960s and 1970s the Beatles,[4] the Rolling Stones, the Who,[5] the Small Faces,[6] the Byrds,[7] the Velvet Underground,[8] the Doors[9] and Pink Floyd[10] admitted to drug consumption and then projected these experiences in songs back to their specific audience but also to the public in general. In the 1960s drug normalisation was considerable with the 'flower power' movement, 'legalise pot' demonstrations; the centrality of psychedelia was shown by the Move's 'Flowers in the Rain' being the first record played on Radio 1 and the Beatles' financial and public support for cannabis was shown through the letter published in *The Times* in 1967.[11]

Drug normalisation was a major feature of popular music in the 1960s and 1970s through coverage in the alternative magazines such as *Oz*. These radical pamphlets did not put forward a blanket acceptance towards drugs; their position could be described as 'critical drug normalization' (Nelson, 1989:92–96). From the 1960s (the Beatles' 'Yellow Submarine', an homage to LSD) to the 1990s (Noel Gallagher's comment that cannabis is like a 'cup of tea'),[12] recreational drugs have been a mainstream feature of popular music. In different decades a range of popular music icons became identified as spokespersons for hallucination. In the 1960s the Grateful Dead's Jerry Garcia was the God of acid. One of the leading figures of drugs during the 1970s was Bob Marley, who symbolised pop musicians who spoke of their drug experience in songs and used images of drug consumption on album covers. Then in the 1980s, in the case of Aerosmith's Joe Perry and Steven Tyler, their nickname of 'the Toxic Twins' told its own story. More recently, on a voyeuristic note, pop musicians have begun to reflect on their drug consumption and also recant their sins publicly; examples include Elton John and David Bowie, and then George Michael and Robbie Williams[13]. Television appearances of pop icons discussing their drug experiences are now common. Ozzy Osbourne's tales of drug adventure are laced with humour and a sense of reflection, while Francis Rossi's[14] public performances of threading a handkerchief in one nostril and out the other, due to long-term cocaine use, turns into a voyeuristic side-show of embarrassment. Meanwhile, other pop icons, such as Brian Epstein, Andy Gibb, Sid Vicious, Marvin Gaye and Kurt Cobain, got caught in a deadly whirlpool of drug consumption without support. Those who survive also become infamous for their attendance at drug rehabilitation centres: Brian Wilson, Marianne Faithfull, Eric Clapton, Keith Richards, David Gahan, Marc Almond, Shaun Ryder, Jason Pierce, Courtney Love, Richard Ashcroft, etc. These drug survivors in turn become reference points for popular-music drug mythology as represented within the music press and daily newspapers.

One area seldom considered by drug prohibition is the production of anti-drug songs by famous musicians. Classic anti-drug songs have bleak reference points, such as the Velvet Underground's 'Heroin', John Lennon's 'Cold Turkey', Curtis Mayfield's 'Freddie's Dead', Steppenwolf's 'Pusherman', Melle Mel's 'White Lines (Don't Do It)', Neil Young's 'Needle and the Damage Done' or 4 Hero's 'Mr Kirk's Nightmare'. The songs are critical of drugs but at the same time they carry a subtext which is also critical of society through their words or the context in which they are delivered. These songs remain classic pieces of popular music with an anti-drug message, in contrast to more direct anti-drug songs such as 'Just Say No', by the *Grange Hill* cast (1986), which is seen as government's anti-drug propaganda. The cultural complexity of anti-drug songs is shaped by the social intricacy of people's lives and their understanding of society. This is reflected in the genre of rap and garage, for example, Public Enemy's 'Night of the Living Baseheads', NWA's 'Dopeman', Two Live Crew's 'In the Dust', A Tribe Called Quest's 'Can I Kick It', Cypress Hill's 'Hits from the Bong', Snoop Doggy Dogg's *Doggystyle*, D12's 'Purple Pills', Ms. Dynamite's 'Natural High' or the drug references peppered in the debut albums from So Solid Crew (*They Don't Know*), The Streets (*Original Pirate Material*) or Dizzee Rascal (*Boy in da Corner*). In these examples drugs are a subject brought from the musicians' experience and reflect their social aspirations. Many of these songs contain negative references to drugs, but at the same time some may support the use of cannabis, for example Nightmares on Wax. Meanwhile, at other times the descriptions of drugs offered are an integrated part of the musicians' personal social background and cultural experience. They are not seeking to encourage use and in many instances are positively encouraging youth to take a 'straight edge'. Thus the topic of drugs within the popular-music song is an integral feature: they represent one source of material alongside others.

To conclude this section it is suggested that drugs have always featured within popular songs. A broad range of pop musicians has consistently spoken about drugs, taken drugs and written songs about drugs or used drugs as a source of creativity to construct a song or piece of music (Whiteley, 1997). In the 1920s Jelly Roll Morton and Louis Armstrong declared their love for 'Mary Warner'[15] and the latter wrote 'Muggles' in 1928, an early homage to cannabis. The Beatles LP *Revolver* (1966) distinctly reveals the impact of drug consumption. On 'Tomorrow Never Knows' John Lennon describes the beauty of hallucinogens. It was no different in the punk era of the late 1970s, when Ian Dury defined the myth of excesses with his song 'Sex and Drugs and Rock 'n' Roll'. Or, in the twenty-first century with Afroman's ironic No. 1 hit 'Because I Got High'. These selected examples demonstrate that songs about drugs in popular music are part of young people's everyday cultural experience, their humour, problems and relaxation. It might appear that in the twenty-first century there is a closer relationship between drugs and popular music, but this appearance is shaped by a series of factors. The popular music industry has grown considerably within the last 50 years. Before 1945 pop was a global product, but now it has become more diversified and intensified in its production (Negus, 1998). Popular music is a mass-market product with a vast array of distinct musical genres. Within these musical genres drugs find expression in the form of experience, warnings, humour and creativity and become part of recreational activities within a youth cultural setting (Toynbee, 2000). On this basis the coverage of recreational drugs within popular music has increased due to the expansion and diversification of the industry.

Four Phases of Youth Culture and Recreational Drug Consumption

Drug consumption as a feature of youth culture is subject to fashion and variation. At certain times a youth culture may be identified with one dominant drug, for example rave culture with ecstasy or hippie culture with LSD, but at the same time the drug most often consumed was cannabis. Thus, certain recreational drugs become selected symbols of the specialised semiotic of a youth cultural style (Blackman, 1995). It is possible to argue that there have been four major movements of contemporary recreational drug consumption within youth culture. These distinct phases of intensive recreational substance use could be described as periods of increased drug normalisation. These can be specified as:

- beat culture and heroin;
- mod culture and amphetamine;
- hippie culture and LSD; and
- dance culture and ecstasy.

The first phase of youth culture and recreational drug consumption is linked to Beat culture. The Beat movement of the 1950s had close associations with the drugs of heroin and cannabis. The Beats located themselves in coffee shops and jazz clubs to perform radical and intellectual poetry. The leading writers of the Beat Generation,[16] Jack Kerouac, Allen Ginsberg and William Burroughs, consciously developed a casual informal style of dress, which altered, according to Ted Polhemus (1994:31), when jazz musicians such as Miles Davis toured Paris in the 1950s meeting intellectuals from the city including Jean-Paul Sartre and Simone de Beauvoir. He states: 'What became known as "Beat Style" was actually Left-Bank style through the dark shades of American jazz musicians.' By the late 1950s Davis had fused French intellectualisation with Italian fashion to promote contemporary modernism linked with drug use and coolness (Carr, Case and Dellar, 1986).

The intellectual literary nucleus of Beat icons produced novels and poems[17] where drugs were an important narrative through which the lives of their characters struggled and sought freedom. They fused Eastern mysticism and existentialism with an altered state through drug consciousness. These authors consumed drugs and wrote drug narratives, although this did not prevent them from being critical of and hostile towards drugs. They saw drugs as a means to enhance an artistic project: Burroughs (1967:276) states cannabis is 'very useful to the artist, activating trains of association that would otherwise be inaccessible ... opiates on the other hand, since they diminish awareness of surroundings and bodily processes, can only be a hindrance to the artists'.

Ned Polsky (1961:166) in his study on the Beat subculture in New York during the late 1950s showed that the majority of the Beats were middle class with a small number of upper-class members. Beats were affluent and possessed time with a disposable income, and Polsky states that 'Beats who use no illegal drugs are few'. The Beats worshipped jazz bebop and were besotted with 'becoming black', as described by Norman Mailer's *The White Negro* (1957), in their experimentation with bohemian values. The Beats' taste for drug consumption became part of their cultural practice and drug prohibition was interpreted by them as punitive. Therefore, freedom to consume drugs became their rallying cry for liberty. Drugs within Beat youth culture became an intimate part of their campaign for expression, individual rights and freedom from oppression. Recreational drugs became an integral part of middle-class individualism and personal liberty. American culture viewed these cultural experimentations with suspicion, but did not see these actions as threatening to the American Dream. In a certain sense the Beats were using intoxicants as their means to investigate the idealism of the American Dream.

The second major movement of contemporary recreational drug use came to public attention through the front page headline of the *Sunday Mirror*, 31 May 1964: 'Exposing The Drug Menace'. It stated: 'A nationwide check reveals that nearly 10,000 teenagers are buying pep-pills and narcotics on the black-market.' Conventional history explains that mod youth culture began in 1964 and this is affirmed by Stan Cohen's (1972) classic study about their media creation, *Folk Devils and Moral Panics*. More recently, a series of ethnographic and biographical texts have emerged which document the origins of mods from the mid-1950s (Hewitt, 1999; Hewitt, 2000; Rawlings, 2000; Lentz, 2002). For Richard Barnes[18] and John Simons[19] the jazz modernist melange of black coolness and French and Italian style became absorbed by mods in 1962, transforming them into a mass happening. The first sign of public recognition came in that year when *Town* magazine interviewed three so-called 'Faces of the London Scene', one of whom was Marc Bolan, aged 14.

Dick Hebdige (1975:89) states in *The Meaning of Mod*: 'Speed was needed to keep mind and body synchronized perfectly.' Drugs were a dynamic feature within mod culture, from dancing to shopping. During the early 1960s A. Linken (1963) and A. Sharpley (1964) undertook a series of journalistic investigations on the all-night dance and coffee bar culture of young people. Linken describes the different types of drug consumption among a range of youth, from university students and the young aristocracy to ordinary adolescent boys who attended grammar schools.[20] Sharpley in a series of articles looks in detail at mod drug use.[21] One of her articles was titled 'My Pep Pill Soho Trip' and speaks of teenagers freely moving from dance clubs to cafés, consuming large amounts of purple hearts. The subject of young drug taking was also covered by cartoonist Paul Temple in the London *Evening News*.[22] Through media coverage and increased government concern drugs became a legitimate discourse whereby young people's behaviour, in particular working-class youth, could be 'objectively' discussed and strategies devised to intervene and demand suitable adjustment. Recreational substance use was now identified as an intentional delinquent action. After mod, drug use by young people was seen as criminal deviance; thus recreational drug consumption became defined as a major social problem and also a professional psychiatric preoccupation (Blackman, 2004).

The third phase of youth culture and recreational drug consumption was part of the hippie counter culture. During the late 1960s and into the 1970s the range of hippie styles of dress, music, ideas, philosophy and living rapidly penetrated wider youth culture and continue significantly today through festivals, protest culture and its critique of Western technocracy (Marcuse, 1964; Roszak, 1970; McKay, 1996; Klein, 2000). In the hippie era the politics of recreational drugs emerged when members of the Beatles and the Rolling Stones were brought before the judiciary accused of drug possession (Shapiro, 1988). As a result of their mass popularity irrespective of the legal judgement these pop icons became drug martyrs. The belief in recreational drug consumption was a key feature of this youth culture, as a result of what Stuart Hall (1968:15) identified as the hippie critique of middle-class society as 'repressed', 'artificial', 'constrained' and 'inauthentic'. He states for the hippie youth culture: 'There is only one way to recover this rich, hidden utopia within the self: through the medium of mind-expanding drugs.'

During the 1960s a leading voice of recreational drugs was Timothy Leary, who become the counter culture's first international drug hero. He was an intellectual from Harvard University, but he was also a drug evangelist who promoted the idea of drug consumption as a valuable experience to improve society. In *The Politics of Ecstasy* he elaborated his idea of 'turn on, tune in, drop out'. The dominant American political establishment viciously disliked Leary's advocacy of LSD. Throughout his life he was hounded by the police[23] and was called by President Richard Nixon 'the most dangerous man in America' (Lee and Shlain, 1992). Leary was a major player in the third phase of recreational drug use through his advocacy for drugs, his connections with elite figures from popular culture and the manner in which he inspired 'the people' of the counter culture to move forward.

Alongside Leary another powerful influence on 1960s and 1970s youth culture was Carlos Castaneda. Both figures came from respectable academic backgrounds and were celebrated as part of an intellectual student community. Castaneda's first work was based on his Ph.D. and published as *The Teachings of Don Juan: A Yaqui Way of Knowledge*. His subsequent books were highly popular and he quickly became a guru for the power of altered consciousness. Castaneda's work was assimilated into the counter culture with its focus on the unreason of Western science and the pursuit of visionary experience and wisdom (Silverman, 1975; Bancroft, 1978; Drury, 1979). The impact of intellectual recreational drug use within middle-class counter cultures settled initially on the elite culture of the university, then moved into popular culture through alternative magazines such as *Oz* and *International Times*, and finally powerfully invaded mainstream culture through popular music. Like Leary and Castaneda, The Beatles also chose to look East and set up camp at the Maharishi Mahesh Yogi's ashram in 1968 (Salzman, 2000). The political resonance of the third phase of recreational drugs was its political connotation that Western culture was deadening the soul and humanity had lost direction. Recreational drug consumption was no longer understood as a criminal problem related to mod youth culture; it was now asserted to be an international political problem that threatened to destabilise Western society through both communism and terrorism (Young, 1971; McCoy, 1991).

The fourth phase of youth culture and recreational drug consumption is contemporary rave. During the 1980s, prior to acid house, the media focused on the dangers of ecstasy,[24] but it was not until the arrival of a new youth culture that the tabloids were able to harness the full potential of youth and drugs into a moral panic.[25] The sex, drugs and rock 'n' roll myth began once again with a new folk devil. In contrast and at the same time, youth culture magazines, for example *The Face, the NME, Melody Maker* and *Boy's Own*,[26] gave detailed and insider perspectives on recreational drugs within acid house and in the 1990s Nicholas Saunders[27] with his book *E for Ecstasy* became the British ecstasy drugs guru.

With the birth of acid house, its development into rave and its further transmutation into dance culture, drug reference points in the era described as the 'chemical generation' have become increasingly normalised. The most effective advertisement for drug normalisation and successful branding of an illicit product in the twenty-first century has been the application of the name 'ecstasy' to the drug itself. Unlike other illegal drugs, ecstasy leads from the front by describing a positive intoxication in the label. The drug requires little by way of explanation for potential users. As ecstasy culture expanded beyond its illegal warehouses into clubs and into mainstream popular music, drug normalisation took the format of band names, including Drugstore, Sheep on Drugs, Dope Smugglaz, the Chemical Brothers, Doves, the Shamen, etc., and also record labels, including Acid Jazz, Bong Load, Chemikal Underground, Loaded, etc. However, there is nothing new in bands seeking to name themselves after drug meaning, as shown by Jim Morrison's adaptation of Aldous Huxley's *The Doors of Perception*, published in 1954.

The central position of recreational drugs within rave youth culture has been well documented by Matthew Collin and John Godfrey's *Altered State* (1997), Simon Reynolds's *Energy Flash* (1998) and Sheryl Garrett's *Adventures in Wonderland* (1998). Furthermore, these cultural texts in themselves have contributed to the consolidation of recreational drugs as part of the drug normalisation process where musicians and DJs describe gigs, festivals and raves in terms of their holistic drug experience. What is apparent in their descriptions of the origins and expansion of ecstasy culture is that it has been romanticised into a narrative of self-description and cultural aggrandisement where reality and fiction become increasingly difficult to distinguish, for example, Wayne Anthony's *Class of 88*, Ben Turner's *Ibiza* and Bez's *Freaky Dancin'*. Since the explosion of ecstasy culture there has been a vast expansion of the drug cultural support system of consumer capitalism. Drug merchandise before this period was primarily contextual in that it reflected the general ideas of the time such as psychedelia in the use of colours or textures. The movement towards more direct drug-related merchandise is connected to the right-wing Thatcherite ideological belief in the free market and individual choice (Collin and Godfrey, 1997). Drug cultural products became another commodity with which to pursue profit. The 21st-century phase of recreational drug normalisation has referentially exploited and used the market potential, creative resources and intellectualism belonging to previous periods of drug normalisation. What is new about the latest phase has been the speed in which corporate commerce got into drugs. Ecstasy culture quickly became incorporated into mainstream capitalism, which uses drugs as a marketing strategy for tourism, computer software, perfume, trainers, soft drinks, etc. (Taylor, 2000).

One of the weaknesses in the drug normalisation theory is its apparently excessive preoccupation with the present. I have attempted to address this issue here by showing historically that each phase of contemporary drug normalisation is critically different. For government and media, drugs during the Beat Generation meant social rebellion. For Mods during the 1960s drugs were 'causally' associated with deviance and criminality. For the establishment, the Hippie understanding of drugs was seen as a direct political and moral threat to society, but by the 1990s, the time of the 'Chemical Generation', drugs were identified as a critical resource to promote consumption, and drugs became a marketing strategy within capitalism to sell commodities for profit (Blackman, 2004). This demonstrates that understanding the different roles played by drugs is fundamental to a more critical assessment of their use by individuals and position within society. It is important that we move away from a narrow prohibitionist understanding of drugs, because substances are more than just a matter for prevention. This section has shown how drugs are an integral feature of contemporary cultural identity, production and consumption. One idea which seeks to build on a more flexible and responsive approach towards understanding drugs in society is the normalisation thesis developed by Howard Parker and colleagues, which is critically addressed in the next section.

Understanding Drug Normalisation

Drug normalisation is an idea elaborated by Howard Parker *et al*. He seeks to describe how illicit drugs have moved from being a symbol of crime and deviance to one where drug consumption is an integral part of young people's recreational leisure pursuits, defined by an opportunity of choice. Today, three major factors shape how we understand what is referred to as 'drug normalisation'. Firstly, the Home Office and police present government statistics of drug arrests and drug seizure which demonstrate the greater availability of drugs. Secondly, government departments, including the Home Office, the Department for Education and the Department of Health, and drug agencies (Drugscope, Release) have produced a vast number of drug policy proposals and drug guidance materials focusing on drug regulation, drug prevention and drug education; and thirdly, tabloid newspapers and television have sensationally and extensively covered media personalities, 'drug barons' and victims of drug scandals, drug deaths and drug-related crime. Government, academic researchers and the media have collectively produced an array of different messages that underpin the notion of drug normalisation. On this basis we can see that the drug normalisation debate is not straightforward.

Critics of the drug normalisation thesis as defined by Howard Parker *et al.*, such as Shiner and Newburn (1999:152), assert that there has been an exaggeration of drug use. For them, the normalisation thesis is 'romantic hyperbole' which misleadingly conflates lifetime use with frequency of drug use. Their basic point is that non-users are the majority and drug-users remain the minority because young people are involved in 'desistance' against drugs. Drug issues, however, are never wholly about statistical information or empirical facts (see Chapter 2). Numerical data about drug problems are always supported by information that cites an emotional appeal or targets people's potential fear of drugs. Within the media facts are used to 'articulate' a social problem; for example, the drug related deaths of Leah Betts, Julia Dawes, Lorna Spinks or Rachel Whitear[28], who featured on the front-pages of tabloid newspapers. These selected social narratives are appeals where empathy and sympathy are combined to convince the reader or viewer that drugs are a major danger to society. Drug problems affect real people and the drug user can be victim and perpetrator at the same time (Blackman, 2004). For government and media, drug normalisation has been taken as an evidence for increased punitive regulation because drug normalisation is defined as drug epidemic (Hunt and Stevens, 2004). This understanding of drug normalisation is questionable, however, as it amounts to a re-caste strategy of 'shock-horror' tactics which are acknowledged to have failed to decrease substance use. This strategy's primary purpose is to heighten 'respectable fears' of intoxicants (O' Connor, O' Connor and Best, 1998). Drug prohibition is using the drug normalisation issue as a political and moral weapon to advance a superior position of rationality and morality, claiming that drug prevention is scientific and objective. Such a positivist approach towards prohibition will fail until it reflects on the words of Jesse Jackson (1991:223) that 'the "wars on drugs" have often been as corrupt as the drug culture itself'. Drug information and the 'Drug War' debate[29] is never straightforward – it is highly charged and subject to misinterpretation through personal accusation and moral campaigns; drug normalisation is a complex social and cultural narrative.[30]

Drug Normalisation Theory

The 'drug normalisation thesis' has emerged over a number of years from the work of Howard Parker. Parker and his research team in a series of publications have interpreted data from longitudinal studies of young people's regular substance consumption. Parker, Williams and Aldridge (2002:943) argue that drug 'normalization is a multi-dimensional tool, a barometer of changes in social behaviour and cultural perspectives'. Thus, Parker's purpose is to use the theory to assess 'sensible' recreational drug taking. The theory of drug normalisation is outlined in Parker, Aldridge and Measham (1998b:152); it specifies that it 'refers only to the use of certain drugs, primarily cannabis but also nitrites, amphetamines and equivocally LSD and ecstasy. Heroin and cocaine are not included in the thesis. Similarly chaotic combination drug use and dependent "daily" drug use form no part of our conceptualization.' They argue that there are six dimensions to the normalisation thesis: drug availability, drug trying, drug use, being drug-wise, future intentions and cultural accommodation of the illicit. In addition, drug normalisation describes the wider cultural process of an apparent increase in the availability of drugs, which indicates an increased acceptance of drug use. Thus, normalisation suggests drug use has become more conventional and integrated into certain people's lives. The evidence put forward for drug normalisation by Parker *et al.* is broadly twofold: statistical data, which specify large numbers of young people who claim to have used drugs, in terms of frequency and regularity, and changes in culture, which they identify as being more drug centred.

Parker (2001) offers more details on the conceptual origins of his idea about drug normalisation, which describes the theory in terms of developments in European sociology, and it is also possible to see how he has been influenced by American sociological writing on deviance by Howard S. Becker and Erving Goffman (who advanced labelling theory). The work of these symbolic interactionists and ethnomethodologists was to problematise the everyday, examine the micro features of people's lives and describe how individuals make their daily negotiations. Parker locates his work within this school of thought, which is concerned with using ideas and languages which can describe people's activities without discrimination. The theoretical problem Parker is advancing derives from David Matza's (1969) idea of bringing the so-called deviant drug user into conventional understanding by suggesting there is a closer relation between deviants and those individuals who are understood to be normal through an examination of shared practices and values. By bringing 'deviant' and 'normal' together Parker has unsettled the sharp boundaries of drug prohibition to assert that illicit drug consumers have been 'spotlighted' for their apparent criminal action in a manner that makes their behaviour appear more distinctive than it really is. The dominant discourses of drug enforcement and regulation such as medicine, psychiatry and international law precisely define and set cultural and legal boundaries. Parker's challenge is supported by Nigel South (1999:9), who argues that drug control policies are dependent on rigorous boundaries which define drug users as 'outside normal cultures'.

The morality of public policy and the objectivity of science articulate an understanding of drug consumers which defines their dual status as both outside and inside society. This double positioning establishes a tautology of 'othering': it enables the legitimate discourses to define drug users as not normal, i.e. outsiders, while at the same time it also has the authority to invoke disciplinary procedures to reform or punish individuals before they are allowed to return to society to become insiders (Foucault, 1977). This section has argued that drug normalisation is an attractive concept and it is an easy term to employ, but it raises major questions for primary drug prevention which are discussed in the next section.

Critical Assessment of Drug Normalisation

It is important to critically assess Howard Parker's theory alongside his ideal of wanting to disturb the boundary between deviant and normal. Adrian Barton (2003:120) argues that Parker's drug normalisation thesis 'carries many challenges for the politician and policy maker'. Drug prohibition has a major problem accepting the normalisation thesis because the so-called 'recreational drugs' listed by Parker, including ecstasy and LSD, are defined as Class A drugs and are regarded as highly dangerous. The British government's formal classification of these drugs actively refuses to accept any degree of normalisation or acceptability. In this sense the theory of normalisation challenges the rationale and justification of the legitimate classification of drugs specified by the United Nations. The normalisation thesis appears to support but also challenge the distinction between so-called 'soft' and 'hard' drugs. By labelling cannabis, LSD and ecstasy as 'soft drugs' belonging to young people's recreational leisure practices Parker opposes their formal classification as Class A dangerous drugs.

Another major challenge to Parker's idea, according to Shildrick (2002:46), is that 'the whole principle of normalization suggests something subjective'. The consequence has been that drug normalisation theory has been criticised for being too expansive, over simplistic, reliant on the distinction between recreational and dependent drug use and exaggerated. The criticism of the theory as being too subjective is directed at Parker's philosophical research methodology. Parker's idea of drug normalisation has been criticised by Shiner and Newburn (1997, 1999) and Ramsay and Partridge (1999) as 'inaccurate' at a methodological level. These critics assert that the normalisation thesis follows too closely the voice of the researched, i.e. drug consumers, in a biographical or descriptive sense and presents the data as naturalistic. Examples of recent empirical studies on young people and drugs – such as Malbon (1999), Hammersley, Khan and Di Hon (2002) and Jackson (2004) – also present the data to show the complexity of drug consumption but at the same time wish to argue through the use of their qualitative data that young people are normal even though they are substance users. The key argument is that participants who consume drugs are assessed to be as normal as the people who do not consume. The theoretical and methodological purpose of Parker's work and other recent studies is to highlight the extent of non-deviant drug consumption through the application of qualitative data and demonstrate the rationality and reason behind sensible recreational substance consumption.

Parker *et al.* (1998b:159) argue that the validity of their account rests on a 'grounded strategy' where truth is seen to derive from the voice with which 'respondents have spoken to us'. Parker's approach is based on symbolic interactionism, and more specifically on the use of Becker's (1963) labelling theory. Shiner and Newburn (1997:512) argue that this theory is an ideological construction; they maintain that data is used to support a pre-existing theoretical position, i.e. 'drug normalisation'. They assert that the normalisation thesis is used as a theoretical backdrop against which 'drug use is seen as being unproblematic by most young people'. They go on to state that 'this trend should not be treated uncritically' (ibid.:526). Shiner and Newburn suggest that the 'normalisation thesis' promotes a sympathetic approach towards drugs because it derives from young people who find drug use acceptable. The implication is that drug normalisation is seen as tantamount to encouraging drug use. Prohibition refuses to accept that illicit drug use is positive or could be seen as part of 'everyday experience'. A key problem for drug prevention is the term itself, 'recreational', applied to drug consumption, because it assumes a positive value in relation to normality. To take recreation is generally thought of as good: it is part of leisure, part of a healthy lifestyle and in this sense recreational drug normalisation is a challenge because it opposes the absolutist notion of drug prohibition (MacDonald and Marsh, 2002).

It is ironic that the theory of drug normalisation should be criticised as being too subjective when historical and contemporary evidence demonstrates that drug prohibition policy has been far from objective and fair. When drug prohibition began as a moral movement in the nineteenth century it did not possess a sacred hold on truth: it demanded conversion to the belief of abstinence as a moral duty. Berridge and Edwards (1987:191) speak of striking parallels between medical and moral propaganda on the subject. They state: 'many doctors most active in formulating concepts of addiction were also active in the moral agitation'. The legacy of the early prohibition movement is an appearance of objectivity where medical concepts are strengthened through moral bias and fabrication.[31] Acker (1995:123) states that drug use 'became closely linked with the threat of social disorder through the elaboration of a psychiatric explanation of addiction'. Here the drug user is defined politically as the total deviant, making moderation impossible as it would undermine the legitimacy of the power structure which produced the theory of prohibition.

Postmodernism, Normalisation, Prohibition and Political Epidemiology

A key part of the normalisation thesis is Parker's analysis of social change linked with understanding society through postmodernity. Beyond the empirical data Parker, Measham and Aldridge (1995:25) argue that 'the availability of drugs is a normal part of the leisure-pleasure landscape'. Furthermore, Parker and colleagues (1998b:27) state that 'changes in young people's attitudes and behaviour are more likely to evolve from aspects of social theory found in the post modernity debate'. There remains, however, some uncertainty about Parker's brush with postmodern theory. He argues that normalisation is consistent with the individualisation thesis developed by Beck (1992). This allows young people's drug taking to be seen as an integral part of contemporary identity and consumption within a capitalist society that gives priority to individual choice freed from tradition. Here we see Parker value some postmodern understandings, but ultimately he seems reluctant to fully embrace postmodernism as this theory may atomise individuals, diminishing the significance of structural inequality.

Shiner and Newburn (1997:156) criticise Parker's theory by stating that the posited link between postmodernity and contemporary patterns of drug use has been exaggerated by a consistent fall in drug use in the 1980s. Ironically, they then state that 'the 1990s have witnessed a reversal of this trend'. Shiner and Newburn do not really engage with Parker's description of wider cultural transformations of the commodification of drugs into mainstream culture (Taylor, 2000). They fail to tackle this aspect of late capitalism and are concerned only with questioning and assessing statistical data which claim a high prevalence of illicit drug use by young people. For them, the postmodern condition is not a causal factor in drug normalisation. While Shiner and Newburn argue that drug normalisation exaggerates drug use, government drug prevention policy has identified drug normalisation or casualisation as a rationale to introduce more 'popular preventives'. Drug prevention utilises the broad framework of ideas set out by the drug normalisation thesis to support the apparent need for more regulation and a punitive drug policy. Thus, drug normalisation has been used to endorse policy initiatives such as drug testing in schools to consolidate prevention (Craver, 2004). In short, as a general reference point drug normalisation is a means to capture and advance the prohibition argument without the use of statistical data. Here prohibition is similar to the spirit of evangelicalism; for the 'anti' and 'against' movement in drug prevention, faith in the desired goal of a drug-free world is seen as sufficient rationale for their arguments. These total beliefs have little room for difference, because the complexities of life and culture, i.e. normalisation, are seen as unnecessary in the drug-free world.

The drug normalisation thesis has been adapted by drug prevention to accommodate its own tautology. The increased dominance of the political enforcement model of drug prohibition and its use of legitimating discourses such as medicine and psychiatry has brought about a loss of complexity in the understanding of drug issues, i.e. normalisation. This process could be described as political epidemiology, which focuses primarily on single causation (Agar, 1997). Currently, drug prevention has little interest in considering the implications of drug differentiation, or wanting to develop a more critical understanding of the relationship between the illegal drugs economy and its legal commercial cultural support systems (Blackman, 1996). Drug normalisation theory was created as a corrective to the stigmatised understanding of young people who consume drugs on a recreational non-problematic basis, who are neither deviant nor criminal. The take-up of the drug normalisation idea has also resulted, however, in the opposite. Drug normalisation has been used negatively to account for an apparently threatening increase in drug availability and also to describe the increased infiltration of mainstream culture with drug reference points.

Conclusion

Pierre Bourdieu's (1996) idea of a 'cultural or social field' is useful to explain the different historical and contemporary positions of drugs. The metaphor enables a more coherent and dynamic picture to emerge. Drug normalisation, drug prohibition and recreational drug use in Bourdieu's terms are part of the drugs 'field', a cultural and social arena where there is opposition and manoeuvring to secure dominance. The drugs field possesses a structured system of social positions occupied by individuals and institutions who struggle over capital irrespective of prohibition or normalisation. The age of mass production in the twentieth and twenty-first centuries brought massive expansion to the culture industries of film, print and popular music. In the last hundred years the range and number of illicit drugs have increased alongside the cultural representations of these intoxicants. During the nineteenth century opium was part of the legitimate colonial trade and in the twenty-first century drug cultural products are now part of mainstream capitalism. The drugs field is a cultural and financial reservoir of economic and moral potential. The acceptance of drug normalisation and the idea of recreational drug use are opposed by drug prevention because from the abstinence perspective they promote positive messages about drug use. It would be inaccurate, however, to describe drug normalisation as being supportive of drugs; it aims to recognise the place and position of drugs within culture itself, not to advocate it. Within the drugs field, Howard Parker's theory of drug normalisation is an intervention which seeks to challenge the hegemony of drug prohibition.

Notes

The title comes from the Pink Floyd song written by Syd Barratt, which reached No. 6 in 1967.
1.   For example 'Jack Shepperd' by W. Harrison Ainsworth (1839).
2.   Other such films include *Cocaine Traffic* (1914), *Damaged Goods* (1915) and *The Devil's Needle* (1916).
3.   First published as *Junkie* by William Lee.
4.   A selection could include 'A Little Help from My Friends' (cannabis), 'Lucy in the Sky with Diamonds' (LSD), 'Happiness Is a Warm Gun' (heroin).
5.   'My Generation' (speed), '5.15 Out of My Brain on the Train'.
6.   'Here Comes the Nice'.
7.   'Eight Miles High'.
8.   'Waiting for the Man'.
9.   'Light My Fire', 'Crystal Ship'.
10. 'See Emily Play'.
11. *The Times* of 24 July 1967, under the heading 'The law against marijuana is immoral in principle and unworkable in practice'.
12. *Sun*, 30 January 1997, *Evening Standard*, 30 January 1997.
13. See tabloid front pages *Daily Star* 21 December 2004, 'Robbie: Why It's Great Doing Drugs'. *Daily Mirror* 21 December 2004 story 'It Was a Great Time I enjoyed Drugs'.
14. Francis Ross is the lead singer of Status Quo.
15. A punning reference to marijuana.
16. The term 'Beat Generation' was first used in 1952 by journalist John Clellon Holmes in an article for the *New York Times Magazine*, 'This is the Best Generation' (16 November), although the term 'Best' had been used in the 1940s.
17. See *The Yage Letters* by Burroughs and Ginsberg (1963) about their consumption of a mescaline-like drug called yage.
18. Barnes (1979).
19. See Lentz (2002).
20. P. H. Connell (1965).
21. `A. Sharpley, *Evening Standard*, 3–6 February and 1 May 1964.
22. P. H. Connell (1965).
23. `In 1967 he was sentenced to thirty years' imprisonment for being in possession of three ounces of marijuana belonging to his daughter, in 1970 he was convicted again for cannabis and sentenced to ten years in prison, in 1973 he was arrested again and he was finally paroled in 1976.
24. *Daily Express*, 25 April 1985, 'How the Evil of Ecstasy Hit the Street'; *Daily Telegraph*, 1 May 1985, 'Ecstasy – the Latest Narcotic Menace', 17 March 1987, 'Yard Stand-by as New Ecstasy Drug Arrives in Britain; *Sun*, 14 April 1987, 'Ecstasy for Sale!'; *Daily Mail*, 14 May 1987, 'Fashion Models in Ecstasy Drugs Raid'.
25. A selection of *Sun* headlines during 1988 and 1989 includes: 'Evils of Ecstasy', Love Drug Stampeded', 'Shoot These Evil Acid Barons', 'Spaced out!' and 'Ecstasy Wrecked My Life'.
     See also the *Sun's* Bizarre column, 12 October 1988, written by former punk fanzine editor Garry Bushell: "It's Groovy and Cool – it's our Acid House T-shirt!"

26. *The Face*, October 1985, 'MDMA We're All Crazy Now'; *Boy's Own*, July 1988, 'Bermond-sey Goes Balearic'; *NME*, 30 July 1988, letters page; *Melody Marker*, 20 August 1988, 'The Road to Utopia'.
27. Jim McClellan, *The Face*, October 1995, 'Spiritual Highs'.
28. Each young woman died in 1995, 1998, 2001 and 2002. Their death was covered by front page headlines.
29. *Daily Mirror* 22 November 2004 'We Are Losing the War on Drugs'. Also, 22 November 2004 *Evening Standard* 'Huge Rise in Cannabis Use'.
30. *Daily Mail*, 31 March 2004, 'Cannabis Law Has Not Freed Police to Do Other Work'; *Daily Telegraph*, 12 January 2004, Cut-price Drugs Hit the Streets'; *Daily Mail*, 11 July 2002, 'A Deadly Threat to All Our Children'; *Sun*, 11 July 2002, 'Dope Trade in Open Air'.
31. Clark 1976:181–208.

Further Reading

Berkhout, M., and Robinson, F. (1999). Madame Joy: The Story of Human Drug Use and the Politics of its Regulation. Sydney: HarperCollins.
Bertram, E., Blachman, M., Sharpe, K., and Andreas, P. (1996). Drug War Politics: The Price of Denial. Berkeley: University of California Press.
Blackman, S. J. (2004). Chilling Out: The Cultural Politics of Substance Consumption, Youth and Drug Policy. Maidenhead/New York: Open University Press/McGraw-Hill.
Plant, S. (1999). Writings on Drugs. Faber and Faber: London.
Royal College of Psychiatrists and Physicians (2000). Drugs: Dilemmas and Choices. London: Gaskell.
South, N. (ed.) (1999). Drugs: Cultures, Controls and Everyday Life. London: Sage.

Study Questions

1. It is a criminal act to sell illicit drugs, but it is legal and profitable to sell drug-related products in shops throughout Britain. How can drug education and drug prevention respond to these social and cultural inconsistencies?
2. The tabloid press, internet websites, cinema, popular music and pulp fiction contain diverse images of drug consumption. How can we critically address the position of drugs within popular culture?
3. Since the 1960s there have been many empirical studies on young people and drug consumption. What have these different investigations shown?

4

The Hardest Drug? Trends in Heroin Use in Britain

Toby Seddon

Introduction

Heroin has arguably been the most debated, mythologised and demonised drug in Britain over the last century. Myths, paradoxes and disagreements abound. In some quarters, heroin is quite simply the most dangerous and destructive drug there is. Damaging to users' health, devastating for their families and disastrous for the communities in which they live. Indeed, for many parents, to find out that their young son or daughter is a heroin 'addict' is their worst nightmare (Dorn, Ribbens and South, 1987).

Others see things differently, suggesting that 'anxieties about heroin are exaggerated' (Carnwath and Smith, 2002:2). They argue that heroin is not especially harmful to health in itself (Stimson and Oppenheimer, 1982:4), pointing to its role in medical practice as a pain relief (Gossop and Keaney, 2004). They also question its addictiveness, citing the consistent evidence that controlled occasional heroin use is possible (Blackwell, 1983; Zinberg, 1984; Pearson, 1987b; Shewan *et al.*, 1998; Shewan and Dalgarno, 2005). For many in this camp, most of the problems associated with heroin are principally a consequence of its illegality.

Somewhat inevitably, given its ability to stir up such strong views and emotions, heroin has long been a symbol of rebellion and 'cool' in popular culture, from William Burroughs in the 1950s to *Trainspotting* in the 1990s. The roll call of writers, artists and musicians who have used the drug is long and illustrious, leading to debates about the connection between heroin and creativity (Carnwath and Smith, 2002:112–15).

Heroin use in Britain today is still relatively rare – national surveys suggest well under 1 per cent of the over-15 population are recent or current users (Condon and Smith, 2003) – but absolute numbers are substantial, with perhaps as many as 300,000 current users (Bramley-Harker, 2001)[1]. Heroin is readily available in towns and cities across the country and is fairly cheap, often sold now in £5 or £10 wraps. It is widely believed to be connected with some of the most serious social problems facing us today, including crime, social exclusion and health inequalities. Heroin is prioritised within the national drug strategy as one of the drugs that causes the most damage to individuals and communities (Home Office, 2002).

This chapter seeks to place Britain's contemporary heroin problem in some historical perspective by reviewing trends in heroin use. A particular focus will be on the 1980s heroin epidemic which, to a large extent, has set the basic pattern for the last 25 years. The chapter begins with a short outline of the early historical context, briefly describing the history of opium and heroin use in Britain up to and including the 1930s. The description of post-war trends is then split into four sections. The first looks at the period from 1945 to the 1970s, the second at the 1980s heroin epidemic, the third at the heroin outbreaks in the mid-1990s and the fourth at the contemporary place of heroin within a polydrug culture. The chapter concludes with a short discussion section which reviews the critical issues and debates raised by this presentation of historical trends in heroin use.

Historical Context: Use of Opium, Opiates and Heroin in the Nineteenth and Early Twentieth Centuries

Opium, which is obtained from the opium poppy, is the base drug from which opiates, including heroin, are derived. Use of opium dates back around 6000 years to the ancient civilisations, where it was known for its properties of inducing sleep, relieving pain and elevating mood (Berridge, 1999:xviii; Stimson and Oppenheimer, 1982:14–15). Evidence of the use of opium in England dates back to at least the fourteenth century and references in the works of medical authors and physicians to the use of opium occur throughout the sixteenth, seventeenth and eighteenth centuries (Berridge, 1999:xxii–xxv).

By the early nineteenth century, the use of opium and opium preparations, such as laudanum and paregoric, had become extensive and widespread in English society (Berridge, 1999). Through the first half of the century, opium and opium-based products could be bought from any grocer's or druggist's shop and, in one form or another, opium 'found its way into every home' (Berridge, 1999:xxix). It provided remedies for a range of common ailments, from coughs and colds to diarrhoea and toothache. There were even soothing syrups for babies and infants based on opium, of which the best known was Godfrey's Cordial, and the practice of 'infant doping' was common (Berridge, 1999:97–105). Opium was part and parcel of everyday culture. It was also an important part of medical practice, used to treat many different conditions. Morphine, an alkaloid first isolated from opium in 1803, started to be widely used in medicine from the middle of the century, including via the newly-discovered hypodermic method of administration (Berridge, 1999:135–49).

From a high point in the 1860s, the last quarter of the nineteenth century saw a gradual decline in the popular use of opium and opium preparations and an increase in the professional control of the drug (Berridge, 1999:225–31). The 1868 *Pharmacy Act* was an important step in regulating for the first time the availability of opium. This was part of a broader process during this period of the general regulation of drugs and medicines, as the medical and pharmaceutical professions became more established. Opium and opiates were not singled out for special or separate treatment (Berridge, 1999).

The last decades of the nineteenth century also saw the arrival of heroin. Diacetylmorphine or diamorphine was first synthesised from morphine in 1874 by Charles Alder Wright working in St Mary's Hospital in London. It was rediscovered in Germany in the 1890s and then marketed as heroin in 1898 by the German pharmaceutical company Friedrich Bayer and Co. for use as a cough medicine (Sneader, 1998; Scott, 1998). In the first years of the twentieth century, heroin was used within medical practice primarily as a cough suppressant and for pain relief. By 1911, however, the *British Pharmaceutical Codex* was warning that heroin, like morphine, could be addictive (Sneader, 1998:1699).

At the beginning of the twentieth century, moves towards setting up separate systems for the control of opium (and some other drugs) started to gather pace on the international stage. A series of meetings, starting in Shanghai in 1909 and ending in The Hague in 1914, set the blueprint for a global drug control system (Berridge, 1999:235–44). Following these international developments, and particularly the Opium Convention signed in 1912 in The Hague, Britain introduced new restrictions on the possession and supply of opium under regulation 40B of the 1916 *Defence of the Realm Act* (Berridge, 1978). This led in the 1920s to a tightening up of legal and professional controls on a wider range of drugs via the 1920 *Dangerous Drugs Act* and subsequent regulations. This marked the introduction of the first significant regulation of heroin.

Against this backdrop of new regulation, heroin use in the 1920s was minimal. A committee convened in 1924 by the Ministry of Health to look at morphine and heroin addiction (the Rolleston Committee) concluded that the incidence of heroin dependence in Britain was still very rare at this time (Ministry of Health, 1926). There was in effect a 'non-existent problem' with heroin (Downes, 1977). Throughout the 1930s up until the outbreak of the Second World War in 1939, levels of heroin consumption remained extremely low. Spear (1969:248), for example, refers to 'a very small circle of heroin addicts in London' in the immediate pre-war years of the late 1930s. A notable feature of this small heroin-using population was that it was drawn primarily from the 'respectable' middle classes and those of 'good' social standing, with a high proportion from the medical professions because of their ready access to the drug (Spear, 1969).

Post-War Heroin Trends: From the Late 1940s to the 1970s

In the immediate post-war years of the late 1940s, there was little change in levels or patterns of heroin use from the situation in the 1920s or 1930s. The population of users remained largely 'professional' in social terms and was essentially stable in size. In 1945, the number of new heroin 'addicts' known to the Home Office was just one and in 1949 there were only three (Spear, 1969:250).

This annual figure did not even reach double figures until 1954, when there were 16 new 'addicts', and this turned out to be the peak for that decade (Spear, 1969). Nevertheless, the 1950s saw the beginnings of what would become a more significant trend in the following decade. Although the number of heroin users remained low, the 1950s saw the first signs of an emerging drug subculture centred primarily on certain coffee bars and jazz clubs in the West End of London. The new heroin users were younger than their 1940s and pre-war counterparts and they were often involved in bohemian lifestyles (Spear, 1969).

This emerging trend accelerated rapidly in the 1960s. There was a sharp upturn in the incidence of heroin use in the first half of the decade (Bewley, 1966) with the total number of heroin 'addicts' known to the Home Office increasing from 68 in 1959 to 342 in 1964 (Spear, 1969:250). As in the 1950s, the new users were mainly young people and there was a strong association with the new drug subculture. Most of this expansion in heroin supply came from doctors' prescriptions, with users selling on their surplus to others. The area around Piccadilly Circus became infamous as a marketplace for pharmaceutical heroin because of the location of the 24-hour pharmacy at Boots there, one of only two all-night chemists in London (Spear, 2002:126–27). A very small number of medical practitioners – the 'script' doctors – appeared to be the source of almost the entire illicit heroin market. An official report at the time famously asserted that 'not more than six doctors' were responsible for the rapid expansion in the availability of heroin (Ministry of Health, 1965: para. 12; Spear, 2002:144–46). One doctor in particular, Lady Isabella Frankau, was responsible for prescribing extremely large quantities of heroin, starting in 1957 up until her death in 1967 (Spear, 2002:127–33). Other doctors at the time became equally notorious, notably John Petro who for a period during early 1967 practised primarily out of the refreshment room at Baker Street Underground station (Spear, 2002:216).

In the last few years of the 1960s, while the rise in use continued, there were some important changes in the heroin scene. In 1967, the first ille-gally-imported non-pharmaceutical heroin – known as Chinese heroin – appeared in the West End of London (Spear, 2002:228). In April 1968, tight controls on heroin prescribing came into force under the *Dangerous Drugs Act* 1967, significantly reducing the availability of prescribed pharmaceuti-cal heroin. Only specially licensed doctors working primarily from the new Drug Dependency Units (DDUs), known as the 'Clinics', were now allowed to prescribe to 'addicts'. Within a short period of time, the illegal imported heroin market would become the principal supply source, as it remains to the present day.

Although the 1960s did indeed see a sharp increase in levels of heroin use (see Table 4.1) and a change in the nature of the using population, it is important to put this in perspective. Pearson (2001) argues that even by the end of the decade, heroin use in Britain remained extremely rare and largely confined to London[2]. At most, it was a regional 'mini-epidemic'. There was certainly nothing at all like the serious heroin outbreaks that had been severely affecting several cities in North America from as early as the late 1940s (Chein *et al.*, 1964).

During the 1970s, the heroin problem in Britain stabilised, particularly during the middle years of the decade (see Table 4.2[3]). A good account of this relatively stable period is provided by Stimson and Oppenheimer

---

Table 4.1

Heroin 'addicts' known to the Home Office, 1960–68

Year	Number of newly-notified heroin 'addicts' in the year	Total number of known 'addicts'
1960	24	94
1961	56	132
1962	72	175
1963	90	237
1964	162	342
1965	259	521
1966	522	899
1967	745	1299
1968	1306	2240

Source: Compiled from Spear (1969).

Table 4.2

'Addicts' known to the Home Office and being prescribed heroin and/or methadone in treatment, 1970–78

Year	Number of known 'addicts' being prescribed heroin and/or methadone
1970	1174
1971	1316
1972	1415
1973	1595
1974	1699
1975	1645
1976	1562
1977	1615
1978	1917

Source: Compiled from Home Office Statistical Bulletin 11/80, *'Statistics of the Misuse of Drugs in the United Kingdom, 1979'*.

(1982) who carried out a ten-year longitudinal study of a sample of heroin users who were attending drug dependency clinics in London in 1969. They describe in detail the operation of the 'Clinic' system and its impact on the heroin-using population during the 1970s.

In 1979, the first reports circulated of the arrival of significant quantities of cheap brown smokeable heroin into the country (Lewis *et al.*, 1985; Pearson, 1987a:65; Spear, 2002:270–71). This was a sign of the dramatic transformation in the British heroin problem that was about to take place.

The 1980s Heroin Epidemic

In the 1980s, Britain's heroin problem was entirely transformed in scale and nature. In the first few years of the decade, cheap and plentiful supplies of heroin became available in many towns and cities across the country. Places like Manchester, Liverpool and Glasgow, which had no previous heroin history, witnessed serious heroin outbreaks (Ditton and Speirits, 1981; Haw, 1985; Pearson *et al.*, 1986; Parker, Bakx and Newcombe, 1988; Fazey, Brown and Batey, 1990). The existing heroin scene in London also expanded and spread to new parts of the city (Burr, 1987). The quantitative scale of the expansion is shown by the figures in Table 4.3.[4]

Table 4.3

New heroin 'addicts' notified to the Home Office during the year, 1980–85

Year	Number of heroin 'addicts' newly notified to the Home Office during the year
1980	1151
1981	1660
1982	2117
1983	3559
1984	4926
1985	5930

Source: Compiled from Home Office Statistical Bulletin 7/90, *'Statistics of the Misuse of Drugs: Addicts Notified to the Home Office, United Kingdom, 1989'.*

The watershed year seems to have been 1979, when there was an influx of heroin into Britain from Iran (Lewis *et al.*, 1985). From 1981, substantial supplies from Pakistan began to enter the market and later on Afghanistan became a significant source of British heroin. This shift in global trafficking patterns and the opening up of new supply routes into Britain was the result of geo-political developments in southwest Asia (Pearson and Patel, 1998:200; McCoy, 2000). As a consequence of this, cheap high-quality heroin became widely available in Britain from the start of the 1980s.

The new heroin users were mainly young unemployed people from the most deprived neighbourhoods and housing estates (Pearson, 1987a). They often became involved in lifestyles based around drug dealing and acquisitive crime (theft, burglary, shoplifting) (Parker and Newcombe, 1987). Consequently, neighbourhoods affected by a heroin outbreak typically experienced a clustering together of social difficulties: high unemployment, high crime rates, heroin dealing and heroin use. This often compounded and exacerbated existing problems of poor housing and poverty and served to worsen what was probably already a reputation as a 'bad' neighbourhood. The arrival of a serious heroin outbreak in a 'problem' housing estate could help accelerate a downward spiral of decline (Pearson, 2001).

For Britain, this clustering together of problems of heroin, crime and deprivation was a new phenomenon, although a familiar pattern to observers from the United States. The early 1980s saw Britain undergoing a severe economic recession and a period of de-industrialisation in which many working-class areas were devastated by high unemployment. Many commentators at the time believed that the heroin problem was a symptom of this wider social and economic malaise (Peck and Plant, 1986). However, the idea that mass unemployment directly 'caused' the heroin epidemic would be mistaken and misleading (Pearson, 1987a). As noted above, the arrival of cheap and plentiful supplies of heroin into Britain at the start of the 1980s was the result of rather more distant events in southwest Asia. Nevertheless, at a local level, strong connections between unemployment, heroin and crime were evident. The processes underpinning these relationships were complex, but in essence revolved around the ways in which some young people in deprived neighbourhoods responded to the problem of mass unemployment during the economic recession. For some, their response was to become involved in aspects of the 'irregular' economy of perks, fiddles and crime, not just as an alternative source of income but also as a way of achieving status and creating a meaningful structure for daily life (Auld, Dorn and South, 1984, 1986; Pearson, 1987a, 2001; see also Preble and Casey, 1969). The supply, exchange and consumption of heroin, as well as involvement in theft and other acquisitive crime, were simply particular areas of activities within this wider 'irregular' economy.

Most of the new heroin users in the 1980s were young men. Robust data on gender are not available but Pearson (1991:189) has estimated that the male to female ratio was approximately 3 to 1. In terms of ethnicity, the new users were overwhelmingly white (Pearson and Patel, 1998:202). This was surprising, given the links described above with deprivation. It would have been expected that minority ethnic communities would have been especially affected by the arrival of the heroin outbreaks – as indeed was very much the experience in North America (Pearson, 2001b:54) – but in fact the opposite appeared to be the case. It has been suggested that the high level of community stigmatisation of drug use may have acted as a cultural 'brake' on the take-up of heroin among young Asians during the 1980s (Pearson and Patel, 1998). Others have argued that this stigmatisation may also have rendered any heroin use in these communities 'hidden' from the gaze of researchers and from the records of the authorities, leading to a distorted picture of the ethnic profile of the epidemic (Akhtar and South, 2000). Nevertheless, it is clear that the penetration of heroin into minority ethnic communities was much less than in the white working-class populations where it became so visible.

In many local areas, the heroin outbreaks were associated, initially at least, with the practice of 'chasing the dragon' rather than injecting (Pearson *et al.*, 1985; Auld *et al.*, 1986; Parker, Bakx and Newcombe, 1988). 'Chasing' originated in Hong Kong in the 1950s and subsequently spread to other parts of southeast Asia in the 1960s and 1970s and then on to some European countries including Britain in the 1980s (Strang, Griffiths and Gossop, 1997). It involves heating heroin on tin foil and inhaling the fumes through a tube. 'Chasing' is an inefficient method of administering the drug compared to injecting but there were a number of reasons why it featured so strongly in the 1980s epidemic. Firstly, the type of brown heroin from Iran and Pakistan that became available at this time was particularly suitable for smoking. Secondly, its cheapness, quality and ready availability made it possible for users to 'contemplate letting some of it quite literally go up in smoke' (Auld *et al.*, 1986:175). In other words, there was not the financial pressure to maximise the 'hit' from an impure, scarce or expensive substance. Thirdly, the practice of 'chasing' was a natural extension of cannabis or tobacco smoking and did not involve transgressing taboos about injecting. This undoubtedly helped heroin use to spread more rapidly within some localities (Pearson *et al.*, 1986:9).

It is worth saying something here about this process of 'spreading' within a neighbourhood. Researchers in North America first developed in the 1970s an outline epidemiology for modelling how a heroin outbreak unfolds within a local community (Hunt and Chambers, 1976; Hughes, 1977). Howard Parker and colleagues tested and refined this model in their research in Merseyside in the mid-1980s and found it to be largely applicable in the UK context (Parker, Bakx and Newcombe, 1988). In this model, two processes are at work within the development of a heroin epidemic. Firstly, *micro-diffusion* through personal contacts. This involves the spread of heroin, and heroin knowledge, along peer and friendship networks. Within a serious outbreak, separate micro networks of this kind develop simultaneously and also join up, rapidly increasing the density of the epidemic. Secondly, *macro-diffusion* occurs when heroin sites spread to neighbouring areas, as dealers and suppliers move or as users migrate to another nearby town or neighbourhood. Parker's study showed how these processes led to the epidemic spread of heroin in the Wirral, which moved during a six-year period from having only a handful of heroin users to hosting around 4000 (Parker, Bakx and Newcombe, 1988).

Parker's research confirmed the earlier finding by North American researchers that there is a common 'natural history' to a heroin outbreak (see also Ditton and Frischer, 2001). In the first few years, there is a rapid period of epidemic growth in which most of those who are going to take up heroin do so. Towards the end of this initial phase, although the number of new 'cases' (the incidence rate) starts to fall, the prevalence rate (the total number of cases) continues to rise as few users give up in the short term. Eventually, prevalence falls as users give up or leave the area or die but it usually comes to rest at a higher 'endemic' level than before the outbreak. Heroin outbreaks therefore have a lasting impact on the localities they affect.

A key point concerning the heroin epidemic in the 1980s is that there were considerable regional variations. Pearson and Gilman (1994:102) argue that it was 'not truly a 'national' problem [...] in many respects it is better understood as a series of local and regional difficulties'. There were several aspects to this local and regional diversity. Firstly, the spread of heroin was patchy in geographical terms. Not all areas of social deprivation were affected by a heroin outbreak. Unell (1987) gives the example of Leeds, situated to the east of the Pennines in West Yorkshire, which, despite an unemployment rate well above the national average, had a relatively small drug problem in the mid-1980s. Pearson and colleagues (1986) in their research in the north of England found this to be part of a broader pattern. Heroin was much more available to the west of the Pennines, in places like Manchester, Liverpool and Carlisle, compared to the east side of the country. Secondly, while overall the epidemic was associated with the practice of 'chasing the dragon' rather than injecting, this was not the case in all areas (Pearson and Gilman, 1994:112). In many localities there were strong taboos about injecting and there was a marked preference for 'chasing' among the new users. However, in places with a prior injecting drug subculture, typically involving amphetamine sulphate, injecting often quickly emerged as the preferred method (Pearson and Gilman, 1994:112–13). Thirdly, there were regional variations in the demographic profile of new users. Parker and his colleagues (1987:156) note that the 3.6 to 1 male to female ratio they found for heroin users in the Wirral was considerably higher than that found by some studies in other areas. For example, in Bristol the equivalent ratio was 2 to 1 and in one London Borough as low as 1.8 to 1. Local and regional variations in the age profile of users were also evident (Parker, Newcombe and Bakx, 1987:156).

To summarise, the 1980s saw the transformation of Britain's heroin problem as a major epidemic that affected many parts of the country. As well as a substantial increase in the size of the heroin-using population, the profile of the new users was very different. They were young, usually unemployed and lived in the most deprived neighbourhoods and housing estates. Their heroin use typically took place in the context of involvement in the 'irregular' economy of theft, handling stolen goods, drug dealing and provision of other illegal services.

New Heroin Outbreaks in the 1990s

For a few years in the late 1980s and at the start of the 1990s, the heroin problem stabilised. This was, however, to be a short-lived period of stability. From around 1992, a new series of outbreaks of heroin use among young people started to occur in several parts of England and Wales (Egginton, Bury and Parker, 1998; Parker, Aldridge and Measham, 1998b; Millar *et al.*, 2001). The first outbreaks between 1992 and 1994 occurred mainly in places with existing minor heroin 'footprints' from the 1980s (for example, Bristol,

Bradford and Hull), but these were followed by major new outbreaks in sites with no previous heroin history. Illustrating this trend of expansion, the number of heroin 'addicts' newly notified to the Home Office increased from 7658 in 1992 to 15,271 in 1996 (Home Office, 1997). By the late 1990s, the majority of urban areas in England had experienced significant upturns in heroin use. At the end of the decade, heroin use and availability in Britain was much more extensive and geographically widespread than ever before (Parker *et al.*, 1998b).

The key question was whether these new outbreaks were simply a repeat or extension of the pattern established by the 1980s epidemic. Would heroin be found in the same kinds of deprived neighbourhoods as in the previous decade and would these new users also become heavily involved in acquisitive offending? Broadly speaking, the answer to these questions was 'yes' but with some qualifications.

The new heroin users in the 1990s were younger than before. In Parker's sample, the average age of trying heroin for the first time was 15½ (Egginton and Parker, 2000:23–24), which is a couple of years earlier than in the 1980s epidemic. This mirrored the broader trend of a fall in the age of onset of drug-trying (Parker *et al.*, 1998b). The 1990s users also appeared to come from a broader range of socio-economic backgrounds than was previously seen (Parker, Bury and Egginton, 1998a; Egginton and Parker, 2000). While the correlation with deprivation remained, some of these young people had relatively conventional and unremarkable upbringings. Once engaged in heroin use, however, their economic fortunes were adversely affected, with high levels of unemployment and reliance on state benefits. This was often accompanied by an increasing involvement in acquisitive crime, especially shoplifting, and drug dealing (Egginton and Parker, 2000:33–34).

Further evidence for a more diverse heroin-using population in the 1990s is highlighted when ethnicity is considered. A series of local research studies in London (White, 2001), Bradford (Pearson and Patel, 1998) and Greater Manchester (Patel and Wibberley, 2002; Akhtar and South, 2000) all point towards the increasing penetration of heroin during the 1990s into some minority ethnic communities, particularly south Asian communities (see also Wanigaratne *et al.*, 2003; Fountain, Bashford and Winters, 2003). For young Asians in the 1990s, of the third or even fourth generation of immigrants, their social and cultural outlook was becoming increasingly British and the cultural bonds that may have constrained heroin use in the 1980s were starting to loosen (Pearson and Patel, 1998; Patel and Wibberley, 2002). Pearson and Patel (1998) describe how this weakening of cultural constraints has occurred, so the underlying processes linking deprivation with heroin problems have started to take a stronger hold. Thus, in Bradford, the 'social and economic circumstances of young Pakistani Asians [...] with few opportunities within the formal economy, suffering unsustainably high levels of unemployment, and experiencing a variety of forms of disadvantage, discrimination and exclusion in all walks of life', together with the wide availability of heroin in the city, adds up to a recipe for a 'truly serious set of social difficulties' within the Asian community (Pearson and Patel, 1998:217).

Summarising, the 1990s saw a new wave of heroin outbreaks across Britain. During the course of the decade, heroin became widely available and used right across the country. As in the 1980s, there were strong connections between heroin, socio-economic deprivation and crime. However, the new heroin users were drawn from more diverse backgrounds than before.

Heroin and Polydrug Use in the Early Twenty-First Century

From the mid-1990s through to the early twenty-first century, heroin has increasingly been used alongside other drugs. This is indicative of a broader phenomenon which has been termed the 'normalisation' of drug use among young people (Parker, Aldridge and Measham, 1998b, 2002; Blackman, Chapter 3). In a nutshell, experimentation with illegal drugs is no longer an exceptional or rare occurrence for young people, with surveys suggesting around 50 per cent will try at least one such drug at some point. Accordingly, today's young heroin users often have extensive polydrug repertoires. The majority will have tried a wide range of drugs – including, for example, cannabis, amphetamines, LSD and ecstasy – but once they take up heroin, the repertoire tends to focus on cannabis, tranquilisers, methadone and crack-cocaine (Egginton and Parker, 2000:21–22).

The use of crack-cocaine alongside heroin is an especially notable development in recent years. Crack first started appearing in Britain in significant quantities from the mid-1990s (Hunter, Donoghoe and Stimson, 1995; Parker and Bottomley, 1996). It is produced by 'cooking' cocaine powder to produce small crystals or 'rocks' which are usually smoked. Like heroin, use of crack appeared primarily in areas of social exclusion and crack users were typically heavily involved in acquisitive offending (Parker and Bottomley, 1996). In the second half of the decade, the coming together of crack and heroin – both within drug markets and in the repertoires of individual consumers (Brain, Parker and Bottomley, 1998) – began to appear as a key feature of the 'heavy end' drug scene. More recent research has confirmed this close connection between crack and heroin use (Egginton and Parker, 2000; Best *et al.*, 2001; Harocopos, 2003; Holloway, Bennette and Lower, 2004; Allen, 2005). The reasons for the links between the two drugs are complex and not altogether certain. One finding from research is that depressant drugs like heroin can be used to manage the 'come down' from crack

(Brain, Parker and Bottomley, 1998). This fits with the picture of heroin users' polydrug repertoires described above which tend to revolve around crack, heroin and other depressant drugs.

One of the impacts of the coming together of crack and heroin is the ratcheting up of drugs bills (Brain, Parker and Bottomley, 1998). Heavy consumption of the two drugs is an expensive business. There is evidence that crack use in particular can lead to very high weekly drug expenditures (Parker and Bottomley, 1996). The polydrug culture in which heroin use increasingly takes place has obvious public health implications too, particularly with drug-trying now starting in the early teens (Parker, 2003:143). It also complicates policy and service responses to heroin, as they can no longer simply be centred around the prescribing of opiate substitutes like methadone (or indeed heroin itself).

Discussion

The historical perspective on the British heroin experience that has been outlined in this chapter throws up some challenges to established positions and viewpoints. Thinking, firstly, about contemporary images and perceptions of heroin, it is evident when looking at British heroin history that the association of heroin with urban deprivation and crime is by no means inevitable or 'natural'. Up until the 1980s, this was not the case in Britain. Indeed, before the 1950s, the typical heroin 'addict' was a middle-class professional. Even after then, in the 1960s and 1970s, the British heroin scene retained a strong middle-class orientation, albeit of a bohemian kind, and links with crime were limited. What we see today as the serious social damage caused by heroin is a relatively recent feature of the British experience of the drug during its 130-year history to date.

Another 'taken for granted' perception of heroin is that it is highly addictive. Yet the evidence suggests that controlled and occasional use of heroin is both possible and achievable (Blackwell, 1983; Zinberg, 1984; Pearson, 1987b; Shewan *et al.*, 1998; Shewan and Dalgarno, 2005). The existence of stable 'addicts' was a consistent feature of the first half of the twentieth century. This body of evidence poses a significant challenge to our understanding of what constitutes heroin addiction or dependence (see Zinberg, 1984; Peele, 1985, 2000; Davies, 1992).

This leads onto an even more controversial issue. If heroin is not automatically addictive or inevitably associated with crime and poverty, is it actually that dangerous at all? In purely pharmacological terms, the answer is probably 'no'. The medical evidence suggests that long-term use of heroin is not particularly harmful to physical health (Stimson and Oppenheimer, 1982:4). Yet we also know that heroin is associated with serious health problems, from abscesses and thromboses, through to hepatitis, HIV and fatal overdoses. How can we explain this apparent contradiction? The key point here is that heroin tends not to be used in ideal conditions. Impure heroin, infected injecting equipment and poor injecting technique present a more common picture of heroin taking and all are associated with potential harms to health. At the most extreme end of the spectrum, fatal overdose is often the result of reckless use of heroin in combination with alcohol and tranquillisers rather than heroin consumption alone. In many cases, failure to carry out basic first aid and to call an ambulance turns an overdose into a fatality (Carnwath and Smith, 2002:144–45).

Perhaps the most vital contextual factor is economic. Heroin-related deaths disproportionately affect the most deprived areas to quite a staggering extent. As Carnwath and Smith (2002:142) observe, 'you would be ill advised to argue that heroin is a gentle drug in the poorer parts of Dublin and Glasgow' where just about everybody knows someone who has died from a heroin overdose. A number of English cities could be added to this list. Michael Marmot (2004) has shown how being poor and living in a poor area has a dramatic negative impact on health, including life expectancy. Similarly, the poorest neighbourhoods tend to suffer most from problems of heroin-related crime and disorder (Pearson, 2001b), including the presence of drug markets (Lupton *et al.*, 2002). The 'dangers' of heroin need to be set in this wider perspective of debates about inequalities and social exclusion and their impact on public health, security and safety.

Reflecting some of these ambiguities and contradictions, the status of heroin has shifted during the course of the twentieth century across the boundaries of 'drug', 'substance' and 'medicine'. It started life, after all, as a cough medicine but has ended up as a highly stigmatised illegal drug. In many respects, even now heroin occupies a somewhat ambiguous position. On the one hand, it is a prohibited illegal drug classified as one of the most dangerous under the Misuse of Drugs Act. On the other hand, under its chemical name of diamorphine, it is widely used in medical practice as a form of pain relief (Gossop and Keaney, 2004). Current debates about the value of prescribing heroin as a treatment for heroin dependence (NTA, 2003; Stimson and Metrebian, 2003; Ashton and Witton, 2003) neatly illustrate this ambiguity and also hark back to the report of the Rolleston Committee in the 1920s (Ministry of Health, 1926).

Taking an even broader view, there is an important international dimension to the heroin problem as well (Auld, Dorn and South, 1984:4–5; Stimson, 1987; Dorn and South, 1987). It was seen earlier in this chapter how geo-political developments in southwest Asia in the late 1970s and early 1980s were significant factors behind the 1980s heroin epidemic in Britain. Today, the vast majority of the heroin available in Britain is derived from opium production in Afghanistan and this production is inextricably linked with development issues (MacDonald and Mansfield, 2001). Afghanistan's position in the 'war on terror' further complicates matters, particularly as it is widely believed that some of the proceeds from drug cultivation and trafficking are used to fund international terrorism (Galeotti, 2001; Scott, 2003). Tackling heroin supply at source will involve engaging with some of the most difficult questions for international development and foreign policy.

What is the future then for heroin in Britain? Anticipating future trends is difficult, although the evidence from the twentieth century suggests at the very least that a downward turn in levels of heroin consumption is fairly unlikely. The post-war North American research, supported to some extent by the British experience, indicates that there may be a longer-term cyclical pattern to heroin epidemics, with outbreaks occurring every 15 to 20 years (Hughes and Rieche, 1995; Ditton and Frischer, 2001; Egginton and Parker, 2000:7). This would suggest that a new heroin epidemic might unfold in Britain from around 2010. Whether or not this speculative prediction turns out to be accurate, heroin seems set to continue to pose some of the hardest challenges for public policy at the start of the twenty-first century.

Notes

The title is derived from Kaplan's classic 1983 book, *The Hardest Drug: Heroin and Pulic Policy*, which remain a key text for anyone trying to make sense of heroin policies.

1. There is no reliable figure for the total number of current heroin users. Edmunds *et al.* (1998:5–6) estimate that 3 per cent per unit of the 4 million people annually using illegal drugs are 'problem' users, giving a total of 120,000. However, not all of these will be herion users. Stimson and Metrebian (2003:11) quote an estimate of 200,000 dependent or problematic way heroin users. The biggest gap in our knowledge is about the number if people using heroin in a non-problematic way which may be substantial. Bramley-Harker (2001) estimates the total heroin-using population to be approximately 300,000, although this figure should be treated with some caution. See also De Angelis, Hick Man and Yang (2004).
2. See Spear (2002:223–27) for further details on the limited spread of heroin outside London during the 1960s. He notes (2002:223) that 86 per cent of the heroin 'addicts' known to the Home Office in January 1967 were in the London area.
3. The figures in Tables 4.1 and 4.2 cannot be directly compared as the system for collating Home Office figure changed in 1968. For more information, see Spear (2002:176–88).
4. The index of notified 'addicts' significantly under-represents the actual number of herion users but the rate of progression in the annual number of new notifications gives an indication of the direction and scale of the trend.

Further Reading

Carnwath, T., and Smith, I. (2002). *Heroin Century*. London: Routledge.
Dorn, N., and Sfouth, N. (eds) (1987). *A Land Fit for Heroin? Drug Policies, Prevention and Practice*. London: Macmillan.

Egginton, R., and Parker, H. (2000). *Hidden Heroin Users: Young People's Unchallenged Journeys to Problematic Drug Use.* London: DrugScope.

Kaplan, J. (1983). *The Hardest Drug: Heroin and Public Policy.* Chicago: University of Chicago Press.

Study Questions

1. Carnwath and Smith (2002:2) argue that 'anxieties about heroin are exaggerated'. How far would you agree?
2. In what ways was the increase in heroin use in the 1960s different from that in the 1980s?
3. Is heroin a useful medicine or a dangerous drug?

5

Drug Markets and Dealing: From 'Street Dealer' to 'Mr Big'

Geoffrey Pearson

Introduction

There is a paradox at the heart of public discourses on the question of illicit drugs. Whereas by far the largest share of public expenditure is devoted towards 'supply side' enforcement matters, research evidence and funding is disproportionately directed towards 'demand side' issues such as patterns of consumption, the behaviour of drug users and treatment. As a consequence, the massive public expenditure on enforcement and intelligence measures against illicit drugs is underpinned by a pitifully thin evidence base. Moreover, such research as exists is largely of north American origin, and heavily slanted towards the low-level retail end of the market.[1] What is required is a more balanced and inclusive approach, which links together different levels of drug markets, from cultivation and production, through various systems of smuggling and drug brokerage, towards 'middle market' domestic drug distribution, and retail supply to consumers.

Accordingly, this chapter adopts a focus on British research and evidence, although comparisons will be made with drug markets in the USA and elsewhere in Europe. The chapter first addresses the different forms that retail-level dealing operations take, discussing the differences between 'open' and 'closed' markets among other things. It then moves to the unique opportunities for drug dealing that emerged within the dance venue and club scene in Britain from the late 1980s through the 1990s and into the new century. In this club scene, friendship networks were fluid and extensive, allowing some small-time dealer entrepreneurs to make a rapid transition into higher reaches of drug distribution systems. Finally, I turn to what is know about middle- and upper-level drug dealers, and the networks of drug brokerage that constitute the 'middle market' that connects up systems of importation and wholesale trading with retail supply. At each point, illustrative case study material will be employed.[2]

Usually viewed as addictive substances with deleterious health and social consequences, from a socio-economic view drugs are principally valued commodities, moreover, commodities with a global reach, and drug markets are a classic form of 'commodity chain' (Wilson and Zambrano, 1994). And, to a large degree, those who participate in drug dealing and brokerage are most usefully viewed as small business entrepreneurs and as rational economic actors (Cornish and Clarke, 1986). This is not the most popular attitude towards drug dealers and 'pushers' in the light of media coverage, but it is one that results from detached, non-sentimental social regard to the issue.[3]

Retail-Level Drug Dealing

Retail-level dealers are those who supply drugs to end-point consumers, sometimes by means of intermediaries where drug users club together to make bulk purchases. Where friends co-operate in such a way to make purchases, the intermediary will often be able to negotiate a discount price with the dealer, thus making a small profit on the exchange. As Lewis *et al.* (1985:286) noted in their study of the heroin market in London, 'the mark-up may be hidden or explicit'. Discussing the recreational drug market, Parker (2000:65) argues that probably most young people in modern Britain purchase the drugs that they consume in this way, through systems of 'networks or chains' which thereby 'protect the majority of young drug takers from direct negotiations with people they regard as real drug dealers'. Quite evidently, people who adopt such an intermediary function occupy an important place in the chain of supply, blurring the distinction between dealer and customer. However, a certain amount of self-deception is involved in these relationships:

> None of these respondents considered themselves real drug dealers. They saw their role as facilitative, as sorting or helping out friends and acquaintances. (ibid.:67)

Retail-level dealing can take a number of forms. For example, whether dealers operate as lone individuals or in teams. Whether it is an 'open' or 'closed' market. Or whether dealers are essentially 'self-employed' or working as a 'runner' for someone who holds the purse strings and makes most of the profit out of the operation. However, the highly complex division of labour described by Johnson *et al.* (1985) in their study of the small-fry involved in the heroin trade in New York's Harlem district – 'steerers', 'touts', 'cop men', 'bag ladies', etc. – has not been noted by British researchers.

The lowest-of-the-low is probably the so-called user-dealer who only sells drugs in order to maintain his or her own drug habit. Here is an example of an extremely simple operation taken from a fieldwork conducted amidst the heroin epidemic of the mid-1980s in the North of England:

> Alan is a young man who lives in a run-down estate in a socially deprived area of a Northern English city. He buys 1 gram of heroin at a price of £70. He takes £25 worth for his own smoke, and knocks out the rest in fourteen £5 bags which he sells to local users. This yields an income of £70, which is then invested in 1 gram of heroin and Alan begins the economic cycle again. (Gilman and Pearson, 1991:101)

Even though his profit margins were low, in terms of the amount of heroin for personal use generated from this operation, Alan's weekly cash-flow of approximately £500 per week translates into a potential annual cash-flow of £25,000 per year. Moreover, some user-dealers in his position were attempting to do that operation three or four times a day, generating a potential cash-flow of £100,000 per year which must be acknowledged as a phenomenal economic achievement in a poor neighbourhood. It is extremely difficult, of course, to manage and sustain a cash-flow of these proportions from such a narrow economic base. Nevertheless, these are the ways in which these supposed 'victims' of the drugs trade, through their subcultural achievement can arrive at the quasi-heroic status in their local neighbourhoods of 'Jack the Lad' (Gilman and Pearson, 1991).

More substantial retail-level heroin dealing operations can generate po-tentially huge profit margins, although in the case of user-dealers there is always a tendency 'to be your own best customer' (Waldorf, 1993) and to consume large proportions of your potential profits.

> Helen was a heroin user who in the mid-1990s inherited a retail-level heroin business when her partner, who was a dealer, was arrested and imprisoned. She bought an ounce of heroin a day from a trusted supplier at £850 the ounce, somewhat below the market rate of £1,000 per ounce. She sold this on in £20 bags with the same purity through a couple of runners and she was glad if she got £1,150 back on the ounce. The typical heroin 'bag' or 'wrap' would contain 0.2 grams to 0.25 grams in this period. At 28 gms to the ounce, these transactions could generate between £2,200 to £2,800 per day in receipts, trans-lated into a profit of more or less £2,000. However, the fundamental business principle of this operation was Helen's heroin habit, although she could not begin to estimate the amount that she smoked: 'I was smoking quite large quantities. I couldn't actually put an amount on it because I was getting it in any amount. I was just, I was just greedy basically with my habit'. She did not add any adulterants (or 'bash') to the heroin, it 'wasn't worth the trouble' but sometimes employed a couple of friends to 'bag up' the heroin (into £20 quantities) who were paid either in cash or heroin. 'Whatever they wanted ... at least two grams. I would supply it and they would use it. It was there basi-

cally'. In addition to Helen's own personal consumption, the baggers up and the runners, there would have been other hangers-on who dropped by her flat for a 'toot' or a 'taste', and overall she and her friends were probably consuming a substantial amount of the heroin that she purchased, in addition to the £300 a day cash profit that she made. This was mainly spent in indulging her own fashion habits, and those of her son who was in his early teens. A more Protestant-ethic and less heroin-chic lifestyle could have generated profits of £500,000 per year or more from Helen's simple heroin operation. (cf. Pearson and Hobbs, 2001:70–71)

A major consideration where retail-level dealers are concerned is whether they are involved full-time or part-time in the drug-dealing lifestyle. In an earlier study of Bristol's black population, Ken Pryce in *Endless Pressure* described the hustle of the marijuana seller or drug 'peddler' (now a discarded term) as essentially a fluctuating, part-time 'side-line' activity:

Because of the 'side-line' nature of this form of hustling, there is a high turnover of the individuals who make a living by peddling. The peddling role constantly shifts from one individual to the next as circumstances (especially financial ones) dictate; therefore one has to be an insider to know who the current peddlers are. (Pryce, 1979:74–75)

With vastly expanded levels of drug consumption since Pryce's study was conducted, it is likely that this depiction is as redundant as his terminology. Higher levels of demand for drugs required more stability and ready access to drugs. Which is not to say that 'serving up' or 'sorting people out' with drugs is a full-time job for many retail-level dealers, although they need sufficient freedom from other constraints to be able to respond flexibly to consumer demand if they are to be successful. Some, such as Alan and Helen described above, were totally committed to the drugs culture through their own heroin addiction. Probably very few involved in the lowest levels of the drug distribution chain are not themselves consumers of the drugs that they offer for sale, particularly where heroin and crack cocaine are concerned, although there are undoubtedly local and cultural variations to this pattern. For example, according to Reuter, MacCoun and Murphy (1990) the typical street-corner cocaine seller in Washington, DC was someone employed in the formal economy, earning an extra $20 per hour through dealing for a few nights each week, in contrast to the $7 per hour earned in the formal economy, and only one-in-ten of them reported having used any illicit substance in the previous 12 months. By contrast, the East Harlem crack sellers studied by Bourgois (1995) were commonly addicted to crack cocaine and heroin and earned relatively little for their work, whereas the kerbside crack dealers described by Jacobs (1999) in the decaying 'Rustbelt' city of St Louis were invariably unemployed, earned on average $2000 per month from drug selling, and although they smoked marijuana and drank alcohol they denied using crack themselves and tended to look down on crack users; but they loved to 'party' and enjoyed the fast life with an easy-come easy-go attitude to money. All three sets of dealers were united, nevertheless, in the exceptional levels of risk that they encountered, whether in terms of arrest or injury.

'Open' and 'Closed' Retail-Level Markets

Among the many variations in drug markets researchers have identified 'open' and 'closed' retail-level markets (Edmunds, Hough and Urquia, 1996; May *et al.*, 2000; Power *et al.*, 1995; Paoli, 2000). 'Open' markets are described as typically those of street-level dealers, there are fewer barriers to entry than closed ones, and they have a fixed geographical location. 'Closed' markets are those where dealers operate from their own apartments, or from rented hotel rooms, and deal only to users known to them by prior appointment. Whether on the street or in an open location such as a public house, however, since successful drug dealers depend on repeat customers and purchases they will tend to generate a reliable group of 'regulars' and to deal only with known faces.

There are, therefore, hybrid forms of open/closed domains for retail drug dealing. Gary, for example, was a part-time cannabis dealer in inner-London who worked both ways: accepting pre-arranged visits to his flat, and also sorting customers out at a local pub, the 'King Cole', although he only dealt with known faces and repeat customers. Indeed, repeat custom was essential to his business operation. Here is a typical scenario:

> Gary is sitting in his usual spot at the end of the bar in the King Cole, nursing a pint of lager and smoking roll-up cigarettes. Immediately behind him is the juke-box, a slot-machine, a cigarette machine, and the entrance to the bar's toilets. This means that there is a constant traffic of people around him, and that customers often have to lean over him to order their drinks from the staff behind the bar. Other people might find this the most inconvenient place to sit at the bar, but this doesn't worry Gary because it enables some customers to have a surreptitious conversation with him and makes his trade less conspicuous. For example, a customer orders a couple of drinks and hands a £20 note across the bar which reliably results in some small change together with two notes, a ten and a five. The small change pocketed, the £15 is slipped to Gary who exchanges the favour with an eighth of cannabis resin wrapped in cling-film. Deal completed. (Pearson, 2001: 179)

Power *et al.* (1995) describe a variety of contexts in which cocaine and crack could be purchased, including open front-line settings that were shunned by some purchasers because of the poor quality of the drugs available, and thought to be the last resort for those perceived to 'have reached the bottom line', 'they are the crackheads'. Another pub-based drug purchasing location offered a split between an 'open' cannabis dealing scene and a 'closed' crack market:

> A man in his thirties acted as doorman and gate-keeper to the pub, vetting those who entered. He had been a cannabis dealer, but now he also sold crack ... Crack was always sold inside the pub, whereas cannabis was sold outside. As this gate-keeping dealer said one evening: 'I have got hashish, if you want anything else then you will have to come inside.' (Power *et al.*, 1995:375)

Completely open 'front line' systems of street dealing are certainly not unknown in the UK, although Power and his colleagues reported that people who regularly bought crack on the front line would do business with the same dealer thus ensuring 'a consistent and reliable supply' (Power *et al.*, 1995:373). Whereas others felt it necessary to have access to a variety of dealers in order to ensure a regular supply. Moreover, the street-corner crack sellers studied by Bruce Jacobs in the US found certain kinds of approach by strangers as risky and unacceptable, and screened out some prospective purchasers by a variety of verbal and behavioural clues (Jacobs, 1996, 1999:104ff.). The distinction between 'open' and 'closed' markets is therefore not by any means so neat as has been described by some UK research. The use of the mobile telephone has furthermore transformed and facilitated drug-purchasing transactions (Natarajan, Clarke and Johnson, 1995). As May *et al.* (2000:16) comment, the use of new technologies such as mobile phones and pagers 'had reduced the need for [the] open market mode of operation'.

The character of local retail drug markets can, and does, change. May and her colleagues emphasised the effects of law enforcement in pushing open markets towards a more closed form, and this can be a significant role of low-level policing in 'harm reduction' terms, since closed markets generally provide less public nuisance to the wider community (May *et al.*, 2000; Pearson, 1992). However, Paoli (2000:61) describes the movement from open street dealing to more closed forms as a consequence of the success of a street dealer who has generated a guaranteed customer base, so that he/she can retire from street dealing to the relative comfort of working from a hotel or private apartment through set appointments. Nevertheless, these changes can also take place through a combination of the mistrustful and sometimes predatory behaviour displayed by dealers and purchasers alike.

In one large northern English city, the heroin scene in the mid-1980s was largely supplied by dealers and user-dealers who operated from their own flats and houses on outlying socially deprived housing estates where the main customer base was also to be found. Following a series of arrests of dealers such as these, in the late 1980s the retail market had re-emerged in an inner-city neighbourhood previously known for 'front line' cannabis dealing, one central location being a multi-storey car park close to a major supermarket. This was essentially an 'open' market. Heroin users arriving from out of town by mini-cab taxi were easily recognisable, by means of local registration plates and insignia, and dealers approached users for comfortable and consensual transactions. This easy peace was disturbed, however, when local youths burst upon the scene with cocoa powder in one pockets and a knife in the other. In order to circumvent this problem that was discouraging the regular customer base, middle-level operators re-located the local market to an adjoining street, in the form of a 'drive-by' service. Predictably, some users exploited this situation and snatched the drugs through the car window, making off with them without paying (cf. Jacobs, 1999). This was found unacceptable to 'middle market' distributors who supplied retail level dealers. So that local distribution re-adjusted once again, finally resting on a system whereby purchasers would drive to a facility such as a pub or launderette with a public pay-phone facility, where they would place an order by telephone, and be served by a 'pizza style' delivery system of youths on mountain bikes. This was before the mobile phone, of course, which has transformed the nature of retail-level drug markets, although generally following the same directions towards pizza-style customer based delivery systems. (Pearson and Hobbs, 2003:337–38)

Drug dealers are not usually thought of as victims of crime, but here we see a low-level form of predatory crime whereby users temporarily victimised dealers (cf. Jacobs, 1999: ch. 4; Jacobs, 2000). Moreover, it was initially law enforcement efforts that dislodged a 'closed' market system on poor, outer-urban housing estates and created the opportunity for an 'open' inner-city market that then further mutated as a consequence of various forms of predatory crime. Drug markets, like many other forms of crime networks, are always mutating (Hobbs, 1995, 2001).

Retail Dealing in and Around the Dance Club Scene

The dance venue scene was one of the most important mutations in the UK drug market during the 1990s. It has represented a different kind of retail-level drug dealing scene since its emergence in the late 1980s and early 1990s initially with the rave scene, consolidating into the overtly commercial late night dance club scene within the night-time economy (Thornton,

1995; Hobbs *et al.*, 2003; Shapiro, 1999; Ward and Fitch, 1998). The initial motor to this was ecstasy, the drug of choice along with amphetamines and LSD 'trips' or 'tabs', for many of those clubbers who attended the 'rave' dance club scene. There were many different forms of this club culture (Thornton, 1995; Malbon, 1999) although the drug dealing systems were broadly similar.

First, there were those entrepreneurial individuals or teams who visited popular dance venues and who touted their wares on the dance floor, whereas other clubbers preferred to buy their supply of drugs prior to going clubbing (Ward and Pearson, 1997). Subsequently, as dance venues commercialised and responded to legislative and regulatory constraints, there was tightened security on the doors of clubs that resulted in dwindling opportunities for entrepreneurial individuals to get their drug wares through searches at entry points. This led to new forms of drug distribution controlled by 'bouncers' who controlled the doors (Hobbs *et al.*, 2003; Morris, 1998; O'Mahoney, 2000; Silverstone, 2003). The change was described in a journalist's account of Tony Tucker, one of the gangsters who controlled the doors of clubs in the vicinity of the Leah Betts tragedy:

> ... [A friend] turned him onto the idea of cashing in on the rapid growth of the club drug scene. Controlling the doors of a club instantly means that you control who sells drugs inside. Tucker began to charge dealers 'rent' of around £1,000 per week in return for granting them exclusive access to the club. (Thompson, 2000:41)

These were 'criminal diversifiers' according to the typology offered by Dorn, Murji and South (1992) of different forms of trafficking operations – namely, those who had started out in more mainstream forms of criminality such as burglary and robberies and who had subsequently discovered the profits to be made in dealing drugs, particularly non-stigmatised drugs such as ecstasy and cocaine. Nevertheless, neat typologies such as these are confounded by the messy actualities in these levels of the drug market. Most importantly, the social ambience of the 'rave' club scene in the late 1980s and early 1990s offered unique opportunities for individual dealers to make a 'killing' and to move into crucial 'middle market' positions. For example, Polly started buying small quantities (say £50) of amphetamine that she could sell on for £100, thereby paying for her own clubbing night out. But soon, friends of friends had started to ask to be sorted out – 'I don't know it just grows ... I suppose where I was working, the places I was socialising, these people ... with their friends ... and they come in, it grows very quickly' – and her business expanded dramatically. Soon, she had adopted a middle-tier role, supplying people who would themselves be selling direct to consumers and other go-betweens to retail dealers. But she also negotiated a deal with a local club dealer for a franchise on the in-club dealing network, and was selling 200 pills herself on the dance floor for an additional £1800 per night profit. For this she was paying the club owner £500 per night:

> ... But I'd got very greedy ... I had more money than anything I could do with and people were still coming to me when I was in the club for single ones ... and then I just got very greedy ... taking out 200 every Saturday night and selling them for £10 each and I might get another £2,000 for that ... But that got really scary ... and I thought Oh my God, dealing like nearly 1,000 a week and this 200 myself, it got really scary actually. I was definitely out of my depth, definitely. (Pearson and Hobbs, 2004:571)

The give-and-take between the commercially controlled doors operation and individual entrepreneurial ventures remains an uncharted territory. A less risky, but nevertheless successful stance was to position oneself one step away from retail-level dance-floor dealing, although again it could be a largely accidental drug-dealing career within the 'friends of friends' culture of the rave dance scene. Paul, for example, was someone who had started from nowhere in the drugs-club scene, but within a few months of asking around about how to access better-quality drugs than the 'duff' tablets he and his friends had been sold at a dance venue, he was selling several thousand ecstasy tablets and other drugs each weekend.

> And then it just went on from there. You know, then their friends want, and *their* friends want, and then it's just escalated ... I was selling two-and-a-half thousand pills in a weekend, four kilos of weed, a thousand drugs, LSD, speed, four ounces of coke ... Their friends want, and friends want, and friends want, and eventually you've got other people who want to start dealing, and then dealers buy from you ... and it's a sky rocket before you even know it. (cf. Pearson and Hobbs, 2004:567)

Buying pills at £2.50 per unit for the several thousand he was purchasing, and selling at £5 per pill in the hundreds that he was selling on to retail dealers, this aspect of Paul's business alone made him £5000 clear profit per week.[4] This kind of rapid ascent within the hierarchy is almost certainly confined to the 'rave' club scene with its particular forms of friendship and quasi-kinship. In terms of other middle-level drug markets, entry into this go-between, middle-man function between wholesale dealers and retail-level dealers might be more difficult to negotiate and require more social and criminal capital.

Middle and Upper-Level Drug Markets: Middle-Men, Drug Brokers and Go-Betweens

Much less is known, in terms of formal research, about middle- and upper-level drug trafficking. Access to trafficking networks is more difficult than access to retail dealers, by reasons of the secrecy required to maintain the security of operations. In what little research has been conducted different approaches have been used. For obvious reasons, few studies have employed ethnographic methods of direct field observation, but these include Patricia Adler's (1985) study of Californian cocaine and marijuana smugglers, and Damien Zaitch's (2002) more recent research into Colombian cocaine traffickers in the Netherlands. Other studies have used prison interviews with convicted offenders (Reuter and Haaga, 1989; Dorn, Oette and White, 1998; Pearson and Hobbs, 2001). Finally, one study in New York employed an analysis of telephone wire taps (Natarajan, 2000).

Public images of 'organised crime', fuelled both by the media and by some law enforcement agencies, are dominated by notions of authoritarian and hierarchical family and kinship-based groups of a 'mafia' type. Whereas, research-based studies have tended to emphasise the importance of more loosely linked networks of independent entrepreneurs, tightly organised clan and kinship-based networks with a global reach undoubtedly do exist. One example would be the Turkish networks that currently control the supply of heroin into Europe, with separate sub-divisions or cells that deal with different aspects of the organisation such as the provision of finance, the purchasing of opium or morphine base from producers or middle men, the processing of heroin laboratories, arrangements for the purchase of precursor chemicals, transportation of the heroin through Europe, warehousing of bulk shipments, trading to lower-level 'middle market' drug brokers, and the laundering of financial assets. For an earlier period, Pino Arlacchi (1986) gave a detailed account of the Calabrian and Sicilian *Mafioso*, and their involvement with different levels of the heroin trade. Broadly speaking, these kinds of organisation seem to have a declining significance in the modern marketplace illicit commodities of all kinds (Zhang and Chin, 2003).

Indeed, virtually single-handed operations are not unknown, reaching from Columbia to Europe, and co-ordinating the importation of large quantities of cocaine and other substances (Barnes, Elias and Walsh, 2000). In between these two scales of operation there is a whole range of flexible, constantly mutating networks of independent traders and drug brokers who make up the 'middle market'. In Zaitch's (2002) account of Colombian drug traffickers in the Netherlands, small flexible networks of *traquetos* operated at the importation levels in a number of different roles, with a network sometimes being put together simply for a single operation. As described by Reuter and Haaga (1989:40, 54) in their study of high-level drug markets, it is more useful to think of drug trafficking at this level as partnerships between independent traders:

> The arrangements described were not so formal and permanent as either legitimate businesses or the traditional criminal organisations described ... Most of the arrangements would be better described as small partnerships ... Hierarchical organisations may exist, but they are not necessary for lucrative careers ... Successful operation does not require creation of a large or enduring organisation ... The trading relationships described by our informants were more like networks than like hierarchical organisations.

Equally, small 'middle market' drug networks – typically, the central figure who holds the cash and governs the business, with one or two 'runners', collecting and delivering drugs from and to various suppliers and customers, and working for a wage or a share in the profits – can operate with the same personnel over long periods of time, until disrupted by law enforcement efforts. The following is a snapshot of some of the activities of one such small business enterprise:

> Alf started working for Frank Robins when he was unemployed and doing odd-jobs, having previously worked in the building trade. Robins offered to pay him £400 a week. He also supplied a car and a mobile phone ... Robins told him he needed a new dealer because his previous one had been arrested by the police when he had also lost £150,000 in drugs seized. It gives some idea of the resilience of Robins' enterprise that he could bounce straight back from this. The basis of Alf's work for Robins as a 'runner' was to collect and deliver drugs to different people at different times, often regular customers, on Robins' instructions. For example, Alf supplied a retail level heroin dealer A who took 1 ounce of heroin every one or two days. There was another heroin dealer B who received 1 ounce daily; B also sometimes took samples of the heroin Robins had been supplied with in order to test its quality for him. Another regular customer was a man C from near Manchester who took 4–5 kilos of cannabis every couple of weeks plus 2,000 Ecstasy tablets. C was a colleague of D, a previous customer of Robins, who was now in prison although C was still allegedly working for D. Then, there was E who regularly received a few thousand Ecstasy tablets and who was known to Alf only as 'Salford Eddie'. Alf usually met customers such as these in pub car parks, or in the car parks of supermarkets or roadside restaurants such as the Little Chef or Pizza Hut. A man called F who was the uncle of one of Robins' associates, G, took 1 kilo of amphetamine base every 2 weeks; and Alf also delivered to Robins' cousin H who had ounces of heroin on a regular basis. Another man called J received twelve 9-ounce bars of cannabis every two weeks, and Alf also used to meet K from the Midlands in a pub car park

every fortnight and supply him with 3-4 kilos of cannabis bush and 1,000 Ecstasy tablets. (Pearson and Hobbs, 2003:337–38)

At these middle and upper levels, drug markets like any other type of commodity market, consist of a series of middleman and brokerage functions – which can otherwise be described as a 'commodity chain' (Wilson and Zambrano, 1994). Precisely how many steps there are-- from importation, through wholesale dealers, to retail sellers and end-point consumer purchases – is a 'grey area', and probably varies between different operations. Drug markets are sometimes described as 'pyramids', but if this is a useful way of describing them, then sometimes they are very flat or shallow pyramids. One experienced cannabis trader explained, for example, how he bought directly from importers, selling to half a dozen men below him who took 5 to 10 kilo loads that they would sell in single kilos to people who were retail dealers. He did not take particularly high profits, typically £25 to £50 per kilo, relying instead on rapid turnover.

'The importers, a typical load for them would be three, four tons. Three tons might sound like a lot of hash, but it'll disappear, thin air, gone. Three or four busy guys like me working off a 3 ton parcel, you'd make that disappear within six weeks, two months … I was doing 70 to 100 kilos a week, selling to five, ten kilo people … I was in the middle'. This operation would yield approximately £2,500 to £5,000 profit per week, with no overheads since the people to whom he was supplying were independent traders. (cf. Pearson and Hobbs, 2001:64)

The supply networks and middle market operations vary for different drugs, and are constantly changing according to market conditions and/or perceived threats from law enforcement agencies. Where heroin is concerned, for example, intelligence sources indicate that 80 per cent of heroin entering the UK is in Turkish control. A load of 100 kilograms imported into the UK might be divided three ways between three independent wholesalers of Turkish origin. At this point, various bit-part players, odd-job men and go-betweens enter the fray, invariably of Turkish origin themselves and maybe connected by kinship to the wholesaler. One man would be recruited to guard the drugs at a safe house, and for this 'baby sitting' role he would be paid by the number of kilos he was taking care of. Another would be recruited as a driver to collect loads of heroin from the warehouse and deliver to customers in loads of 1 to 5 kilos who would themselves supply down the chain to smaller operators.

Steve, in his mid-40s, was a career criminal who has spent a lifetime in drugs and crime. Throughout the 1990s he was involved in heroin, and for some years he bought from a Turkish connection in north London. He was trading one or two kilos per week at £21,000 per kilo, and selling in ounce, multi-ounces and part-ounces at £800 to £1,000 per ounce. He always bought from the same source. Heroin was being imported in 20 to 30 kilo loads, and he might be allowed to buy a part-load of five kilos. 'Obviously, I say the same source, I never met the man. My person was the person who just sat in-between, contacted the Turk ... it was mostly Turkish.' (Pearson and Hobbs, 2001:60)

An alternative system of importation employed by south Asian traders based in the UK is to bring in the drug by air in passenger's baggage.

One such network was compact and family-based and consisted of second-generation Pakistani UK residents, working to an uncle who was first generation, and other elder members of the kinship group resident in both Pakistan and the UK. In all there were five or six people involved. They imported heroin in 10 to 15 kilo loads by air through couriers recruited in Pakistan. After one courier panicked and left the baggage at the airport, transport systems were changed. Baggage handlers at a UK airport were recruited to intercept the suitcase at arrival and to arrange for it to be removed from the aeroplane and to circumvent customs. For this service, the corrupt baggage handling team, who were white, would be paid £5,000 per kilo ... Couriers were still recruited in Pakistan, although this new arrangement meant that the couriers took very little risk, because his/her job was simply to get the suitcase onto the plane. The new transport system was very difficult to co-ordinate, however, because the suitcase had to get onto a plane in Pakistan, which would arrive to coincide with the shift-working system of the baggage team ... Their distribution was to Pakistani dealers and low-level distributors in a number of towns and cities scattered across the UK who would typically buy one or two kilos. (Pearson and Hobbs, 2001:60–61).

The importation system for cocaine mirrors that for heroin precisely. It is either shipped in bulk loads by sea from South America in large via the Galician coast of north-west Spain or direct into Rotterdam harbour (Labrousse and Laniel, 2001:117ff.). Or it arrives in 'small-but-often' loads carried by air passengers acting as 'mules', either carrying drugs in baggage or involving 'stuffers' and 'swallowers' who internally ingest the drugs: either by Colombians into Amsterdam, or by Jamaicans from the entrepot Caribbean into British airports (Zaitch, 2002; Platzer, 2004; Pearson and Hobbs, 2001:20–22 and 62–63). Although these are the main forms of the importation of heroin and cocaine into the UK, many other routes and nationalities are involved in different ways (Observatoire Géopolitique des Drogues, 1996).

A further twist is that there appears to be an increasing trend for British middle-market traders to deal directly with Turkish and Colombian warehousing systems based in continental Europe, and to import heroin and cocaine into the UK on their own behalf – thus circumventing wholesale and warehousing systems in the UK.

Mr. A owned clubs and pubs in a Yorkshire city, with two men handling distribution for him, Gary and Carl, supplying customers in the home city, but also in Glasgow, Liverpool and sometimes London. He imported 30,000 Ecstasy tablets on a regular basis from the Netherlands, plus one or two kilos of cocaine. George was later recruited as a driver. George describes his part in the operation: 'He, well depending on the scale of things, he did move quite a lot of drugs … around 30,000 Ecstasy a week … He would probably be giving these people 5,000 Ecstasy tablets and they would be giving him the money later … He didn't only deal in one type of drug, he dealt in probably three or four different types – cannabis, Ecstasy, cocaine and amphetamines – he didn't deal with heroin or anything like that … As I say, what I started to do was run to collect money and I would go up to Scotland and I would meet people, I would collect money for them. I would go over to Liverpool and collect money for them. But that was about as far as my involvement was going … So I mean OK he would make 50 pence a tablet, on each tablet, so he was probably making near on £20,000 a week for what he was doing, moving it on. He also sold hash, weed. He probably would be selling 50 kilos, 60 kilos a week of weed. Then amphetamine, cocaine as well to the point … he wasn't dealing a lot of cocaine, but he was dealing in ounces …' (Pearson and Hobbs, 2004:573)

We have only sparse knowledge of how UK crime networks link up with warehousing systems and middle-men drug brokers in continental Europe, and in particular the Netherlands, where for a variety of reasons connected with shipping tonnage and airspace volume drug trafficking networks tend to converge (Zaitch, 2002). Only a snapshot can be offered, of someone trading with a criminal network very much like Mr A's in the north of England.

Alfonso was someone who, working out of Amsterdam, supplied drugs to people in the UK, Italy, Spain and elsewhere. 'These people used to come over from England to buy drugs. The main drug was Ecstasy, but people were coming wanting cocaine … People used to buy from me 30,000 Ecstasy and 1 kilo of coke. They'd be supplying it to people buying 1,000 to 2,000 at a time, and they'd be distributing it to people buying 100, 200 … I could easily sell 50,000 a week. There's a market …' Alfonso was close to a pill manufacturer, buying through an intermediary at approximately 50 pence each and selling them on at £1 each. Cocaine was less profitable at his level of the market. 'I'm investing 50 to make 60 [thousand guilders], but with Ecstasy I invest 50, I get 100 back.' (Pearson and Hobbs, 2004:574)

That is, for an investment of £15,000 Alfonso could make a return of £30,000 with ecstasy. He had established his lucrative connection with the English gang through a chance meeting in Ibiza.

> I've always been a party animal, so ... we'd already met in Ibiza ... It goes on and on and on ... They start asking questions, am I interested in this, can you help me, of course I can. So little by little it goes on like that ... You know, drugs is a criminal thing, but it didn't feel like that, I was just doing business. You want to buy something, I can sell it, make a profit ... There's lots of people want drugs. You want it, I can get it. I was just more or less a middle man. (Pearson and Hobbs, 2004:574)

Alfonso worked on this basis, regularly supplying tens of thousands of ecstasy tablets to half-a-dozen customers, purchasing drugs for his customers on demand. He did not warehouse drugs at all, and nor did he deliver, they always had to be collected. As one police officer based in Rotterdam explained:

> This can take place at remarkable speed. Traffickers book a night in the Hilton and order pills in the evening which are subsequently produced and ready to be picked up the next morning after breakfast. (quoted in Gruppo Abele, 2003:32)

With fleeting exchanges such as these, within a buoyant global market, it is little wonder that enforcement agencies struggle to keep abreast of the drug market.

Conclusions: A Fragmented Picture

The over-riding impression is of the highly fragmented nature of drug markets, with different actors playing different roles at different times, none of them able to draw the 'big picture'. Participants in drug distribution networks only know as much as they need to in order to perform a particular task. A core aspect of the culture of serious crime networks is not to be 'nosey' by asking too many questions. Given that it is often the 'small fry' who are caught up and arrested in enforcement operations, those with the most limited understanding of the network within which they function, this further confirms the sense of fragmentation.

Sometimes, this fragmentation is carefully constructed by well-capitalised individuals who coordinate the network, by placing 'cut-outs' between themselves and the drugs, creating highly compartmentalised functions for each step or process in the commodity chain, in which each participant has no knowledge of other compartmentalised functions. This use of intermediaries and go-betweens is employed by risk-adverse operators who never adopt a 'hands on' approach with drugs themselves (Dorn, Oette and White, 1998).

At other times, the fragmentation is a consequence of the business requirements of the operation. As one man who controlled the transport link in the importation of cannabis explained:

> I had the transport link, the driver who brought the stuff across from wherever. And I had this man who wanted to buy ... well, not the man himself, but someone acting on his behalf. I was sitting in the middle. Once the arrangement was in place, my main worry was that the man who wanted to buy didn't meet up with the transport end. Because once they met, that left me nowhere. So I always had to be the go-between ... Like I said, I was the middle man, that's where I made my money, took my cut. (Pearson and Hobbs, 2004:566)

For whatever reason, then, the fragmentation is carefully constructed and maintained. This makes for very real difficulties in conducting research into drug markets and drug dealing. It is hardly surprising that small-fry retail dealers, or the 'pond-life' as they are sometimes described by enforcement agents, have little understanding of the market structures above them. Nevertheless, as I hope to have shown, the nature of middle- and upper-level drug markets is itself constructed out of various aspects of brokerage, with middle-men and go-betweens easing the flow between independent traders and entrepreneurs. As we have summed it up elsewhere:

> Our response ... has been to aim for a variety of aims and perspectives – those of people above (whether offenders or enforcement officers) looking down; people below looking up; people looking from the periphery of a network inwards; people at the centre of a network looking outwards, etc. This means that the picture is rather like a large jigsaw – but a jigsaw in which each piece comes from a different set. (Pearson and Hobbs, 2001:58)

Notes

1. For a select bibliography of research on drug markets and drug dealing, see Pearson and Hobbs (2001).
2. Unless otherwise stated, the bulk of this case study material is taken from two research projects, published as Pearson, Gilman and McIver (1986) and Pearson and Hobbs (2001) together with related publications.
3. On 'sentimentality' in sociological and criminological research, see Becker (1964:4–6).
4. These prices reflect market conditions in the 1990s. With the subsequent collapse in the retail price of pills claiming to be ecstasy, to as low as £2 per unit in the UK, this has changed the nature of the business and blown a hole in the upper levels of the ecstasy market (Gruppo Abele, 2003:37).

Further Reading

Lewis, R., *et al.* (1985). 'Scoring Smack: The Illicit Heroin Market in London, 1980–1983', *British Journal of Addiction*, 80: 281–90.

Pearson, G., and Hobbs, D. (2003). 'King Pin? A Case Study of a Middle Market Drug Broker', *Howard Journal of Criminal Justice*, 42(4): 335–47.

Power, R., *et al.* (1995). 'A Qualitative Study of the Purchasing and Distribution Patterns of Cocaine and Crack Users in England and Wales', *Addiction Research*, 2(4): 363–79.

Parker, H. (2000). 'How Young Britons Obtain Their Drugs: Drugs Transactions at the Point of Consumption', in M. Natarajan and M. Hough (eds), *Illegal Drug Markets: From Research to Prevention Policy*. Monsey, NY: Criminal Justice Press.

Waldorf, D. (1993). 'Don't Be Your Own Best Customer: Drug Use and San Francisco Gang Drug Sellers', *Crime, Law, and Social Change*, 19(1): 1–15.

Study Questions

1. What are the typical varieties of retail drug supply system, and what influences the form that these assume in terms of the following: customer behaviour, law enforcement activity, and retail business requirements?
2. To what extent, and why, did the dance club scene of the 1990s offer unique opportunities for drug dealers to expand their business operation?
3. What are the main geographical sources for illicit drugs, and how is the middle market organised that links up systems of importation with retail supplies to consumers?
4. Is the notion of the drug 'pusher' at all useful, or are drug dealer/consumer relations better thought of as consensual exchanges?

Part Two
Policing, Control and Care

6

Drugs and Crime: Exploring the Links

Tim McSweeney, Mike Hough and Paul J. Turnbull

Introduction

The conclusion that there are links – albeit complex ones – between some forms of illicit drug use and crime has been consistently reached by many studies conducted across different locations and populations over a number of years. Indeed Welte, Zhang and Wieczorek (2001) have described this finding as 'one of the reliable results obtainable in criminology'. It also forms a key tenet underpinning recent drug and crime reduction strategies in the United Kingdom. However, the exact nature and direction of this link is still unclear (Best *et al.*, 2001; Simpson, 2003).

In keeping with much of the current drugs/crime debate in the UK, we have focused here upon the links between drug use and property crime (offences like burglary, shoplifting, robbery and other theft). We have not explored the links between alcohol and crime (Deehan, 1999; Engineer *et al.*, 2003; Richardson and Budd, 2003) or drugs and violence (Anglin and Speckart, 1988; Dobinson and Ward, 1986; Goldstein, 1985; Harrison and Backenheimer, 1998; Jarvis and Parker, 1989).

This is not then an exhaustive review. The research evidence exploring and describing the links between drug use and crime has already been comprehensively reviewed elsewhere (see Hough, 1996; Hough, Mc Sweeney and Turnbull, 2001; Seddon, 2000; Stevens *et al.*, 2003 for recent reviews). It is not our intention to duplicate this work. Instead we aim to pull together some of the key ideas and experiences to emerge from the more recent British research and provide an overview of the accumulating research evidence to describe some of the different interactions between drug use and offending behaviours that have been observed.

We shall begin by briefly outlining four different types of link that could plausibly exist between drug use and crime. This chapter will then focus primarily on key pieces of recent British research – but will also consider relevant international work – conducted across four distinct populations. This will include studies that have sought to examine:

- the nature and extent of illicit drug use and offending behaviour in the general population;
- drug use in the known offending population;
- offending behaviour among problematic[1] drug users in contact with drug treatment services; and
- patterns of drug use and crime among criminally involved drug users.

This will help to unravel some of the aetiological processes at work and assist in highlighting the important role of other complex and inter-related social, economic and cultural factors. In doing so, we shall call into question the use of a unidirectional model to explain the link between drug use and crime and thus reveal a much more dynamic and interactive relationship.

Types of Link

As will be discussed below, there is a large degree of overlap between those using illicit drugs and those who are involved in crime, with a pool of people who both use drugs and offend. Hough, Mc Sweeney and Turnbull (2001) have suggested that this link can arise in a number of ways:

- Illicit drug use may lead to other forms of crime. Sometimes referred to as the 'economic necessity' model, the link arises from the need to generate funds to buy drugs or as a result of the dis-inhibiting effects of some drugs.
- Crime may lead to drug use. For example, crime can provide both the money and the contacts to buy drugs or serve as a palliative for dealing with the stresses of a chaotic, criminal lifestyle.
- There could be a more complex interaction whereby crime facilitates drug use and drug use prompts other forms of crime.
- There may be an association arising from a shared common cause – but no causal link at all between offending and drug use.

The fourth model is perhaps the least researched and developed. It suggests that drug use and crime are likely to share some causal roots without themselves being causally related. For example, economic deprivation, inconsistent parenting, low educational attainment and limited employment prospects are considered risk factors not only for chaotic or dependent drug use but also for heavy involvement in crime.

Hough (1996) has noted that these models are not mutually exclusive or incompatible with others as different explanations may be more appropriate at different points throughout a drug using career. He describes how in some cases problem drug use may trigger theft as a means of fund raising; while others might never have become drug-dependent if crime had not provided them with the means to buy large amounts of drugs. Some people will both be involved in crime and also use illicit drugs without there being any causal connection whatsoever between the two.

It will also become clear that most drug users are – and remain – in control of their use; many such users are also involved in crime, but drugs are not to blame for this. There is a small minority of drug users who are dependent in their use and chaotic in their lifestyles; there is a strong probability that these people will finance their drug use through property crime.

Drug Use and Offending in the Overall Population

A large number of people engage in illicit drug use in developed countries throughout the world but most do so in a relatively controlled way, with cannabis being the most widely used drug. According to United Nations estimates, 185 million people world-wide – approximately 5per cent of those aged 15 years and over – have consumed an illicit drug (UNODC, 2004). The 2002/2003 BCS estimates that 36 per cent of the adult (16–59) population in England and Wales have used illicit drugs at some stage in their life, and 12 per cent have used illicit drugs during the previous 12 months. This represents around four million people who will have used illicit drugs during the last year. Around one million will have used Class A drugs. Use is largely concentrated among the young: 47 per cent of people between the ages of 16 and 24 have used an illicit drug at some time in their life and 28 per cent will have done so during the last year (Condon and Smith, 2003). However, levels of drug use are higher among 20- to 24-year olds than among 16- to 19-year olds.

With around three million users during the last year, cannabis is by far the most frequently consumed illicit drug in England and Wales. Amphetamines, cocaine and ecstasy were the next most commonly used drugs (by 2 per cent of the adult population respectively). Use of heroin and crack is rare. However, there has been an increase in the use of cannabis, crack and cocaine since the 1996 BCS sweep, leading to an overall increase in Class A and any illicit drug use during this period.

Results from a national survey of over 10,000 secondary school children aged 11–15 years questioned during 2003 revealed that 21 per cent had taken an illicit drug during the last year; 12 per cent had done so during the last month. Cannabis was the most frequently used drug with 13 per cent of pupils aged 11–15 having used during the last year. One per cent had used heroin and/or cocaine at some point during the last 12 months. Four per cent had taken a Class A drug during this period. The likelihood of being offered drugs appears to increase sharply with age, from 19 per cent among 11-year olds to 65 per cent among 15-year olds (Department of Health, 2004).

The Youth Lifestyle Survey (YLS) provides an estimate of the extent, frequency and nature of self-reported offending among a sample of 12- to 30-year olds in England and Wales, taking into account background and lifestyle (Flood-Page *et al.*, 2000). It makes broadly similar but slightly higher estimates than the BCS. The YLS identifies the family, school and peer group as being important influences on a young person's likelihood of offending and highlights lifestyle factors such as drug use and frequent drinking as the most important predictors of offending. The YLS found that about a fifth of young people admitted to some form of offending and concluded that self-reported drug use was the strongest predictor of serious or persistent offending, with the odds of offending for drug users being nearly five times higher than for non-drug using respondents. Drug use (at least once a month) was also found to be the most predictive factor of involvement in offending for older men (aged 18 to 30 years).

Recent research also suggests that young people identified as 'vulnerable' are much more likely to experiment with drugs at an earlier age. Their circumstances may also expose them to the range of risk factors associated with the problematic use of substances (Goulden and Sondhi, 2001). A number of studies have addressed the prevalence and nature of substance use among these vulnerable groups including young offenders (Hammersley, Marsland and Reid, 2003; Newburn, 1998), excludees (Powis *et al.*, 1998), children looked after by local authorities (Ward, 1998; Biehal *et al.*, 1995; Ward, Henderson and Pearson, 2003), the homeless (Wincup, Buckland and Bayliss 2003; Klee and Reed, 1998) and children of parents who misuse drugs (Lloyd, 1998).

However, for the majority of young people, there is no persuasive evidence that there is any direct causal linkage between offending and drug use. The association between drug use and offending in surveys like the YLS is perhaps better understood as being 'deeply embedded in other social processes since ... drug use is both about risk taking ... [and] ... about using "time out" to self-medicate the impact of the stresses and strains of both success and failure in "modern" times' (Parker, Aldridge and Measham, 1998b: 151–52).

Parker and colleagues' longitudinal studies have described evolving patterns of drug use among young people in the north-west of England (Measham, Aldridge and Parker, 2001; Williams and Parker, 2001). Experience of illicit drugs was widespread in their samples and most funded drug use through legitimate means. In developing their concept of normalisation Parker *et al.* explain the extensive growth in availability, experimentation, use and acceptability of illicit drugs by today's youth with their respondents making a sharp distinction between acceptable and unacceptable drugs – with heroin and crack in the latter group and use of these drugs was low. There was only a very small minority who were heavily involved in crime, dependent drug use and other forms of delinquency.

Subsequent research has described how 55 per cent of 18- to 34-year olds accept that using drugs is a normal part of some people's lives while two-thirds have a friend or family member who uses illicit drugs (Stratford et al., 2003).

Drug Use in the Known Offending Population

There were 1.42 million offenders sentenced by the courts during 2002 (Home Office, 2004) while recent government estimates indicate that a group of around 100,000 offenders are currently active and might be considered as prolific (MacLeod, 2003). Illicit drug use is much more prevalent among known offenders than the wider population. Dependent or problematic use of drugs is also much more common. A large number of offenders have been identified as regular users of illicit drugs and many regard themselves as dependent, often attributing their offending behaviour to their use of drugs. Research has consistently shown how the criminal justice systems of developed countries throughout the world have disproportionate levels of contact with drug users. For example, a large proportion of arrestees in England and Wales, the United States and Australia test positive for one or more drugs at the time of arrest (59, 68 and 69 per cent respectively) (Taylor and Bennett, 1999; Fitzgerald and Chilvers, 2002).

The NEW-ADAM survey (Bennett, 1998, 2000; Bennett et al., 2001) involves drug-testing and interviewing samples of arrestees in different locations throughout England and Wales. The latest sweep of the survey found that 65 per cent of all arrestees tested across 16 different sites (1435) were positive for some form of illicit drug, with 24 per cent testing positive for opiates and 15 per cent for cocaine. The average weekly expenditure on drugs for heroin and crack/cocaine users was £290. The main sources of illegal income during the last 12 months were property crime (theft, burglary, robbery, handling stolen goods and fraud/deception) followed by drug dealing and undeclared earnings while claiming social security benefits. Heroin and crack/cocaine users had an average annual illegal income of around £15,000 – compared to an average annual illegal income of £9000 for all interviewed arrestees. Many (78 per cent) past year heroin and/or crack cocaine users acknowledged a link between their drug use and offending. Bennett concluded that drug use and in particular the use of heroin and crack/cocaine is associated with higher levels of both prevalence and incidence of offending.

Arrest referral schemes have existed in some UK locations since the 1980s. By 2002, all 43 police force areas in England and Wales were operating these schemes, though most were still in early stages of development. National estimates indicate that around 180,000 problematic drug users enter the criminal justice system through custody suites each year (Sondhi, O'Shea and Williams, 2002). Between October 2000 and September 2001 arrest referral workers in England and Wales screened 48,810 drug-using offenders and revealed an estimated expenditure of £550 million per year on illicit drugs (£11,000 per individual). In London these schemes contacted 10 per cent of all arrestees (11,793 contacts from a total of 121,021 arrests made) between April 2000 and March 2001 (Oerton *et al.*, 2003).

In addition, findings from an evaluation of new powers available to the police in England and Wales to drug test arrestees in specific target offence groups revealed that at least half of all arrestees in six of the nine pilot areas tested positive for heroin and/or cocaine use. In one London site 65 per cent of arrestees tested positive for heroin and/or cocaine use (Deaton, 2004).

Hearnden and Magill (2004) interviewed 82 burglars to discover why they first became involved in crime and how they selected potential targets. Just under one in four stated that they had become involved in burglary in order to fund their drug use. Raising money for drugs was also reported as the main motivation for more recent burglaries. Of the 57 offenders asked, 34 recalled that at its height their daily expenditure on drugs was costing them more than £100.

A significant minority of offenders subject to community supervision have also been identified as problem users. Estimates from various English probation areas range from 7 per cent (May 1999) to 37 per cent (ILPS, 1995). In the US, nearly 70 per cent of probationers report past use of illicit drugs and just under a third had used in the month before their most recent offence (BJS, 1998).

Similarly, different sections of the prison population in England and Wales experiences higher levels of drug use than the general population (Strang *et al.*, 1998; Singleton *et al.*, 1998). Recently the Home Office commissioned an extensive programme of research that described high levels of drug dependence among women, young male and minority ethnic prisoners (Ramsey, 2003). The research also revealed that 73 per cent of 1900 recently sentenced male prisoners interviewed during 2000 had used an illicit drug in the year before imprisonment, and more than half of them considered themselves to have a drug problem. A similar number were able to establish a link between their drug use and offending behaviours.

Such trends are consistently replicated across US (Robins and Reiger, 1991; Peters *et al.*, 1998; CASA, 1998), Australian (Butler, 1997; Kevin, 2000) and European (Turnbull and McSweeney, 2000; Stover, Von Ossietzky and Merino, 2001) prison populations.

Offending among the 'Problem Drug Using' Population

Only a small minority of illicit drug users go on to develop potentially problematic patterns of use (Hough, 1996; Godfrey *et al.*, 2002). Problematic use tends to focus on – but is not exclusive to – drugs of dependency such as heroin, cocaine (especially when smoked as crack) and amphetamine. Gauging the number of problematic users is difficult because of the various definitions and measurement used, and thus estimates have varied (Meltzer *et al.*, 1995; Edmunds *et al.*, 1998; Edmunds, Hough and May, 1999; Frischer *et al.*, 2001; Bramley-Harker, 2001). One of the most recent estimates (Godfrey *et al.*, 2002) suggest that there are between 280,000 and 500,000 problem Class A drug users in England and Wales – at least 7 per cent of the 4 million who use illicit drugs each year. It is also apparent that the circumstances of many of these problematic drug users expose them to a range of risk factors associated with other forms of social exclusion, increasing susceptibility to major physical and psychological health problems and often exacerbating personal, economic and legal difficulties (Gossop *et al.*, 1998; MacGregor, 2000).

During 2003/04, there were estimated to be between 125,900 and 154,000 problem drug users in contact with drug treatment services and general practitioners in England (National Treatment Agency, 2004; Druglink, 2004). However, it is estimated by Godfrey *et al.* (2002) that up to one-third of all problematic drug users will never contact treatment services. The Audit Commission (2004) and Sondhi, O'Shea and Williams (2002) have described a range of possible reasons for drug users not contacting drug treatment services. These include:

- a lack of motivation and 'not being ready';
- past negative experiences of treatment;
- concerns about confidentiality and suspicion of criminal justice based initiatives like arrest referral;
- denial, stigma and fear of exposure;
- for women, childcare and protection issues;
- low self-esteem and peer pressure to maintain a drug using lifestyle; and
- limited choice, inflexible appointment systems and restricted opening hours.

While there is no persuasive research evidence of any causal link between drug use and crime for the vast majority of illicit drug users (Hough, 1996, 2002), the large amount of money spent by the minority of problematic or chaotic users to finance consumption has been consistently highlighted by several studies in different locations and over a number of years. The largest prospective longitudinal cohort study of treatment outcome for drug misusers ever conducted in the UK, the National Treatment Outcome Research Study (NTORS) found that the 1075 users it tracked were, prior to intake, buying drugs with a street value of £20 million per year. Sixty-one per cent of the NTORS sample reported committing crimes other than drug possession in the three months before they started treatment; in aggregate they admitted to 71,000 crimes in this period. The most commonly reported offence was shoplifting. (Gossop *et al.*, 1998). Ten per cent of the sample accounted for three-quarters of the total acquisitive crimes committed. By contrast, half reported that they had not committed any acquisitive crime in the three months prior to starting treatment (Stewart *et al.*, 2000).

A smaller study of 221 methadone reduction and maintenance clients in London found over four-fifths had been arrested for some criminal offence in the past (Coid *et al.*, 2000). However, offending prior to treatment had not always been undertaken solely to fund drug-taking. Despite this, two-thirds believed there was a strong link between their current offending and their drug habit and half claimed that their current offending served solely to fund their drug habit. Best *et al.* (2001) examined 100 people entering drug treatment in London. Consistent with NTORS and Coid *et al.*, they found slightly more than half of the sample reported funding drug use through acquisitive crime. This study also demonstrated how those involved in crime often report more frequent use of crack and a greater expenditure on drugs.

Harocopos *et al.* (2003) tracked a cohort of 100 London crack users over an 18-month period. At intake, levels of drug use and involvement in crime were high. In the month before the interview these crack users reported an average daily expenditure of £100 and most financed their use through crime. However, those respondents who were abstinent from drugs at follow-up were significantly less likely to offend than those who continued to use. These findings are consistent with results to emerge from 4–5 year follow-up interviews completed with NTORS participants, suggesting that crack users report a greater involvement in acquisitive crime than non-users (Gossop *et al.*, 2002).

There is also an extensive research literature in the US which suggests that many problematic users are involved in criminal activity (Nurco, Kinlock and Hanlon, 1995; Anglin and Perrochet, 1998; Luigio, 2000).

Patterns of Drug Use and Offending among Criminally Involved Problem Drug Users

The shift in strategy and policy, apparent in the UK since 1997 for the treatment of criminally involved problem drug users – from a public health and harm reduction agenda to one with a criminal justice driven focus – can be attributed in part to the increasing acknowledgement of the relative ineffectiveness of conventional responses such as imprisonment in tackling drug use and drug related crime, and an acceptance that the provision of community-based treatment alternatives is a more cost effective approach than the use of custody and has fewer detrimental effects (Home Affairs Committee, 2002; ACPO, 2002; Social Exclusion Unit, 2002; Allen, 2002). As a consequence legislation introduced since the late 1990s has substantially extended the ability of the police and courts to coerce drug dependent offenders into treatment.

There is now quite a significant body of research examining patterns of crime and drug use among problem users who are identified as such as they pass through the criminal process. Much of this work has involved evaluations of criminal justice-based referral and treatment programmes targeting this group. The studies show that these problem drug users commit large amounts of acquisitive crime. For example, drug using offenders on probation in London were found to be spending an average of £362 per week on drugs prior to arrest primarily raised by committing acquisitive crime, notably shoplifting. In the month before arrest, over half (51 per cent) of these probationers were using both heroin and crack (Hearnden and Harocopos, 2000).

The evaluation of a range of arrest referral schemes designed to refer offenders to treatment also found similar levels of expenditure on drugs funded through property crimes such as burglary. Again most reported polydrug use with 97 per cent using either opiates or stimulants or both (Edmunds, Hough and May, 1999). More recently, Oerton and colleagues (2003) described the characteristics of 12,000 problem drug users identified by arrest referral workers in London. The offence profile of these arrestees varied and included shoplifting (21 per cent), drug offences (17 per cent), other theft (12 per cent) and burglary (10 per cent). Four-fifths (80 per cent) had previous convictions. Many had used heroin (55 per cent) and crack cocaine (49 per cent) in the month before their arrest. Average weekly expenditure was £391. For those using both heroin and crack cocaine weekly expenditure rose to £632. Half (51 per cent) reported no previous contact with treatment services.

Turnbull and colleagues described the drug use and offending behaviour of those offenders given drug treatment and testing orders (DTTOs) in three English sites. Three-fifths of those given the 210 pilot orders had never received any form of help or treatment for their drug use (Turnbull *et al.*, 2000). Of the 132 drug-using offenders interviewed most (120 or 91 per cent) had been using opiates on a daily basis before arrest. They reported committing several types of property crime on a daily basis in order to fund an average expenditure of £400 per week on drugs. Almost half received their order following a conviction for shoplifting. Subsequent research examining the impact of DTTOs in London and Scotland has described similar patterns of involvement in drug use and offending behaviours among criminally involved drug users (Best *et al.*, 2003; Eley *et al.*, 2002).

Discussion: The Type of Links Observed between Drug Use and Crime

The socialisation perspective in criminology (Dunlap *et al.*, 2002) has been used to describe how drug use and criminality can become accepted and thus be perceived as natural, normal and even inevitable. The literature also suggests that 'lifestyle' and 'subcultural' factors are important in explaining why those who try illicit drugs are also more likely than others to get involved in other forms of law-breaking. The search for novelty and excitement, and enjoyment of the rewards of risk-taking are defining aspects of youth culture (Parker, Aldridge and Measham, 1998b). It is hardly a surprise that large minorities of the population engage in the – relatively controlled – risks of both recreational drug use and minor crime at some stage of their adolescence and young adulthood; particularly at a time when 'the trajectories of young [people] are becoming more diverse, uncertain and for some more problematic' (ibid.:25).

For those whose offending – and drug use – is more persistent and less controlled, other explanatory factors also need to be called into play. In the first place, chaotic drug users and persistent offenders – in contrast to controlled drug users and occasional petty offenders – have limited social and economic resources and limited exposure to legitimate 'life opportunities' (see e.g. Harrison 1992; MacGregor, 2000). The majority are from deprived backgrounds, with inconsistent parenting, poor access to housing and health care, low educational attainment and limited employment prospects. Hough, Mc Sweeney and Turnbull, (2001) have argued that given the scale of participation described by surveys such as the BCS, controlled drug use can have no obvious association with social exclusion. Chaotic or dependent use, by contrast, does appear to share that constellation of risk factors that also predict heavy involvement in crime – and exposure to many forms of social exclusion.

If these risk factors predispose people both to uncontrolled drug use and to involvement in persistent offending, Walters (1998) and De Li Periu and MacKenzie (2000) have discussed how reciprocal causal relationships can begin to emerge, whereby criminal involvement both facilitates and maintains drug use, and drug use maintains involvement in crime. While some researchers, such as Hammersley *et al.*, (1989) and Burr (1987), have argued for subcultural explanations of the close linkage, the accounts of the offenders themselves are often more consistent with a pathological perspective, where dependence provides the motive for continued and escalating involvement in acquisitive offending, as the following quote from an interviewee sentenced to a DTTO in London illustrates:

Q: You've mentioned the drugs side of things, what about the crime side, because one of the arguments is that a lot of people were involved in crime long before they ever got into using drugs heavily. So even if you solve the drug problem there are still going to be people who are offending just to get by?

A: Not for me cos I mean…all right I was doing crime but nothing like to the extent of what I was doing, you know. So no, mine's gone hand in hand. I mean if I could solve my drug problem then that would be my crime problem out of the window.

Hough *et al.* (2001) recently reviewed this growing body of evidence and called into question the 'addiction model' often used to describe a unidirectional relationship between drugs and crime whereby illicit drug use leads inexorably to dependence and thence to crime. For example, some studies have shown how heroin users are able to exert a degree of control over their use of heroin and thus avoid involvement in crime (Pearson, 1987). While Hammersley *et al.* (1989:1040–41) have noted how 'day-to-day crime was a better explanation of drug use than drug use was of crime [with] income from crime leading to greater expenditure on drugs'. For others it appears that dependent drug use may well have predated and precipitated acquisitive offending, while for some, the onset for involvement in crime preceded their first use of drugs (Pudney, 2002; Harocopos *et al.*, 2003). A review of US research by Deitch, Koutsenok and Ruiz (2000) concluded that roughly two-thirds of drug using offenders report involvement in crime before the onset of drug use. Research also suggests, however, that criminal and drug-using careers often develop in parallel; acquisitive crime providing people with enough surplus cash to develop a drug habit, and the drug habit 'locking' them into acquisitive crime (Edmunds *et al.*, 1998).

This is not to deny the wide range of other causal factors which may underlie both drug use and offending given that the predictors of uncontrolled drug use and of persistent offending appear remarkably similar (Farrington, 1994; Goulden and Sondhi, 2001). Seddon (2000) has argued that it is useful to consider problem drug use and persistent offending as expressions of broader delinquent behaviour that share causal roots. However, it is also important to understand how, once established, the two behaviours can be mutually sustaining. In other words, drug dependence tends to amplify the offending rates of people whose circumstances may predispose them to becoming persistent offenders (Harrison and Backenheimer, 1998; Ball, Schaffer and Nurgo, 1983); and equally, persistent offending may amplify levels of drug use.

Government has just launched a major Drug Interventions Programme designed to get statutory and voluntary sector agencies to work together to tackle the social factors associated with drug misuse and crime. It has recently allocated almost £0.5 billion to this programme over three years; if successful, it has the potential to substantially reduce levels of crime (see Department of Health, 1996; Hough, 1996; Marsden and Farrell, 2002 for recent reviews of drug treatment effectiveness). However, it is also important to ensure that criminal justice interventions are not seen as a panacea for tackling the wider problems of drug use and drug related crime. Maintaining the lifestyle changes, which treatment may enable, requires long-term commitment to multi-disciplinary intervention that effectively addresses and tackles the wider risk factors that both initiate and perpetuate the complex cycle of persistent offending and problematic drug use (Audit Commission, 2004).

Conclusion

Around 4 million people use illicit drugs each year in England and Wales. Most use involves the relatively controlled consumption of drugs such as cannabis, ecstasy and cocaine. People who try illicit drugs are more likely than others to commit other forms of law-breaking. However, there is no persuasive research evidence of any causal linkage between drug use and crime for the vast majority of illicit drug users. The most recent estimates suggest that there are between 280,000 and 500,000 problem Class A drug users in England and Wales who have chaotic lifestyles involving dependent use of heroin, crack/cocaine and other drugs. A small proportion of problem users – unlikely to exceed 100,000 in number – finance their use through crime and are extensively involved in the criminal justice system. Frequent estimates suggest that this group of users spend in the region of £400 each week on drugs, despite limited legitimate incomes. Shoplifting,

burglary and selling drugs are common fund raising strategies. This group also report long parallel careers in offending and drug use. The majority of those who steal to buy drugs were involved in crime before their drug use became a problem for them. Many have numerous previous convictions and served prison sentences. Very few report any previous experience of, or contact with, treatment services. If appropriate drug treatment and integrated support is given to this group, a minority can be expected to reduce their offending levels.

Note

1. The ACMD (1982) define problematic users as those experiencing social, psychological, legal or physical problems arising fro m their use of drugs.

Further Reading

Bean, P. (2004). *Drugs and Crime*. Second edition. Cullompton: Willan Publishing.
Barton, A. (2003). *Illicit Drugs: Use and Control*. London: Routledge.

Study Questions

1. In what ways is it assumed that drug dependence and crime are related?
2. Has recent government drug policy focused too much on crime?
3. 'A significant proportion of crime is though to be drug-related, and if we get to grips with dependent drug use, we could halve the crime rate'. Discuss both parts of this statement.

7

The Police and Drugs

Chris Crowther-Dowey

Introduction

The policing of drugs within society has created considerable debate, particularly the proposition that the drugs laws exacerbate the problems caused by drugs. It has been argued that through the social control of drug users four central problems have arisen. Firstly, the prohibition of, and attempts to regulate, drugs markets have sometimes worked against the police service's need to balance its capacity to control and care for populations who drift in and out of states of dangerousness and vulnerability. Secondly, the black market gives organised criminal gangs and dealers considerable power in determining the street level working of the drugs economy. Thirdly, there is no regulated quality control and hence the health-related risks for drug users have risen. Illegal drugs are not regulated and among other things there is no control over their strength and purity. Not least, there is the risk of transmitting HIV/AIDS through the sharing of infected needles. Fourthly, the policing of drugs is an expensive enterprise and in some cases (i.e. cannabis) the drugs laws are unpopular partly because the police lack the resources to respond to a host of other more pressing social problems. In light of this, contemporary policing of drugs is fraught with difficulties in terms of balancing justice, economic and health priorities.

This chapter will focus upon these difficulties and discuss the ways in which policing drugs has changed in Britain, drawing on Brixton as a case study. There are two main parts to the discussion. The first part provides a brief historical overview of the policing of drugs through the use of stop and search beginning in the 1970s. Brixton, an area in the south of the Metropolitan Police District (MPD), is important because of the riots taking place there in 1981 and the consequent reappraisal of police policy and practice. In recent times, cannabis has been policed in innovative ways, particularly through the Brixton drugs experiment. This was followed by the home secretary's reclassification of cannabis from a class B to a class C substance in early 2004. It is shown that elements of this twenty-first century experiment had, in fact, been carried out informally 20 years ago. After examining developments in Brixton the next part of the chapter considers the situation nationally, including a discussion about harm-reduction strategies. Attempts to reduce harm comprise drug arrest referral programmes (ARPs) and DTTOs, and are largely driven by a concern with HIV/AIDS (TDPF, 2004:12). In some areas of police activity the organisation has adopted a more caring attitude, however policing has not entirely moved away from a more coercive approach to law enforcement. Finally, the chapter will conclude with the argument that the legalisation or decriminalisation of drugs is unlikely in the foreseeable future and that the police will continue to pursue a dual strategy of law enforcement and harm reduction. In the last analysis, however, the policing of an unregulated and criminalised drugs market cannot realistically aspire to reduce the harm caused to public health and civil society by drug misuse. Initiatives emphasising harm reduction may go some way towards addressing the health needs of drug users, but the organised criminal cartels responsible for distributing 'hard drugs' will remain relatively unscathed, adding further to the exploitation and immiseration of drug consumers. The safety and security of law abiding citizens will also be under threat as violence escalates between rival suppliers in an increasingly competitive drugs market.

The Lambeth Cannabis Pilot Scheme

There is a relatively long and troubled history of policing in Lambeth, a relatively deprived community. As well as being poor, the borough of Lambeth is a geographical area associated with the redefinition of contemporary police policy and practice, especially in the last quarter of the twentieth century. Lambeth attained particular notoriety following the occurrence of the Brixton riots in 1981 and the response to this unrest from the late Lord Scarman (Scarman, 1981)[1]. Prior to these disturbances this territory was characterised in quasi-military terms as a 'Front Line' (Keith, 1993); a zone of potential police–community conflict. It was a location where an undercurrent of tension and sometimes hostility existed between a group of predominantly work-less and marginalised young black men and an essentially white, sometimes racist, police force. The source of this unease centred on the police's insensitive approach to tackling crime and disorder, and for the purposes of this chapter, principally through the occasional raids of the streets and 'shabeens' (social clubs) to disrupt a sometimes busy drugs market place.

While there is evidence to show that the trading of soft drugs such as 'ganja' (cannabis) was commonplace, and the presence of 'hard drugs' was an undeniable reality, the police's response to crime, including drugs-related criminality, is best characterised as hard and aggressive. Throughout the

1970s and 1980s over-zealous policing and significant evidence of racist banter and behaviour among rank and file officers resulted in the criminalisation, demonisation and ultimately alienation of significant numbers of the policed population (Bowling and Phillips, 2002). The media and government's production of stereotypical images of black criminality also added to these widespread negative representations (Hall *et al.*, 1979). By April 1981 the police's intensive and mass usage of their powers to stop and search suspected drug suppliers and users on the streets resulted in a major riot. The stop and search issue is discussed later in this chapter.

Brixton: From Policing Against towards Policing with Communities

There is no space here to discuss in detail the Brixton riots and subsequent events (see Crowther, 2000). The highly influential official inquiry commissioned by the government at that time, written by Lord Scarman (1981), raised some important issues about policing in general, but specifically the policing of drugs in modern Britain. Scarman's report covers a potentially overwhelming brief and in many ways stands as an account of the condition of the work-less classes in London's poorest communities. It is his examination of police work that is important here, in particular his decision to revisit the core functions of the Metropolitan Police identified back in 1829 by Sir Robert Peel. Peel stated that there are two tasks the police must undertake: firstly, peacekeeping or the maintenance of public order; and secondly, the prevention and detection of crime. Both of these activities are important, but Peel prioritised the former, and crucially it was noted that pursuing the latter could jeopardise the realisation of the former. A pertinent example of this is the Metropolitan Police's reliance on the so-called sus laws introduced in the nineteenth century as part of the 1824 *Vagrancy Act*. This piece of legislation underpinned the police's decision to stop and search young African-Caribbean males to search them for drugs.

Even though it is indubitable that the police are required to enforce the law (i.e. the *Misuse of Drugs Act*, 1971) one of the first lessons students of the police and policing are taught is that the literal interpretation and absolute enforcement of all laws at all times and in all places is impossible, mainly because there are simply not enough police officers with sufficient resources. In addition, operational policing is influenced by other factors such as the discriminatory stereotypes mentioned above, but also by non- or extra-legal policy frameworks. Perhaps the most significant issue, though, is police discretion (Choongh, 1999; Reiner, 2000), amounting to a degree of subjectivity and selectivity in the maintenance of the rule of law. Following the discovery of cannabis the following disposals are

possible. The offender may be informally warned or arrested. After an arrest is made a decision is taken as to whether or not the offender should be cautioned or charged. In Brixton the police exercised their discretion in a way that was perceived to be illegitimate and unjust, and the police lacked the consent of sections of the policed (Scarman, 1981). There was also a perception that differential policing had an adverse effect on decisions about whether to issue a fine, a court discharge or other sentence following prosecution and conviction (Bowling and Phillips, 2002). In short, the riots occurred, in part, because of the efforts of the police to impose hard crime control strategies, such as anti-drugs legislation, at the expense of keeping the peace.

The Police and their Power to Stop and Search

Among Scarman's proposed solutions to the apparent police crisis was the repeal of the 'sus' laws to avoid any repetition of the Brixton riots. This led to the eventual reform of the police's powers to stop and search, achieved through the passing into law of the *Police and Criminal Evidence Act* (PACE) in 1984. It is necessary to rehearse this here because stop and search, albeit a sometimes crude and blunt instrument, is a key part of the police's toolkit for dealing with drugs. PACE is still extant today, but a more recent official report, namely MacPherson's (1999) inquiry into the police's flawed investigation of the tragic murder of the young black teenager Stephen Lawrence, has led to some further reforms of the police's powers to stop, search and make an arrest.

A police officer may stop and talk to any person in any public place if they suspect they are in possession of, importing or producing drugs. Any conversation that takes place should be used to determine if the officer's grounds for suspicion are justified. This suspicion must not be based on the perceived ethnicity, sex, age, the past history or general appearance of the suspect. Most stops are conducted with people when they are on foot, but the police can also stop motor vehicles and request to see the driver's licence. If a vehicle is unattended and the police have reason to suspect that a car contains drugs they can carry out a search without the owner of the vehicle being present.

If a person is to be searched, in most cases the police must gain consent. The exception to this rule is when the police have 'reasonable suspicion' (i.e. behaviour associated with drugs offences) or if the organisation has been given a tip-off that a person has committed a drugs-related offence. Given concerns about police discretion and evidence of racism among the rank and file officers, and the 'institutionally racist' nature of the organisation, the police must inform the suspect of the legal reasons for stopping them and why they wish to carry out a search (Rowe, 2004). For example, they need to explain why they stopped the person and be specific about what they are looking for. There are some safeguards in place for the suspect, not least the right to complain if they are dealt with inappropriately. Furthermore, the suspect needs to have their legal rights explained to them. The police officer initiating the stop must also provide their name and the identity of the station where they work. In public places, suspects may only be asked to remove their coat, jacket or gloves to enable an officer to search for narcotics. Any other searches for drugs need to take place outside of public view, and more intimate searches need to undertaken by an officer of the same sex as the suspect. The police enjoy additional powers under the *Misuse of Drugs Act* (1971) and they are able to take a suspected person to a police station without making a formal arrest if they wish to do a more thorough and detailed search. Intimate and more invasive searches for drugs in body orifices may be authorised by a police superintendent who has reason to believe a suspect has concealed a class A drug (i.e. cocaine or heroin). Such a search may only be conducted by either a doctor or nurse in a medical environment. Following the interaction the person who has been stopped has the right to request a record of the search, which they must be able to see within a year of the incident.

Buildings may also be subjected to a search for drugs. The police may enter and search premises at a reasonable time, with the consent of the occupier. The occupier has a right to see a warrant or a written statement outlining their rights. If the occupier invites the police inside, the officers present can search for drugs, even if the original purpose of the arrest was unrelated. The police have additional powers enabling them to enter and search premises where consent is not required. For example, they may go into a building to make an arrest if they can see an offence is taking place, such as the consumption of drugs or an attempt to dispose of evidence such as illicit substances.

From Law Enforcement to Peace Keeping

The change to stop and search was just one component of a broader recommendation. According to Scarman, peace keeping is more important than crime fighting, sometimes meaning that the police do not apply the letter of the law, particularly if in doing so they might create serious disorder and violence. This suggestion was generally accepted by the then home secretary, Lord Whitelaw, but also among senior police officers (Reiner, 1991). What, then, were the consequences of Scarman for the police's attempt to regulate the use and supply of drugs on the streets of Lambeth?

It is important to acknowledge from the outset that Scarman was not calling for the abandonment of the rule of law, but rather a different set of approaches for addressing drugs-related crime. Rather than tack-ling criminality through the use of force and hard policing styles, there was a reorientation of police policy and practice. In Lambeth there was a four-pronged approach to the management of crime and disorder, consisting of

- multi agency approaches to police work;
- intelligence-led policing strategies;
- the visible presence of uniformed officers and
- police-community consultation.

Taking the first of the above, an emphasis was placed on multi-agency work, based on the assumption that the causes of and solutions to criminality are not just the responsibility of the police. For example, in the case of drugs the police co-operate with other agencies in the public sector, including health and education, signalling the police's shift away from a job based exclusively on exerting control through the legitimate use of force to a job which also focuses on the provision of care and support. Moving on to the second point, rather than deploying large numbers of officers to raid premises in the hope that they would pick up drug dealers, the police decided targeted surveil-lance would probably produce better results. These alternative methods were introduced to avoid any of the unnecessary aggravation frequently caused through the face-to-face encounters linked to police officers' use of stop and search (Bowling and Phillips, 2002). By positioning covert cameras in areas where alleged drug dealers are known to operate, the police were able to gather more reliable intelligence or evidence to identify suspects and offenders. Thirdly, instead of deploying specialist police units like the Special Patrol Group (SPG), Scarman (1981) argued that there should be a highly vis-ible police presence, but these officers should patrol in a non-confrontational way, acting as deterrents rather than enforcers. Finally, the above would be realised through public consultation. The mechanisms for this established by PACE (1984) and have been formalised via the crime and disorder audits introduced by the *Crime and Disorder Act* (Home Office, 1998).

The four approaches mentioned above were key features of the anti-drugs policing strategies introduced by the police commander, Alex Mar-noch, in post-riot Lambeth. This officer accepted Scarman's counsel and he developed a policing style which was more consultative than confron-tational. Police work is best done when the police converse and commu-nicate with the people they police. The logic of this approach is that the police need the consent of the community if they are to effectively address crime problems, such as selling and misusing drugs. In contrast to his predecessors, Marnoch actively discouraged his officers from making arrests for the possession of cannabis for personal use, especially on or near to the 'Front Line' (Keith, 1993). If any arrests had to be made he instructed his officers that this should be conducted away from this tension ridden area to avoid increasing the potential for any conflict and full-scale riots like Brixton 1981. In Marnoch's view, the unthinking and uncritical enforcement of the drugs laws was likely to be counter-productive and create more social harm than public good. The legalisation or decriminalisation of cannabis was not on the public policy agenda but there was a different understanding of how drug misuse should be resolved.

Thus, in the early to mid-1980s the police began using new methods of policing drugs, but these were not altogether unproblematic. One outcome was that the prioritisation of peace keeping and the subsequent residualisation or decreased use of crime fighting tactics allowed the drugs trade to expand, especially the market for 'hard drugs'. At times, the police were not able to distinguish the anti-social behaviour associated with the use of cannabis and alcohol from the more serious threats posed by organised drug gangs selling potentially more harmful drugs that can cause ill health and inter-personal violence (Keith, 1993). When the police did use coercive methods the outcome was the displacement of drug-related crime to other parts of the MPD. In addition, the idea of allocating officers to an area to ensure a visible police presence still left communities feeling exposed to unnecessary surveillance and over-policed.

The Late Twentieth-Century Legacy

Thus far it has been established that the policing of drugs in Lambeth, and many other areas like it, has been burdened with difficulties. So far, there are three inter-related points that need to be made clear. All drugs classified under the *Misuse of Drugs Act* (1971) are illegal and the police are required to apply the letter of the law, albeit under the influence of discretion and policy directives. The use of drugs may pose an immediate threat to the physical and psychological health of individual users. More than that, drug users may harm the communities in which they live due to users' anti-social behaviour and involvement in various crimes to fund their respective habits (see Chapter 4). Suppliers may also cause social harm, as rival gangs become embroiled in turf wars to maximise their control and influence over global and local, or 'glocalized', drugs markets (Winlow, 2002). Such a situation requires the police to respond to the supply and use of illicit substances in social settings where inter-personal and communal violence are never far away.

Lambeth Cannabis Warning Scheme: Contextual Factors

The story above perhaps helps explain an event that occurred in December 2000. A police officer in Brixton was arrested and charged because of his failure to deal with cannabis properly. He had exercised his discretion, as many officers had done previously, but on this occasion a criminal charge was made. It is not surprising that the colleagues of this officer reacted in they way they did. To ensure that they did not end up being arrested and charged, they stated that they would arrest every individual who they found in possession of cannabis. Shortly after this incident, Commander Paddick was appointed to lead and manage policing in Lambeth. Paddick was concerned by this event and investigated possible ways of responding to cannabis without exposing his officers to the danger of arrest. As well as this legal conundrum, Paddick identified a range of political and economic problems with arresting people for cannabis use. Some of his arguments were also found in a report published before his arrival, entitled *Clearing the Decks* (Metropolitan Police Service, 2000). He argued that arresting people for cannabis placed a considerable burden on the police's limited resources. More than that, the outcomes in the prosecution process did not justify the investment of resources. For example, the results of arrests were frequently cautions, small fines (i.e. £50) or conditional discharges at court (PSS Consultancy Group, 2002).

The problem of finite resources experienced in Lambeth were part of a more general problem faced by the police service throughout the other 42 forces in England and Wales, specifically the influence of the 'New Public Management' or 'managerialism' (Long, 2004; Neyroud, 2003). These ideas gained ascendancy throughout the public sector during the 1980s and while they refer to a set of complex political rationalities some broad tendencies can be identified. In essence, providers of public services must satisfy the government and the wider public that their activities are 'cost effective', provide 'value for money' and are evaluated according to effectiveness, efficiency and economy. The police are now required to adopt a more business like style of service in order that they are able to deliver more economic, effective and efficient services. The significance of the 'Three Es' can be seen through the emphasis on value-for-money, performance targets and auditing, quality of service and the consumer. The introduction of market and private sector values also constrains professionals through the introduction of national standards and objectives, systems to measure financial accountability and increased external scrutiny and monitoring (Crowther, 2000).

To address this problem Paddick explored various possibilities, including an idea called the 'seize and warn scheme'. This concept was based on the Commander's appreciation of Lambeth's history, and an acceptance of Scarman's view that arresting everyone they stopped and searched who possessed cannabis would put the already fragile police–community relations under considerable strain, possibly culminating in yet another major outbreak of public disorder.

There were further continuities with the 1980s, inasmuch as Lambeth was affected by the problems of ill health and violence, sometimes caused by drug dependence. According to community leaders, not just the police,

crack cocaine and heroin, along with gun-related violence and street robberies blighted the quality of peoples' lives in this locality. There was a view
in the community that these harder drugs should become police priorities
rather than cannabis. In addition, community representatives argued a shift
of emphasis along these lines would conceivably curb the police's continued, often poorly conceived usage of stop and search against African-Caribbean youth.

The controversial changes suggested by Paddick clearly presented problems. An obvious criticism is that the police may have given the impression
to the wider public, particularly those who do not use drugs, that the police
are abrogating their responsibility to enforce the law and protect the public
from the harm caused by an unregulated drugs market. Moreover, Paddick
did not have the authority to implement a pilot without the approval of his
superiors. In short, it was necessary to broach the subject with the community and the higher echelons of the police organisation. Paddick announced
in *The Evening Standard* (29th March 2001) that the police in Lambeth were
considering taking a softer line and not arresting people for cannabis.
Following this the police met on three occasions with the Lambeth Police
Community Consultative Group. Throughout these discussions the Group
made it absolutely clear that they were opposed to drugs, but that they
supported the philosophy underpinning Paddick's plan (Dapp, 2002).
Paddick's bosses adopted a similar position, and despite some scepticism,
it was seen that the court results did not fully justify the cost of prosecuting
people. Indeed the way drugs are currently policed is placing the criminal
justice and penal systems into a state of permanent crisis (TDPF, 2004:8).

Implementing the Lambeth Cannabis Warning Scheme

By 4th July 2001 the Lambeth Cannabis Warning Scheme was implemented,
initially for 6 months (*The Evening Standard*, 4th July 2001), but it actually
ran for just over a year until 31st July 2002. On the 1st of August 2002
the police's discretion to arrest individuals in possession of cannabis was
returned to them, raising questions about the need for an exit strategy
(Metropolitan Police Authority, 2002:3). The rationale of the initiative was
to reduce the time spent dealing with individuals caught in possession of
cannabis, thus freeing up time for the police to respond more effectively to
serious offences, including Class A drug offences, burglary, gun crime and
robbery (PSS Consultancy Group, 2002). What actually happened?

Immediately prior to the initiation of the scheme it was necessary for
an officer to devote considerable time filling in forms, which acted as a
disincentive and frequently led to officers 'turning a blind eye'. Any adult

who was found to be in possession of small quantities of cannabis for personal use had the substance confiscated from them. There were two outcomes: individuals admitting this offence were given a 'formal warning'; and those who did not admit to committing the offence were issued with an 'informal warning'. In both instances, the course of action taken avoided the making of an arrest (Metropolitan Police Authority, 2002).

As part of the pilot, police officers were told that if young people were found to be in possession of the drug, it must be confiscated. Young people were automatically referred to the YOT. These teams were set up by the 1998 *Crime and Disorder Act* (Home Office, 1998) to provide 'joined-up' inter-agency solutions to problems with complex causes. In the case of cannabis possession, the individuals referred to YOTs would be offered counselling, support and advice. More than that, the parents of the young person concerned were also invited along to receive similar support.

The Impact of the Lambeth Scheme

The response of senior Metropolitan Police officers to the Lambeth scheme was positive and the then deputy Commissioner of the Metropolitan Police, Ian Blair declared the scheme 'undoubtedly a success – in statistical terms'. Mike Fuller, the deputy commissioner in charge of drugs strategy, was also positive referring to the project as 'a godsend' (*The Guardian*, 2 July 2002). To put these views into context it is necessary to scrutinise the impact of the scheme.

The PSS Consultancy Group (2002) evaluation focused on the impact of policing activity on drugs in Lambeth and adjoining boroughs. It examined data about offences and disposals, as well as gleaning police officer's perceptions through a questionnaire survey and focus groups.

A key priority of the pilot was to reduce the pressure the policing of cannabis placed on scarce resources. The police achieved this goal and more time was available to enable the police to focus on more serious offences. For example:

> During the 6 months of the evaluation, Lambeth officers issued 450 warnings. This released at least 1350 hours of officer time (by avoiding custody procedures and interviewing time), equivalent to 1.8 full time officers. A further 1150 hours of CJU staff time was released by avoiding case file preparation. (PSS Consultancy, 2002:1)

The Warning Scheme was still bureaucratic though, because officers had to fill in a crime report, a stop and search form and possibly a criminal intelligence sheet. They also had to produce a written record of what happened to the seized drugs. Despite the considerable work involved there was an 110 per cent increase in the number of interventions concerning cannabis and 1390 warnings were issued in contrast to 661 arrests in the previous year (MPA, 2002:6) The MPA suggested that the PSS calculations above may be an underestimate of the total resource saved, but the time saved works out to be the equivalent of 1.8 officers per annum or up to 2.75 more officers if the increased enforcement activity is also integrated into the costing methodology (MPA, 2002). The availability of more resource may account for the finding that:

> Lambeth also increased its activity against Class A drugs relative to adjoining Boroughs. (PSS Consultancy Group, 2002:1)

It would appear from the above points that the pilot had been of some success. The costs of controlling cannabis supply had been reduced and some police time had been liberated to direct more resources towards combating the sale and trafficking of Class A drugs. For example:

> There was an increase in police activity in relation to class A drug trafficking enforcement in Lambeth, which increased 19% (89 in 2000, 106 in 2001), when compared with a 3% increase on adjoining boroughs. The increased performance against class A trafficking continues to be sustained, particularly against crack cocaine. The total number of drug offences, which denotes arrests, increased from 1367 to 1733 (26%) during the period from April – March 2001-2, when compared with the same period the previous year. Arrests for drug trafficking have also increased from 288 to 344 (16%) during this period. This would indicate that one objective of the pilot scheme has been achieved, which was to release officers' time to carry out more class A drug enforcement. (MPA, 2002:10)

Despite the 'statistical' success story, Vauxhall MP, Kate Hoey vehemently opposed the scheme and argued that it had caused far more harm than good by giving the message to children that 'cannabis is no worse for you than sweets' (*The Guardian*, 2nd July 2002), thus obfuscating the risks the substance poses to young peoples' physical and psychological health. This view was backed up by anecdotal evidence from other residents living in the areas.

The evaluation also focused on the perceptions of police officers. Some officers still felt that the public did not understand the aims and objectives of the policy. Some of the officers surveyed also voiced concern that the policy had resulted in the restriction of their powers to address drug offences and that a valuable source of intelligence was being lost. Indeed, the majority of officers felt that the policy would lead to an increase in general drug use in Lambeth and for this reason the policy should not be rolled out to the rest of the MPD (PSS Consultancy Group, 2002:2).

The community also had views on the scheme which were gathered by a Police Foundation instigated survey delivered by MORI. The report found that there was much concern that some young people might be more likely to come into contact with and misuse drugs as a result of this scheme. Lambeth police were naturally worried about these concerns and conducted a survey of local schools, finding that neither the experiment nor the home secretary's discussion about reclassifying cannabis had led to any increases in dealing or the confiscation of cannabis at schools. Some critics argued that the borough had become a site for 'drug tourists' making use of a lax enforcement strategy, but this claim was not borne out by the evidence. There was also a belief that the experiment signalled the legalisation or decriminalisation of cannabis, demonstrated by Deputy Assistant Commissioner Mike Fuller's comment: 'The public were very unclear about what was happening and thought drugs were being legalised and this wasn't the case' (*BBC News*, 21st March 2002). This suggests that communication about the strategy could have been improved. The market & opinion research internatonal (MORI) poll found that there was more support for the scheme among white rather than black and Asian residents (*BBC News*, 21st March 2002). Finally, there was no evidence of formal complaints being made by members of the public against the warning scheme pilot.

As indicated above, on 1st August 2002 the police reverted back to the original policy of making arrests for the possession of cannabis. During this period, however, public debate had been preoccupied with the reclassification of cannabis and it was appreciated that simply returning to the ways things had been done before could create tensions between the police and community.

The Reclassification of Cannabis

A significant date in Britain's history of the policing of drugs was 10th July 2002 The home secretary announced the reclassification of cannabis from a class B to class C drug (Home Office Press Release, 10th July 2002). Research had indicated that this reclassification would result in some financial savings and give police officers more time to patrol and respond to calls for public assistance. There may be slightly fewer serious crimes detected, but the savings in police time elsewhere would compensate for this. There would also be non-economic benefits, specifically fewer adversarial contacts between the police and young people (May *et al.* 2002).

After taking advice from the Advisory Council on the Misuse of Drugs (ACMD) the home secretary was made aware that cannabis could not be decriminalised and had to remain illegal because it is a harmful drug. It was acknowledged that cannabis carries health risks of both an acute and chronic nature and can also lead to dependency. It was agreed, however, that cannabis was not as harmful as either class A (i.e. heroin, crack) or class B (i.e. amphetamines) drugs and for that reason cannabis, including resin, should be reclassified as C. The government has therefore adopted a clear position: cannabis is illegal and poses risks to the health of users. In practical terms, though, it was not feasible to criminalise adults possessing cannabis, mainly because resources are finite and class A drugs needed to be prioritised. Cannabis was reclassified from a class B to a class C drug on 29th January 2004. As a controlled drug, the production, supply and possession remains illegal but the penalties imposed have been altered. The maximum penalty for producing and dealing all class C substances is now 14 years. The maximum penalty for possession has been reduced from 5 years to 2 years imprisonment, but for adults the aim is to avoid making an arrest. This is typical for class C drugs. The preferred penalty for possession is confiscation of the drug (in the case of adults) and a warning unless there are aggravating factors, such as: public disorder associated with the use of cannabis; if a person smokes cannabis openly in a public place; if a young person aged 17 years or under is found in possession of cannabis; people who are in possession of the drug in close proximity to places such as schools, youth clubs or children's play areas. Young people (under 18) offending for the first time will be arrested where they will be given a formal warning or reprimand. If the perpetrator re-offends they will be given a final warning or be charged.

Obviously the Lambeth pilot scheme was only tried out in one area of London and therefore too much should not be read into this. It is therefore necessary to get some sense of other developments in the policing of drugs nationally, in particular the use of harm reduction strategies.

Harm Reduction

Arrest Referral Schemes

On making an arrest the police have various courses of action they may follow in cases when an arrestee is either suspected of, or known to be, a drug user. For example, a range of Arrest Referral Schemes (ARS) was introduced in 2000. Prior to the introduction of these schemes the police provided a range of services for individuals with drugs-related problems. Firstly, in some police stations custody staff distributed information about support available for drug users on a non-coercive basis. Secondly, some police stations had a dedicated drugs worker, who was either present on the premises or on call. The role of this member of staff was to assess and refer individuals with a drug problem to appropriate treatment programmes. Thirdly, the police had powers on making an arrest to either defer a caution or take no further action if a suspect agreed to seek treatment for a substance misuse-related problem (Dorn, 1994; Chatterton, Varley and Langmead-Jones, 1998; Edmunds *et al.*, 1998; Edmunds, Hough and May, 1999).

On 1st April 2000 the Home Office's Crime Reduction Programme provided funding to launch a significant number of ARS as part of an overarching strategy to protect communities from drug related and anti-social and criminal behaviour (Home Office, 2000). They are there for the purposes of public health harm reduction and to give treatment and social care, mainly because less drug use improves physical and psychological health. The main function of ARS is twofold. Firstly, they target offenders with drugs-related problems and refer them to take up appropriate services. Secondly, and this will only be confirmed through self-report data and arrest figures, ARS aim to deliver specialist drug treatment services to reduce crime.

In the spirit of the *Crime and Disorder Act* (Home Office, 1998) ARS are multi-agency initiatives involving the police, local drugs services (in the form of Drug Action Teams (DATs) and Drug and Alcohol Action Teams (DAATs) as well as other 'gateway agencies' (Sondhi, O'Shea and Williams, 2002). ARS operate independently of the police and are used at the point of arrest to offer, mainly adult, arrestees an opportunity for a coherent treatment programme at an earlier stage than they originally were. The majority of ARS (81 per cent in the first year and 83 per cent in the second year) may be found in police stations with 13 per cent in the courts and 7 per cent in other venues (O'Shea, Jones and Sondhi, 2003). When an arrestee is booked in at a police station it is the custody officer's duty to inform the arrestee that an ARS is available in the station. If the arrestee takes this opportunity they then see an independent drugs worker who will conduct an independent assessment. Alternatively, appropriate staff carry out 'cell sweeps' and adopt 'cold calling' tactics to establish contact with arrestees suspected of using illegal drugs. On the basis of this initial interview the individual may be referred for drug treatment services or other programmes such as employment, social services or housing. There are four tiers of service. Tier 1 is in the health service domain, including Accident and Emergency (A and E) and general medical services. In the second tier, services include needle exchange and outreach. Tiers 3 and 4 provide more specialist services, including structured community-based residential services for substance misusers.

Although there is evidence that fewer arrests were made of individuals who have received ARS services (Sondhi, O'Shea and Williams, 2002), some users, however, would appear to be missing out on services. Black and Asian problem drug users are one group, as are young, dependent users of crack who fund their habit through street robberies and female sex workers who are similarly dependent on this drug.

Furthermore, it is necessary to take into account the influence of the new public management and managerialism (Home Office, 2002; Long, 2003; Neyroud, 2003), and the extent to which it has led to a significant reallocation of resources, thus making the regulation of drugs markets and substance misuse increasingly difficult (Crowther, 2002). For example, the ARSs are targeted, which means effectively that some arrestees are missed out. Also, ARS are not always offered on a 24 hours basis and if custody suites are busy, then it is not always feasible to provide support. It is therefore necessary for a more realistic theoretical appreciation of the more complex relationship connecting drugs-related crime and policing, which appreciates that control and care are not always fully achieved (Crowther, 2004).

There are other initiatives delivered at later stages of the criminal justice process.

Criminal Justice-Administered Treatment

After the police have dealt with an offender there are various possible outcomes for the latter, including conviction and sentencing. If offenders are sentenced to either a custodial or community-based punishment there is provision for individuals with a recognised drug problem. Police budgets, however, are sometimes redirected towards schemes run by non-police agencies. This is linked to a general trend in criminal justice policy over the last decade or so, which has seen an attempt to direct offenders with a drug habit towards treatment programmes, mainly involving the offender abstaining from drug use. An example of kind of provision mentioned in the previous paragraph is the DTTO, a sentence was designed to reduce the harm caused by drug misuse. The DTTO is a community sentence involving the probation officers supervising and monitoring offenders as part of an attempt to address drug misuse. Under a DTTO an offender is required to undergo treatment to reduce or eliminate their problem with drugs. The treatment lasts no less than six months, but for no more than three years. The courts cannot specify the nature of the treatment, although it must be provided by an institution recognised in the order. Throughout the duration of the order the offender is required to undergo tests on a regular basis to assess if there has been any drug use in the treatment period. The offender must also stay in contact with their supervisor, notify them of their movements, and be available for regular appearances at court, if required.

The thinking behind the above has been criticised, not least because criminal justice agencies are administering what are to all intents and purposes health services. Besides, the courts are determining the use of the DTTOs without any consultation between the offender or patient and a medical profession. For example, there is urine testing which is not only intrusive but also involving a degree of compulsion. Above all, breaches of the sentence may result in a custodial sentence. The rhetoric may be all about treatment and harm reduction but this is the velvet glove concealing the iron fist of further criminalisation (TDPF, 2004:13). The official response has also been tepid with the National Audit Office (2004) reporting high reconviction rates for offenders.

Conclusion

This chapter has explored some debates that centre on the policing of drugs in British society. During the last quarter of the twentieth century, the police have sometimes taken a relatively tough stance on the supply and possession of drugs, especially by employing the coercive powers of stop and search. Unfortunately, in applying stop and search, rank and file officers have been shown to exercise their discretionary enforcement of the drugs laws in a discriminatory way against some socially disadvantaged, ethnic minority groups. This culminated in the inner-city riots of 1981 and a reorientation of police policy and practice, moving away from policing *against* communities towards a more explicit peacekeeping function. Subsequently, the police have been required to respond more cautiously to crime by working more closely *with* communities and other agencies to respond to criminogenic conditions. The supply, possession and use of drugs continued to be treated as a crime, although cannabis is deemed to be less of a priority and rigid enforcement was replaced by a non-discriminatory discretion. Following the urban unrest of 1981, the police concentrated their anti-drugs strategies primarily on 'hard drugs' because of the serious damage their supply and use causes to society, but also to maintain effective policing. The police had some success in dealing with the cannabis conundrum in the first few years following Lord Scarman's report. Class A drugs, however, are much more difficult to police, especially because of the risks to health and wealth being posed by the unregulated supply and demand of crack cocaine and heroin. The policing of these drugs also failed to fully stop continued conflict between patrolling constables on the beat and young black men.

At the turn of the twenty-first century, the issues discussed above still confronted the police in Lambeth, but there were additional problems brought about by those changes in government policy embodied by the principles of managerialism. An already difficult task of regulating an expanding drugs market was worsened by the state demanding more effective service delivery with fewer resources to do the job. The Lambeth cannabis pilot scheme was used to illustrate how the police could maintain the rule of law effectively and economically by reconfiguring policing priorities. This experiment became intertwined with a national, government-led debate about reclassifying cannabis (which resulted in this drug becoming a class C substance). The limits to what the police may do in response to drugs have long been recognised and over the last few decades the need for alternative approaches to crime control has been developed. Instead of depending solely on punitive methods, the aim also has been to formulate harm-reduction strategies to tackle drug dependency in the case of 'hard drugs'.

In short, there has not been a major shift in government thinking and there is no expressed commitment towards the legalisation of drugs. The police have proved a greater willingness and capacity to perform a wider range of duties beyond crime management and reduction, and harm reduction is a core component of contemporary policing. Despite the police service taking on some practices that are novel in the context of traditional policing styles, the organisation must still respond to an unregulated and disorganised drugs market run by organised criminal networks. The stated aim of reducing harm may improve the welfare of some drug misusers, but initiatives like DTTOs are ultimately concerned with criminal justice rather than health priorities. While various statutory agencies struggle to determine their respective roles and responsibilities in relation to drugs, the criminal production and supply of heroin and crack cocaine is likely to continue to cause serious harm to the lives of people in the communities affected by these drugs.

Note

1.   Similar riots across Britain in the spring and summer of 1981 were bracketed off from Scarman's remit.

Further Reading

Jacobson, J. (1999). Policing Drug Hot-Spots. London: HMSO.
Lee, M., and South, N. (2003). 'Drugs Policing', in T. Newburn (ed.), The Handbook of Policing. Cullompton: Willan.
Lupton, R., Wilson, A., May, T., Warburton, H., and Turnbull, J. (2002). Drug Markets in Deprived Neighbourhoods. London: Home Office.
Newburn, T., and Elliot, J. (1998). Police Anti-Drugs Strategies: Tacking Drugs Together Three Years On. London: Home Office.

Study Questions

1. Outline the main problems drugs present to the police service.
2. What can the police do to control: (a) drugs trafficking; (b) drugs dealing; and (c) offending that is related to the misuse of drugs?
3. Can the police service also reduce drug-related crime?

8

Drugs Education

Alison McInnes and Amanda Barrett

Introduction

Despite the paucity of evidence proving the effectiveness of drugs education for young people, successive UK governments have placed it at the centre of drug control strategies. Public health issues connected to illicit drug use invariably involve legal, ethical, moral and religious controversy (Mort, 1987) and the objectives of drugs education - either to promote harm minimisation or abstinence from drugs – remain contested ones. This chapter focuses mainly on drugs education in schools, particularly UK provision, with some reference to wider, mass media-based education campaigns and evidence from other countries.[1]

What is Drugs Education?

The charity Drugscope defines drugs education as 'the acquisition of knowledge, understanding and skills, and exploration of attitudes and values which facilitate young people to be able to make informed decisions about their own and other people's use of drugs' (www.drugscope.org.uk). At present there is a statutory requirement for schools to provide drugs education to children and young people and surveys show that parents and carers desire drugs education for their children (DfES and DoH, 2003).

Drugs education can include any intervention, such as using the mass media, schools, youth work and peer education. The main aim is to produce a measurable shift in children and young people's knowledge about, attitudes to and use of drugs. The main drugs education approaches include media (propaganda) campaigns; giving factual information (to school children and their parents); the acquisition of social, personal and lifestyle skills; peer education; harm minimisation initiatives and the promotion of healthy living.

The government policy document *Tackling Drugs to Build a Better Britain* (Home Office, 1998a) identifies the importance of young people being able to handle any drug-related problems they may encounter and ultimately being able to resist drugs. The policy recognises the need for information, skills and guidance to be provided in ways that are sensitive to age and circumstances. In UK schools, drugs education is taught as part of the Personal, Social and Health Education (PSHE) of the National Curriculum in Science and increasingly in Citizenship lessons. The key aims are to provide school children with opportunities to increase their knowledge and understanding of the risks of legal and illegal drugs; explore their own and others' attitudes and values towards drugs and drug users; and to develop their personal and social skills so that they feel able to communicate effectively, recognise choices, make decisions and access help when needed (DfES and DoH, 2003).

The National Healthy School Standard (NHSS) launched by the Department of Education and Employment (DfEE) in 1999 established drugs education (including alcohol and tobacco) as one of its key themes. It states that all schools should be 'interested' in drugs education by April, 2004. Moreover, all Primary Care Trusts (PCTs) should employ drugs workers with the provision of delivering the NHSS in schools. OFSTED will oversee that schools are carrying out the NHSS (but this is not a mandatory aspect of school provision and does not form part of school assessment). One requirement is that all schools must have a planned drugs education programme and a named member of staff responsible for drugs education provision.

In 2004, the Department for Education and Skills (DfES) prepared further guidance for schools in respect of drugs education. This sends a clear message that illegal drugs on school premises are not acceptable and gives head teachers a clear 'one strike' option to permanently exclude school children involved in dealing drugs on school premises, even for a first offence. At the launch of the guidance, School's Minister Stephen Twigg, reiterated that 'we are committed to a zero tolerance policy towards drugs in schools and many schools are already doing excellent work on drugs education. Nearly all schools now have drug policies and OFSTED tells us that the quality and quantity of drugs education has never been better' (www.dfes. gov.uk).

The Failure of Drugs Education

Despite the plethora of national and local initiatives, agencies and programmes in the UK designed to educate children and young people about drug use, to deter them from it, or at least reduce the harm that might come from drug use, drug prevalence surveys suggests that their effectiveness is, at best, mixed. In Chapter 2, Newcombe reviews such findings in detail. He points, for instance, to national surveys of drug use among 15 to 16 year olds in Europe that show the UK to have the highest rates of self-reported, life-time drug use. In this context, it is unsurprising that researchers talk of the 'normalisation' of drug use among British youth (see Blackman, Chapter 3 and Shildrick, Simpson and MacDonald, Chapter 1). Rather than leading to a scaling down of drugs education initiatives, Blackman (2004) argues that this increasing prevalence of youthful drug use has, over the past ten years, spurred UK government's efforts towards drugs education and drugs prevention.

In this section, we consider the effectiveness of schools-based drugs education programmes, pointing up some of the general and particular problems that interventions have encountered. Current health policy in the UK emphasises the need for drugs interventions to be evidence-based; i.e. established through rigorous assessment of not only 'what works', but what does not work (Cohen, 2002). Yet, Dorn (1981:281) has argued – startlingly – that 'no known method of drugs education can be said to reduce drug use'. Coggans *et al.* (1989), Bagnall (1991) and May (1991) have also concluded that those drugs education programmes that have been evaluated have at best been ineffective and may indeed have been counterproductive. Much available evidence suggests that providing young people with information on drugs does not necessarily lead to behaviour change (Plant and Plant, 1992). More specifically, OFSTED (2002) claimed that drugs education lessons in schools fail to provide adequate opportunities for school children to explore their attitudes to drug use and to develop the skills they need to make informed decisions.

De Haes (1994) concludes that evaluation studies repeatedly show that the effects of drugs education programmes are often weak and can produce both positive and negative results. One particular example of the general problem can be found in the classic work of De Haes and Schuurman (1975). In a study of 1035 14 to 16 year olds in Rotterdam (The Netherlands) they investigated which of the three approaches to drugs education was the most effective. Participants were sorted into classes which were subjected over a two-week period to a 'warning approach' (i.e. one that emphasised the dangers of drug use), an 'informative approach' (i.e. that aimed to impart knowledge about drugs), or a 'person-oriented approach' (focusing on values, social skills and problem solving). There was also a control group who received no drugs education programme. Those in the 'warning' and 'information' approach classes showed increases in correct *and* incorrect answers to questions about their drug knowledge. Only the 'don't know' answers diminished.

De Haes and Schurmann concluded that, as a result of these appro- aches, 'honest uncertainty' about drugs had transmuted into 'misplaced confidence'. As far as behaviour was concerned, none of those pupils who were drug users changed their behaviour, regardless of which approach was used. The researchers also measured pupils' *first* use of drugs in a seven-month period after the baseline study. In the 'warning' group 7.3 per cent of pupils went on to use drugs for the first time (compared with 2.6 per cent for the 'person-oriented' group, 4.6 per cent for the 'information' group and 3.6 per cent for the control group). De Haes and Schuurman (1975) concluded that 'substance-oriented' drugs education programmes, whether purely 'informative' or 'warning-based', have a *stimulating* effect on drug experimentation, but that 'person-oriented' approaches can reduce drug use.

Approaches to Drugs Education and Prevention for School Children

Universal Versus Targeted Approaches

The Health Advisory Service (HAS, 2001) reviewed evidence relating to drugs education and prevention. It highlighted the need to develop strategies that enhance protective factors and reduce risk factors and which aim to delay initiation into drug use and that are age appropriate. 'Universal' and 'targeted' interventions are therefore cited as two methods of delivering drugs education. The former – such as health education programmes for all school-age children – do reach large numbers of people, but evidence to support their effectiveness is limited (HAS, 2001). The latter approach requires 'at risk' individuals to be identified in order to target prevention strategies at those most likely to engage in drug use. The DfES (2004) offers guidance to schools in identifying individuals vulnerable to using drugs, including the potential risk and protective factors. While schools can provide a valuable role in enhancing protective factors, reducing the impact of risk factors and supporting those in need of specialist intervention, concerns are raised around methods of detection and stigmatisation of identified individuals. The launch of the DfES guidance led to considerable media interest in detection methods, namely, the use of sniffer dogs, searches and random mandatory drug testing (MDT).

In a culture where drug incidents in schools have been managed punitively (such as by excluding pupils), fewer young people might be expected to admit to using or trying drugs, due to fears of the consequences. Given a context of the normalisation of drug trying among the youthful population (Stead *et al.*, 2000), screening methods to identify 'at risk' individuals are likely to give false positive and negative results, potentially exposing them to stigmatisation and recrimination. In this context, schools are faced with the real dilemma of providing a culture where those in need of help feel at ease to disclose without fear of recrimination, balanced with the need to fulfil substantial responsibilities of detection. Of course, the introduction of sniffer dogs into schools and random drug testing raises questions about effective practice (e.g. sniffer dogs are trained to pick up the scent of drugs on individuals but those individuals may not, in fact, have been the actual carriers or users of such drugs). They also raise more serious, ethical questions about human rights (e.g. in relation to informed consent from children and young people to be searched/ tested, rights to privacy and so on) (Marks, 2004).

These concerns are perhaps most apparent in recent UK political support for, and initial moves towards, random drug testing of school pupils (via the provision of urine samples) (McKeganey, 2005). In his review of the ethics, practicalities and likely effectiveness of such testing, McKeganey itemised the problems associated with this most recent example of a punitive, 'zero-tolerance' approach to children and young people's (potential) drug use. Most obviously and echoing general refrains in the field of drugs education, he points to the very limited independent, rigorous evaluation of the likely impacts of such initiatives. McKeganey reminds us that occasional use of cannabis is the most likely finding of such testing and he queries the extent and nature of the positive help that might come to children and young people identified in this way. He also notes a range of other significant worries about a policy/practice move in this direction, including the potentially high financial costs; ethical issues about who to test, informed consent, observation of tests and confidentiality of results; the possible risk that some pupils might, as a consequence, switch to less easily detectable 'harder' drugs'; the possible detrimental impact on trust between pupils and teachers; and the unpredictable responses of schools and pupils to drug testing and its results.

Abstinence Versus Harm Minimisation

Much of the recent history of UK and US drugs treatment (see Webster, Chapter 9) and education policies can be understood as a struggle between approaches that emphasise care, education and harm minimisation on the one hand, and those that promote control, prevention and abstinence on the other. It is worth noting that in these countries the use of illegal or socially disapproved drugs have been approached in far more draconian ways than have legal drugs such as cigarettes and alcohol. The former have been regarded as targets for total abstinence, rather than being subject to controlled use (Plant and Plant, 1992). Ironically, the harm caused by legal drugs – to users, their families and communities – is often far greater (Royal College of Physicians, 2001).

As Blackman (2004:156) points out, 'prevention is based on the idea that information on drugs should be *against* drug use, whereas drugs education considers drug information should be *about* drug use'. His argument is, however, that drugs education approaches have become dominated by implicit (often explicit) prevention assumptions. He contends that, whatever their particular emphasis and approach, fundamentally all drugs education programmes commence from a problem-oriented perspective on illicit drug use and contain an eventual goal of prevention (even if harm minimisation is an explicit objective along the way). The following, key extract from a DfEE policy document on good practice in drugs education schools illustrates this thinking: 'schools alone cannot "solve" the *problem* of drug use in society [but] an effective programme of drugs education in schools can be an important step in *tackling it*' (DfEE, 1998:3, emphases added). Few would disagree with the contention that abstinence-based approaches have won out over the ones which rather than seeking to control and eliminate youth drug use, aim to provide objective, neutral information about drug use and reduce the harm that can *sometimes* come from it.

Harm minimisation or reduction approaches work from the point of view that illicit drug use (and the use of legal drugs) has become a normalised feature of contemporary, *mainstream* youth culture, (rather than merely the preserve of a particularly vulnerable, risky or at risk segment of the youth population) (Parker, Aldridge and Measham, 1998b). Because young people typically perceive themselves as being invulnerable to the harm caused by drugs (Elkind, 1985) and because the 'risky' behaviours adopted by some young people are fostered by powerful factors that are difficult to counter (Plant and Plant, 1992), harm minimisation takes what it therefore sees as a rational and pragmatic approach. They advocate practices which attempt to reduce or eliminate the negative consequences of substance use, regardless of whether the user wishes to abstain (Strang, 1993). This philosophy currently dominates the provision of *community-based* substance misuse services in the UK (even if stopping drug use is the ultimate, eventual goal). Of course, complete abstinence from the use of dangerous substances could be argued to be one pole of a harm minimisation continuum (with, for instance, medical interventions to combat the effects of drug overdose at the end of the spectrum). In reality, however, the philosophy and practices of harm minimisation tend to be at odds with and in conflict with approaches that preach abstinence.

Although the DfES (2004) guidance on drugs education in schools alludes to the use of harm minimisation (with its references to exploring risks and personal decision making), primarily it promulgates an abstinence approach to drugs education. One example of the difficulties that can come from this approach – and the conflict between the two philosophies – can be seen in the way that schools manage drug incidents. Schools can legally dispose of cannabis found on their property (for instance, by flushing it down the toilet) and thereby seek to lessen the potential criminalising consequences of the incident. The DfES (2004) guidance states, however, that schools must report an incident like this to the police and keep the cannabis locked in a safe. If the school keeps the cannabis on school premises for 48 hours or more, however, the school can be charged with possession. Moreover, autonomy over how best to respond to the drug incident is taken away from the school with the result that the incident – and the young person in question – may become criminalised.

Proponents of the harm minimisation approach argue that its opposite (abstinence programmes) fail to equip children and young people to function in a society where the use of illicit substances is widespread and where 'drug offers' are increasing (Parker, Aldridge and Measham, 1998b). Young people already engaged in drug use may not be receptive to abstinence-based approaches, especially if they find their (pleasurable) experience of drugs differs radically from the 'negative' picture painted in abstinence campaigns. In a context where abstinence messages and practices prevail, young users of drugs may choose further to avoid revealing their drug using behaviour to drugs practitioners, teachers and others (thus widening the gap between users and drugs services).

Despite some research evidence to support the effectiveness of harm minimisation, calls for it to be the basis of universal interventions to prevent haphazard, inaccurate, 'trial and error' acquisition of knowledge (Saunders and Marsh, 1999) – UK drugs education policy has steered away from this approach. It would seem that political anxiety and preference – reflecting fears that the public might conceive of harm minimisation approaches as encouraging drug use – has, in this case, overcome the current British government's stated emphasis on policy being evidence-based.

Media Campaigns

Outside of schools-based education programmes, mass media-based campaigns have also tended towards taking an abstinence stance. Some of the first drugs education programmes (Fluke and Donato, 1959) included abstinence-based media campaigns intended to induce fear of drug use. Early drugs education methods relied on scare tactics and moral exhortations that linked the use of drugs to alarming physical and moral degeneration. The Federal Bureau of Narcotics introduced an early example of this method by producing the drugs education film *Reefer Madness* (after marijuana was outlawed in the US; see Blackman, Chapter 3).

More recent campaigns in the UK and US repeat this emphasis upon warning young people of the dangers of drug use, relying on shocking imagery and exhortatory messages (e.g. 'just say no') so as to scare recipients of these messages away from drug use. In the UK, the emergence of HIV/AIDS in the early 1980s led to negative images and press sensationalism in mass media campaigns, which provided false messages and misinformation that proved difficult to dislodge: 'Take heroin and before long you'll start looking ill, losing weight and feeling like death. So if you're offered heroin, you know what to say. Heroin screws you up'.

The 'Heroin Screws You Up' and the 'Don't Die of Ignorance' AIDS campaigns in England and Wales have been severely criticised (Plant, 1987). Neither campaign had the support of researchers, clinicians, drug agency workers or health educationalists. As such, they can best be understood as political campaigning (rather than scientifically based, education programmes). They contained dubious messages and were not evaluated in a credible way (Marsh, 1986). The notionally unattractive pictures of heroin users were adopted as teenage pin-ups and had limited effect, as young people tended to interpret the messages as applying only to 'junkies' and not to themselves (Coggans *et al.*, 1990). A propensity for adolescents to believe in personal invulnerability (Elkind, 1985), together with the evidence they may have of their own, friends' or even parents' (see Rogers and McCarthy, 1999) *non*-problematic use of drugs, can lead to young people either avoiding the negative messages of mass media campaigns or disputing their credibility.

Even before the media campaigns of the 1980s, the Advisory Council on the Misuse of Drugs (ACMD, 1984:35–36) warned that:

> Whilst we accept the need, in appropriate circumstances, for education to include factual information about drugs and their effects, we are concerned about measures which deliberately present information in a way which is intended to shock or to scare. We believe that educational programmes based on such measures on their own are likely to be ineffective or, at worst, positively harmful.

Thus, mass media approaches to drugs education have tended to exaggerate the dangers of drug use, limited discussion of the complexity of drug experiences (including the potential pleasures and benefits of drug use) and perpetuated inaccurate stereotypes of drug use(rs). At the same time as apparently ignoring De Haes and Schuurman's (1975) conclusions about the ineffectiveness of (and possible negative effects of) 'warning' approaches to drugs education, it is near impossible to measure exactly the potential consequences of such campaigns. As such, they have been heavily criticised. Swadi and Zeitlin (1987) summarise the problems associated with them and why they are likely to be ineffective. This happens in particular when they give incomplete, inaccurate or incomprehensible information that does not address individual 'problem-solving' in respect of drug behaviour (such as resisting 'peer pressure').

Finally, Plant, Peck and Samuel (1985:126) suggest that it is 'important to distinguish between an educational campaign and an exercise in exhortation or propaganda ... Exhortation or propaganda may involve the provision of factual material but may also advise or attempt to convey a specific message'. Most explicitly the message is that 'complete abstinence is best' and implicitly, it is that the government is taking action in respect of what it sees as a social threat – rising youthful drug use (Plant, Peck and Samuel, 1985). 'Propaganda' – the promotion of information and viewpoints that are 'misleading or dishonest' (Oxford English Dictionary, 2000) – is perhaps a better way to describe these campaigns than 'education' (www.drugscope. org.uk).[2]

Drug Information, Peer Education and 'Life Skills' Programmes

In contrast to mass media, abstinence-oriented campaigns, didactic drug information programmes aim at providing school children with factual knowledge about the use of drugs.[3] Dorn and Murji (1992:38, emphases added) identified that:

> both information-type programmes and general values and living skills programmes seem, on the evidence, to be equally ineffective in terms of restraining initial drug use. Information may, however, have a role in restraining post-initiation *escalation* of use and in *harm reduction*.

Many school-based drugs education programmes relying on information giving approaches are either untested or fail to meet their stated objectives (Swadi and Zeitlin, 1987; Coggans *et al.*, 1991). Echoing Dorn and Murji's conclusions, the *National Evaluation of Drug Education in Scotland* (Coggans *et al.*, 1991) identified that school-based drugs education does not appear to affect either illegal or legal drug use and was most successful in raising levels of knowledge.

Many *skills-based* prevention initiatives have focused upon social skills, specifically the ability to resist peer pressure and say 'no' to offers of drug use, despite attempts at persuasion by peer group members. The DfES (2004) guidance refers to the long held belief that young people require education on 'how to resist pressure to do wrong'. In 1994, Coggans and McKellar challenged this 'inadequacy theory' (i.e. that young people were initiated into drug use and continued using, due to their inadequate skills at declining the offer and responding to pressure). Blackman (2004) provides a more sustained critique of this and other orthodox assumptions in drugs education.

Although there is evidence to show an *association* between drug use and peer factors, causation has not been established. In many cases it has merely been assumed that 'peer pressure' leads to experimentation with drugs. This has become entrenched in mainstream thinking. The hypothesis of 'peer pressure' depicts young people as passive individuals, powerless to resist their peers who lead them to experiment with substances. This implies that young people begin using substances as a result of being unable to refuse drugs or deal with pressure from others, despite wanting to resist using. This is one of a number of 'inadequacy theories' attributing substance use as being due to the absence of particular skills or traits.

Coggans and McKellar (1994) challenge assumptions about peer pressure, preferring instead notions of 'peer preference' or 'peer assortment'. These concepts view young people as actively selecting their own peer group based upon their 'beliefs, attitudes and aspirations' (ibid.:16). This *may* include choosing a peer group that provides access to drug trying experiences. Coggans and McKellar explore the complex and interacting nature of peer factors in the development of young people, their lifestyle choices and motives in a way that moves beyond the simplistic view of 'peer pressure' encapsulated in some drugs education approaches. Their stance chimes with some more recent research on youth transitions and, within these, drug-using careers. Simpson (2003), for instance, provides a nuanced, detailed reading of the drug, crime and drug-crime careers described by his north-east England informants. He shows how popular and common-sense viewpoints (e.g. that drug use leads to crime, that peer pressure causes initial use etc.) brush over the diverse, complicated and shifting biographies described by his interviewees (see also MacDonald and Marsh, 2002). Perri 6 and colleagues also insist that drugs education strategies must '*engage* with local youth cultures' (1997:45, emphasis added) and seek to understand the motivations of young people, rather than presuming that these are known in advance.

Peer education has become a fashionable way of delivering drugs education programmes, partly because of the assumptions concerning peer pressure described above. It can be defined as 'young people who are trained to support and deliver ... education and can be very popular with young people and teachers. It is a way of providing information in an environment in which young people feel accepted and secure' (DfES, 2000:28). The value of peer education is briefly mentioned in the DfES (2004) guidance without reference to the evidence source. As with the majority of drugs education programmes, there are difficulties involved in evaluating peer education and Lloyd *et al.* (2000:121; cited in Blackman, 2004:165) concludes that peer education is 'largely ill defined and unproven'.

The Drug Prevention Initiative (1996) evaluated a *Youth Awareness Programme* (YAP), using a series of in-depth interviews with workshop participants and individuals that were not taking part in the programme. Among its insights, the study found little evidence of young people actively seeking out drug information and tending to rely on everyday contacts. Thus, young people require 'accurate drug information' that is accessible with 'minimal effort'. The evaluation noted that young people are also likely to encounter both 'positive' and 'negative' experiences of drug use. Unless discussion of negative experience (e.g. the potential harm to health) is balanced by acknowledgement of the positive (e.g. the pleasures of use), young people are likely to question the credibility of the information and the 'messenger'. The YAP evaluation examined the issue of credibility in depth and highlighted the importance of 'person based', 'experience based' and 'message based' credibility. This suggests the need for the peer educator to be credible as a person, in terms of age and approach, have experience that the target group can relate to and have a realistic and coherent message to impart. Abstinence-based approaches were found to undermine all aspects of credibility.

Life Skills Training (LST) is a 'substance abuse prevention/competency enhancement programme designed to focus primarily on the major social and psychological factors promoting substance use/abuse' (www. lifeskillstraining.com/LST1.htl). It is taught in a series of lessons to 11–14 year olds. Botvin (1990) originated the concept of LST and conducted a large-scale, six-year longitudinal study that showed that those school children who received the LST programme in their schools had lower rates of cigarette smoking, drunkenness and cannabis use than those not in the programme. As well as being very resource intensive (e.g. in terms of teachers' time), there is, however, no proven, causal link between LST programmes and processes and the measured outcomes. To establish such a connection, a study would require the existence of control groups who were subjected to a similarly intensive, long-term non-LST drugs education programme (e.g. a basic drugs awareness course) and results that showed significantly better outcomes for the LST groups.

Another broad-spectrum LST programme, *Students Taught Awareness and Resistance* (STAR), was developed at the University of California (Pentz *et al.*, 1986). The drugs component forms just one part of a wider life-skills approach. This programme is also said to have a significant impact on delaying the onset of drug use (Hurry and Lloyd, 1997). *Drug Abuse Resistance Education* (DARE) has also been evaluated extensively in the US and has been shown to have an impact on attitudes to drugs. In the US, DARE is usually delivered in the final year of primary school and taught by uniformed police officers. In Mansfield in the UK, DARE was evaluated by Whelan and Moody (1994) in three schools with a group of 9 to 10 year olds. One school implemented the programme with the other two schools acting as comparison schools. They concluded that with reference to drug use, no general patterns of development in knowledge and attitudes were found to have resulted in pupils who received the DARE intervention, as compared to those who had not received the intervention.

McGurk and Hurry (1995) evaluated *Project Charlie* ('Chemical Abuse Resolution Lies in Education'), another major life skills drugs education programme, first developed in the US. It was implemented in primary schools in Hackney between 1991 and 1993. *Project Charlie* incorporates the principle elements of a drugs education programme into its curriculum. It is a broad-based, drugs education approach which includes skills acquisition (e.g. in respect of decision-making, peer selection, drug resistance), enhancement of self-esteem, the provision of information and so on. It was developed in Edina, Minnesota in the late 1970s, in response to that community's concern about drug use. The programme has undergone three major revisions, with the latest completed in 1992 (as Blackman, 2004, points out the regular revision of the content and design of programmes such as this makes evaluation and comparison of outcomes difficult).

The target group is wide, spanning the elementary (primary school) years (5 to 11 years old). The stated goals of *Project Charlie* are: to promote abstinence from drugs for school age children; to delay the onset of experimentation with drugs; to limit the eventual drug use in terms of amounts, frequency and situations; to inhibit the development of drug use (McGurk and Hurry, 1995). *Project Charlie* was evaluated by Hurry and Lloyd (1997) when school children exposed to Project Charlie in 1992 were followed up in 1996 and compared with a group who had not participated. They found that the programme had a continuing impact, predominantly in terms of lower levels of experimentation with both illegal drugs and cigarette smoking. Participants were more likely to resist 'peer pressure' than the control samples in the study. In conclusion, Hurry and Lloyd (1997) argued that *Project Charlie* (and other well-delivered, primary school drugs education programmes) *can* have a delaying effect upon the onset of illegal drugs and cigarette smoking.

Project Charlie is aimed at children in primary education, whereas *NE Choices* is a multi-pronged approach focusing on children in secondary education. The dilemmas and problems encountered in accurately evaluating drugs education initiatives are highlighted in the findings of Stead *et al.*'s (2000) evaluation of *NE Choices*. The initiative, targeting school attendees aged 13 to 16 years, set out to reduce prevalence of drug use in the target population, by delaying the onset of drug use, reducing frequency of use and reducing polydrug use. Despite favourable responses from participants regarding their satisfaction and interest in the programme, the evaluation was unable to provide evidence to support achievement of the four main aims of the programme.

Problems encountered by the research team included the numbers of participants unwilling to disclose key information due to fear of adverse consequences. As a result, responses could not be traced from baseline to follow up, meaning individual change could not be mapped and vital data became unobtainable. Young people were unlikely to disclose substance use because they anticipated a punitive response. In evaluating *NE Choices*, Stead *et al.* (2000) suggest that commencing drugs education with 13 year olds was too late. Similarly, the DfES (2004) guidance now advocates commencing drug prevention at five years old. The rationale here is for 'primary prevention'; anti-drug, abstinence messages and norms may be more easily inculcated into those who are so young as to be very unlikely to have experienced, or witnessed, the 'positive' aspects of drug use.

Conclusion

The chapter has provided a brief review of some of the most significant forms of drugs education and examples of key projects and programmes that illustrate these. A dispassionate reading of the research and evaluation literature suggests that – across *all* methods of drugs education from the mid 1970s onwards – programmes have had no more than marginal effects on children and young people's attitude and behaviour, in relation to drug use. The research evidence suggests that perhaps too much has been expected from drugs education as a tool to prevent drug use.[4] The DfEE's review of good practice in drugs education puts a positive gloss on this picture of limited success (1998:13):

> We do not wish to raise unrealistic expectations of what drug education can achieve. A pragmatic and realistic approach is needed by all – acknowledging that no conceivable approach will stamp out drug-taking altogether. However, there is a growing body of knowledge about the subject, and we are beginning to understand the complexities and know more about what works. Although it is a complex area and there are many lessons involved in the decision to take drugs, it is becoming clearer that drug education, based on lessons from research, delivered in the proper context and in the appropriate way has the potential to reduce drug misuse or at least to delay the onset of experimentation.

Blackman (2004:154–55) is more scathing in his assessment of the current state of play in drugs education policy:

> Given the negative assessment of the effectiveness of different drug education interventions, it is important to ask: why does drug education continue? The unconvincing results of these drug education programmes seem unlikely to halt their delivery. The problem is located as being located elsewhere: for example, the failure is not the drug education programme but the lack of creative and interactive teaching methods; or the weakness is linked to the underlying theoretical model, which requires revision or the failure is dismissed because there has been no detailed and systematic evaluation. The continued legitimacy of drug education seems to rest on a strange combination of science and faith … the apparent popularity of drug education seems to derive from a self-belief in public prevention morality.

If we are to continue with serious, credible programmes of drugs education the evidence that we do have suggests that 'warning-based' approaches that seek to frighten children and, young people away from drug use are ineffective and worse, can be counter-productive. Programmes that provide information and life-skills to participants have had more success (De Haes, 1994) but here successful outcomes have, overall, tended to be ones connected to the delay in onset, rather than prevention, of drug using behaviour (Cohen, 2002). A key problem within different types of approach has been that their fundamental stance – that all drug use is dangerous and to be prevented – clashes with the 'everyday knowledge' of young people that, in fact, drug using experiences can (also) be pleasurable and apparently non-problematic. If current social trends towards increased use and normative tolerance of recreational drug use continues (see Chapter 2) it is possible that we may see 'a more liberal future' (Barton, 2003:147) in respect of UK drugs education policy, as more and more of the population becomes, at least one-time, drugs users. If so 'the influence of harm reduction will increase' (ibid.) as policy and programmes more fully orient themselves towards ensuring that school children and young people emerge from their drug trying experiences as unscathed as possible (Health Development Agency, 1997).

Notes

1. For the purposes of this chapter, 'drugs' refer to the alcohol and cigarettes as well as the illegal drugs. 'Children' refers to people under the age of 11 years and 'young people' to those aged 11 to 18 years old (DfES and DoH, 2003). Drug use can be defined as 'drug taking through which harm may occur, whether through intoxication, breach of school rules or the law, or the possibility of future health problems, although such harm may

not be immediately perceptible. Drug use will require interventions such as management, education, advice and information and prevention work to reduce the potential for harm' (SCODA, 1999:vii).
2. Mass media campaigns can, however, have value if targeted properly. The Royal College of Physicians (1986) notes that although UK anti-smoking campaigns had produced short-lived effects, they had raised public awareness of a serious health issue. Moreover, the British public are less likely to drink and drive as a result of campaigns on this issue (Plant and Plant, 1992).
3. While apparently more liberal in approach, critics have argued that education information and life-skills strategies also contain within them an implicit drug prevention goal. As Blackman (2004:152) puts it 'decision-making approaches speak about choice but it is clear that the assumption of an "informed choice" is pre-established as "No"'.
4. One of the most ambitious targets for drugs education can be found in the objectives of the government's Connexions service. It aims to help reduce the proportion of 13 to 19 year olds using illegal drugs by an astonishing 50 per cent by 2008 (DfEE, 2000).

Further Reading

De Haes, W.F.M., and Schuurman, J.H. (1975). 'Results of an Evaluation Study of Three Drug Education Methods,' International Journal of Health Education, 18, supplement.

Department for Education and Skills and Department of Health (2003). National Healthy Schools Standard: Drug Education. London: DfES and DoH.

Department for Education and Skills (2004). Drugs: Guidance For Schools. London: DfES Publications.

Study Questions

Within small groups, agree ground rules prior to commencing this study activity regarding confidentiality and group behaviour.

Your own experience in school or college of drugs education

1. Discuss within your group your own experiences of drugs education in primary, secondary and further education. Explore any possible impact this education had on your drug using behaviour and that of your peers, including:

   * Prevalence of drug use
   * Age of onset of drug use
   * Frequency of drug use
   * Mixing of drugs (including alcohol and cigarettes).

Drugs, sex and other risky behaviours

2. Identify risky behaviour which young people can engage in and devise harm minimisation strategies to manage these risks.

Drug Policy

3. Critically analyse, in relation to current policy guidance, the drug policies in place during your own period of primary and secondary education.

A glossary of commonly used acronyms in drugs education

ACMD	Advisory Council on Misuse of Drugs
DARE	Drug Abuse Resistance Education
DAT	Drug Action Team
DfEE	Department for Education and Employment (now DfES)
DfES	Department for Education and Skills
DoH	Department of Health
DPAS	Drug Prevention Advisory Service (now Regional Govt. Office Drug Teams)
DPI	Drug Prevention Initiative (became DPAS)
LEA	Local Education Authority
LST	Life Skills Training
NHSS	National Healthy School Standard
MDT	Mandatory Drugs Testing
OFSTED	Office for Standards in Education
PROJECT CHARLIE	Chemical Abuse Resolution Lies In Education
PSHE	Personal, Social and Health Education
SCODA	Standing Conference on Drug Abuse (now DrugScope)
STAR	Students Taught Awareness and Resistance
YAP	Youth Awareness Programme

9

Drug Treatment

Colin Webster

Introduction

Compared to knowledge about heroin dependency and its treatment, knowledge about treating stimulant, crack and cocaine dependency is in its infancy. What is known suggests that the treatment of cocaine and crack dependency has poorer outcomes compared to the treatment of heroin dependency (Gossop *et al.* 2002, 2003; Neale and Robertson, 2004). Although heroin use is seen as the most problematic drug abusing behaviour, cocaine and particularly crack cocaine use are quickly catching up as a focus for concern. Nevertheless, most resources in the drug treatment field continue to be devoted to addressing heroin use, and this chapter mostly focuses on the treatment of heroin addiction.

The aims of the chapter are structured around the question whether drug treatment should be voluntary or coercive, and this theme runs throughout. The chapter begins with an outline of the international context. While drug treatment policies and approaches are constrained by international agreements, they are also contested between and within different national settings. At the same time approaches may converge or diverge across these national settings as one country's approach influences another's approach. Secondly, contemporary British drug treatment policy is considered in terms of the different ideologies, particularly from America, that are influencing it. Thirdly, the history of the 'British system' of drug treatment shows how contemporary drug treatment shares continuities and discontinuities with a legacy of indecision and dispute, about whether drug addiction, its control and treatment, should primarily be understood as a moral, medical or criminal problem. Fourthly, the evolution of British treatment policy has followed a path increasingly dictated by a rapidly growing prevalence of problematic drug use, to the point where the treatment system has not been able to cope with this growing problem. Fifthly, debates about whether drug treatment should be voluntary or coercive are reviewed, particularly in respect of the consequences for the effectiveness of treatment. Finally, evidence about the effectiveness of drug treatment is evaluated in detail, to identify the factors and conditions that make successful treatment most likely.

141

A cursory glance at recent drug treatment literature reveals that current debates are dominated by the question of whether drug treatment should be voluntary or mandatory. Specifically, whether drug users should be treated and supported according to the principle that they volunteer for treatment or, whether they should be identified and coerced into treatment by the criminal justice system, early on in their drug using career. The conditions under which people enter treatment – voluntarily or coercively – is said to be key to the success or failure of subsequent treatment. Others argue that whether users enter treatment voluntarily or not, it makes little difference to treatment outcomes. However, this debate is indicative of an important recent shift in treatment approaches and philosophies, from an emphasis on user's health and social needs and reducing harm, to a more coercive approach that emphasises reducing the criminal harms that users enact upon others to feed their habit. After presenting evidence proffered by those on both sides of the debate, the chapter explores reasons why this shift in drug treatment policy is occurring. I also argue that the dichotomy between treatment that is chosen and that which is coerced is likely to be in practice a false dichotomy because coercion is also a strong element in supposedly, 'softly, softly', non-criminal justice, harm reduction approaches. Similarly, 'tough' criminal justice led approaches are likely to contain elements of voluntary engagement because if drug treatment is to be at all effective it requires a longer-term and more pragmatic approach than the diktats of a court order.

Although evidence focusing on the effectiveness of drug treatment is reviewed, 'effectiveness' depends on the wider direction and purpose of drug treatment policy, which requires an understanding of the historical, economic, political, social, national and international contexts, in which policy operates, and which influence policy. These various contexts reveal that drug treatment policy and practice are not straightforward matters of medical/ clinical judgement and effectiveness, or a neutral technical matter of 'What Works'. The ways in which growing drug dependent populations are treated, cared for, contained, controlled and managed raises issues that are value laden, and in the end, are political issues. Different and often opposed approaches to drug treatment arise within and between different national and historical contexts, according to moral and political perceptions of the purposes of treatment and the nature of the threat to social order, that dependent drug users are said to pose. The chapter concludes that treatment on its own will fail unless social support, such as housing and employment, are offered to users, and the underlying conditions that give 'poverty drugs' their appeal, are addressed (MacDonald and Marsh, 2002).

More immediately, we should not lose sight of the central question in discussions of drug treatment. That is, 'what constitutes 'effective' drug treatment, and under what conditions is effective treatment likely?' Baldly put, the purpose of drug treatment is to reduce and eventually eradicate dependent drug use and addiction – abstinence – and its associated social, health and crime problems. Although treatment must overcome seemingly intractable, and complex, medical, health, psychological and social processes and causes at the individual level, investment in treatment means that 'for every extra £1 spent on drug misuse treatment, there is a return of more than £3 in terms of costs savings associated with lower levels of victim costs of crime, and reduced demands upon the criminal justice system' (Gossop, Marsden and Stewart, 1998).

The International Context

Drug treatment – whether within the tutelage of the criminal justice system or without – has become the preferred method of tacking drug abuse in western societies. Few societies can ignore the fact that demand drives supply, and it is hoped that by influencing demand, treatment will undermine supply. The scale and value of the international criminal drug economy means that drug trafficking is the most important aspect of global criminal networks (Castells, 2000). In 1994 it was estimated that the global trade in drugs amounted to about $500 billion a year, larger than the global trade in oil. A substantial proportion of 'narcodollar' profits is laundered and about half of the laundered money is reinvested in legitimate activities influencing the legal economy. Economic globalisation and new communications and transportation technologies have greatly facilitated the supply of illicit drugs. Castells (2000:177) summarises the problem:

> Drug traffic is the paramount business, to the point that the legalization of drugs is probably the greatest threat that organized crime would have to confront. But they can rely on the political blindness, and misplaced morality, of societies that do not come to terms with the bottom line of the problem: demand drives supply. The source of drug addiction, and therefore of most crimes in the world, lies in the psychological injuries inflicted on people by everyday life in our societies. Therefore, there will be mass consumption of drugs, for the foreseeable future, regardless of repression. And global organized crime will find ways to supply this demand, making it a most profitable business, and the mother of most other crimes.

Previous attempts to directly interdict the cultivation, manufacture and supply of drugs in their countries of origin, or through policing drug imports in countries of destination, have proved relatively unsuccessful in preventing supply. A perverse example is the way that the 'War on Terrorism' has undermined the 'War on Drugs'. Since the Taliban were ousted from Afghanistan, local heroin production has again risen to levels reaching those attained in the pre-Taliban era. In the later phase of Taliban rule heroin production was forcibly repressed.

Although an increasing international consensus has emerged that the only realistic strategy for tackling drug misuse must involve social interventions and treatment (Andell and McManus, 2002 cited in NACRO, 2003; Audit Commission, 2002; EMCDDA 2003), there is little agreement about the mechanisms by which treatment is delivered, or whether treatment should be voluntary or coercive.

To begin with, different countries possess conflicting drug policies and treatment approaches; while at the same time, international legal agreements proscribe certain treatment approaches, such as the legalisation and controlled prescription of heroin. In this respect, as in so many others, American pressure towards prohibition and international agreements about proscribing heroin prescription arose very early on. Globalisation has meant that drug treatment and drug control policies can 'transfer' from one country to another. For example, drug treatment policies in Britain have in part been influenced by American approaches, although this convergence is complex (see Newburn and Sparks, 2004). As political and economic systems become more similar, such influences are bound to occur. However, divergence can also occur and we should not expect that strategies and policies would necessarily take on substantially similar forms across a range of countries.

O'Malley (2004) cites Australia's rejection of an American-style War on Drugs. America's coercive and socially exclusionary criminal justice-based approach to drug control has meant that many drug offenders receive lengthy prison sentences (Tonry, 1995). In contrast, Australia's national policy of drug harm minimisation is based on a socially inclusive strategy, aimed at integrating dependent drug users into society. The American system of compulsory random drug testing is used to exclude people from the labour market and prosecute users through the criminal justice system, whereas Australia's drug testing policy uses relatively neutral and voluntary techniques, aimed at long-term goals of locating and minimising harm and risk. America's coercive approach dates back to the mid 1980s. Abandoning the medical prescription of opiate substitutes like methadone, which was used on grounds of harm reduction, US policy shifted to using methadone to contain 'addicts', until this was abandoned in favour of imprisoning them. This shift mirrored the general move in the criminal justice system from rehabilitation of offenders to containment and incarceration (Rosenbaum, 1997). Australia's policy of prescribing opiate substitutes, however, was designed to stabilise and maintain addicts without the need to use heroin, to lower health risks and risks associated with injecting heroin, and to reduce the pressure to commit property crime in order to buy drugs, and to allow users to take up paid work more easily. Australian treatment policy recognises that coercive and inappropriate drug policy responses may serve to exacerbate the drug problem. The British system of drug treatment lies somewhere between America's and Australia's approach, as we shall see.

According to O'Malley (2004) these differences in approach can be explained by the different assumptions each society holds about drug users. In the United States, 'addicts' are 'demonised' and 'pathologised', as both irrational and irresponsible, whereas drug policy in Australia and New Zealand assumes that drug users make, mostly, rational, morally neutral, drug-taking choices, and 'users' (rather than 'addicts') are addressed in terms of the adverse risks created by drug consumption, and are offered drug treatment choices. As a consequence, Australia minimises coercive criminal justice responses or deploys such responses as a conduit to treatment or therapeutic practices rather than as a means to punishment or incapacitation. Clearly, despite similarities in political and economic systems, America has not been 'successful' in 'exporting' its punitive approach of 'exclusion and abandonment' (O'Malley, 2004). It would of course be wrong to interpret international drug treatment policy as America versus 'the rest'. For example, Sweden's prohibitive and repressive approach and the Netherlands's liberal and tolerant approach point to sharply opposing styles of drug control and treatment in a European context (Chatwin, 2003). Besides, all such comparisons carry within them a tendency to ignore or hide the complexity and heterogeneity of approaches, and changes in policy, within countries.

Where the issue of convergence and divergence of different national drug treatment policies *is* important is in the convergence of similar tensions and debates within drug treatment policy across national contexts. Within the US, Australia, Europe, and Britain 'neo-liberal' ideologies dominate social and public policy, including drug treatment policy. These societies can be characterised as being made up of an alliance or hybrid between neo-liberalism which emphasises a small and enabling state, 'freedom of choice through the market' and 'freedom of the individual', and a socially authoritarian conservatism (neo-conservatism) emphasising a strong intrusive national state, duty, obedience, self-denial, strict discipline and punishment (O'Malley, 2004). While neo-liberalism emphasises individual 'autonomy' and 'rational choice', neo-conservatism emphasises social discipline. It is the tension between, and different emphases given to, these influential ideologies that determines the shape of drug treatment policy in any given society. Neo-conservatism emphasises authoritarian, coercive and penal approaches, whereas neo-liberalism emphases therapeutic interventions. Both ideologies are linked by a shared opposition to the welfare state, seen as generating dependency and as economically draining, yet for neo-liberals users appear as informed choice-makers within a rational choice framework rather than as welfare-dependent. At the same time, and consistent with a neo-liberal framework, treatment programme evaluation

Drug Treatment

and effectiveness are constant concerns, imposing economic responsibility and accountability, while contractual outsourcing of drug treatment to private and charitable agencies has replaced or supplemented state-based provision (O'Malley, 2004). The next section illustrates these contemporary ideological tensions and conflicts within drug treatment approaches and policy in relation to British drug treatment approaches.

Contemporary British Drug Treatment Policy: Neo-Conservatism, Neo-Liberalism and the Audit Society

Recent pronounced shifts in the direction of British drug treatment policy, towards a more criminal justice approach, might suggest that policy is being influenced by American-style neo-conservatism. America's full conversion to neo-conservative drug treatment ideology occurred in the 1980s with President Reagan's 'War on Drugs' rhetoric. Although still organised around enforcement, British government's drugs policy in the 1980s and 1990s continued to emphasise 'harm reduction', and community-based prevention and treatment strategies, as demonstrated by a number of official reports at the time: *Tackling Drug Misuse* (1985), *Tackling Drugs Together* (1995), *Tackling Drugs to Build a Better Britain* (1998). After Labour's re-election in 2001, the locus of drugs policy moved from the Cabinet Office back to the Home Office, and the new National Treatment Agency (NTA) started work, based in the Department of Health. It appeared that during this time a consensus emerged around creating a shared agenda between criminal justice and treatment approaches, which rejected the traditional bifurcated approach, between penal and health/welfare approaches. The new chief executive of the NTA stated: 'It is sound criminal justice policy to invest in drug treatment.' (cited in South, 2002:928). The government's second drugs strategy *Tackling Drugs To Build a Better Britain* (Home Office, 1998) brought in a further agenda. This was a more sustained attempt to build in performance targets and generate an 'audit culture' around the delivery of drug treatment. At the same time, 1999 guidelines on the clinical management of drug users gave advice to the medical profession on how best to implement the drug strategy, which augured a more interventionist approach towards clinical judgement in the area of drug treatment (Department of Health, 2002, 1999).

If neo-conservative ideology seemed not to influence the British drug treatment system at this time, then which ideology was driving the system? The next section details the history of the 'British system' of drug treatment. To briefly jump ahead, this early period was influenced by classical liberalism, which depicts and 'allows' individuals the freedom to regulate and govern their own lives (Foucault, 1977, 1991). By the twentieth century these perceptions changed as drug users and others became associated with wider fears about 'fitness', social fragmentation, individualism, increases in crime and unemployment. Classical liberalism was seen to have failed and the state took on a greater responsibility for guaranteeing individual freedom from threats of social disorder, while establishing the parameters of 'correct' behaviour (Rose, 1996; Garland, 1985). This 'welfare liberal' phase was characterised by both the proliferation of 'experts' – social work, psychiatric and medical – in the field of drug treatment and elsewhere, and a more punitive, penal response, to dependent drug use. Several authors (see Garland, 2001; Rose, 1996) have recognised that since the 1960s and 1970s, these penal welfare approaches associated with welfare liberalism have given way to neo-liberal forms of governing perceived threats to social order.

In drug treatment this meant placing less emphasis on social contexts of drug use (e.g. poverty), state protection and rehabilitation of drug users, and more on prescriptions of individual responsibility. Neo-liberal ideology emphasises devolving responsibility for 'self-government' (self-control) to individuals, families and communities, and has been accompanied by exposing professional practice to fiscal accounting, audit and evaluation, and in some cases replacing professionals with 'grass roots' 'experts' (Power, 1997; Muncie and Hughes, 2002; Webster and Robson, 2001). Similarly, drug treatment systems emphasise that drug users must be held responsible for their actions, and that families and communities rather than the state take primary responsibility for drug prevention and treatment. At the same time, the state seeks to activate non-state agencies and organisations, and encourage inter-agency co-operation and local initiative. Although the state may issue centrally controlled drug treatment directives and guidance (through the Home Office, NTA and Health Trusts), responsibility for their implementation is passed down to local bodies, and ultimately, to drug users themselves. This recent period based on neo-liberal ideology, resting on a simultaneous devolution and centralisation of policy, has entailed the 'joining up' of welfare, harm reduction, health and justice approaches across a myriad of agencies and institutions.[1] A 'bottom-up' approach starting from families, communities and schools is supposed to compliment a top-down approach based in policing, criminal justice, drug treatment and drug prevention (Andell and McManus, 2002).

Supposedly 'independent' local DATs were given the task of drawing all these approaches and agencies together. DATs co-ordinate, manage and contract out drug treatment to different agencies through funding agreements that separate the purchase and provision of services. The overlaying and overseeing of drug treatment by DATs has led to what Muncie and Hughes (2002), Power (1997) and others have called the 'new managerialism', which stresses the need to develop a connected, coherent, efficient and above all cost-effective series of policies and practices. In the drug treatment field, managerialism is ostensibly governed by pragmatism and therefore side-steps dispute about fundamental treatment philosophy, instead emphasising the achieving of results ('What Works'), while ignoring the quality of processes by which these results are achieved (Bean and Nemitz, 2004). The setting of explicit targets and performance indicators enables auditing of efficiency and effectiveness, and encouragement of multi-agency co-operation (McLaughlin *et al.*, 2000). For example, through crude government and local target setting (numbers in treatment) agencies are asked to state their outputs (the numbers treated) and coverage (resources expended in achieving these outputs). However, little information is gathered about the substantive outcomes of treatment (how many reduced or stopped drug use as a result of treatment, and for how long?). Power (1997), in his study Audit Society: Rituals of Verification, has analysed and documented some of the more perverse elements of this 'audit culture' across public and private sector organisations. A major consequence in respect of drug treatment is that complex issues of philosophy and effectiveness become depoliticised and subjected to the logic of financial audit.

Apart from the obvious pressures this puts on drug workers to meet targets rather than client needs, one practical consequence can be mentioned here. When agency effectiveness is measured by the simple expedient of 'getting people into treatment' (the current main priority of the NTA and the criminal justice system), this can in practice lead to a 'revolving door' of treatment rather than effective treatment (Webster and Robson, 2001). The way this 'works' (or more accurately, doesn't work) is that individual users are enrolled on treatment programmes, usually of too short a duration to be effective. They may stay on the programme, or dropout, or be dropped from the programme. The usual reason why treatment is withheld after beginning a programme is that the 'client' is deemed to have 'breached' the programme by not 'complying' with the conditions or rules laid down, i.e. they have failed a drug test and are shown to be using illegal drugs, or have 'topped up' their methadone prescription with street heroin (Best *et al.* 2001a, 2001b). Other reasons range from not attending regularly, to disagreeing with the treatment approach (e.g. unrealistic expectations that the user achieve abstinence through a rapidly reducing prescription). However, entry onto a programme, whether or not the programme was sustained or had 'successful' outcomes, is itself 'counted' as a 'success'. Although the drug treatment service fulfils its target (of getting people into treatment), very little has been achieved. Furthermore, the same individual may, at a later date, return for treatment and be counted as another separate 'output', in terms of fulfilling the organisation's targets. Because dependent drug use is a 'chronic relapsing condition', users may return several times, each event being counted as a target met. This multiple counting of the same individual makes a mockery of measures of effective drug treatment.

This essentially neo-liberal approach to drug treatment, and some of its perverse outcomes, have only very recently begun to give way to a more coercive neo-conservative agenda, exemplified by current debates about coercive and authoritarian approaches found in mandatory drug testing for all those arrested, and court-based DTTOs. Although at the moment, the drug treatment system remains a hybrid of a diverse and expanding array of strategies that are capable of drawing in the criminal and non-criminal, neo-liberal and harm reduction responses to drug misuse seem on the wane. Funnily enough, in this scenario, as Muncie and Hughes (2002) wryly comment, 'addicts' are deemed not rational and responsible enough to be fully engaged with their treatment, but are deemed fully rational and responsible if they offend.

The British System of Drug Treatment and Control

The system of drug treatment based in historical peculiarities and traditions found in Britain continues to influence the shape of contemporary drug treatment. Britain was the first nation to systematically trade opium as an international commodity. Britain had invested heavily in the export of opium from China and India and engaged in two 'Opium Wars' (1839–42 and 1856–58) to wrest control of this profitable trade. Therefore domestic control over opiate use in Britain was limited. The British state monopolised the legal trade in opium, and then made its trade, supply and use illegal, in the context of worries about the ability of British soldiers to fight in the First World War. Moral opposition to opiate use, however, had been growing for some time, and use came to be seen as a medical 'problem'. From these early beginnings, the treatment and control of dependent drug use incorporated a mixture of political, moral, medical and criminalising judgements. The 1868 *Pharmacy Act* removed morphine and opium derivatives from general stores and gave pharmacists the monopoly of dispensing (South, 2002). Further attempts to bring the treatment of opiate dependent users under medical control in the 1888 *Inebriates Act* and 1890 *Lunacy Act* failed. The 1913 *Mental Deficiency Act* allowed for the first time, the detention of 'moral imbeciles' on grounds that addiction and intoxication can lead to 'insanity' (Pearson, 1991). Subsequent medical, moral and political debates about control measures 'waxed and waned' until the phasing out of opium exports from China and India in the early years of the twentieth century (Pearson, 1991; South, 2002). It was at this time that an ideological framework emerged, within which and since, views about treatment and control have become polarised between the medical view of drug use as 'addictive' or a disease, and a moral view of it as a vice to be controlled by punishment (South, 2002). In 1916 the *Defence of the Realm Act* made unauthorised possession of cocaine or opium a criminal offence. It is highly significant that the first penal response to drug use in Britain was enacted in the moralising climate of a wartime emergency rather from a reasoned debate.

Acts in 1916 and 1920 laid the foundations for the 'British system' of drug control and institutionalised a fundamental conflict in approach, which continues today, between a medical framework emanating from the Ministry of Health and a penal framework emanating from the Home Office. These foundations were consolidated in the *Dangerous Drugs Acts* of 1920 and 1923, which confirmed possession of opiates and cocaine as illegal, except when prescribed by a doctor. From henceforth, while the Home Office would control these drugs and their new status as illegal, the Ministry (later Department) of Health would oversee prescribing. This moralising, medicalising and criminalising legacy and its significance is often forgotten in contemporary debates about drug treatment. Leaving aside drug control, the British system of drug treatment has its origin in the 1924 Rolleston Committee and subsequent 1926 Report, which allowed for the prescription of morphine and heroin to enable gradual withdrawal, or to 'maintain' a regulated supply to those unable to break their dependence, or who would otherwise suffer serious disruption in their lives (South, 2002; Pearson, 1991).

Even at this early stage and subsequently, the British system diverged from the path taken by the US, where the connection between narcotics addiction and criminal activity was felt to be much stronger. Unlike the US where punitive approaches to enforcement and treatment defined the response to drug use, in Britain the addict population was considered to be middle class, middle aged, small and receding, and therefore offered no threat to social order. Although South and others (2002:926, Pearson, 1991; Dorn and South, 1992) have argued that at this time medical approaches were dominant, they 'were in fact shadowed and influenced by strong moral and penal positions'. Nevertheless, most drugs legislation between 1920 and 1964 reflected the Rolleston approach, in the context that Britain was perceived not to have serious problems with illegal drugs. From the 1960s onwards changed conditions brought a gradual change to this relatively benign homegrown approach. A major reason for this change was the growing prevalence of illegal drug use among populations believed to be either subversive and/or a criminal threat to law and social order. Although much more marked in the US, this was eventually to lead to a closer, but far from complete, convergence with US style enforcement and treatment policy.

Prevalence and Treatment

An important reason why British and US drug treatment experiences and policy diverged can be stated simply in terms of the size of the perceived problem, and associated drugs-crime relationship. Change in the size of the drug using population was an important element in why changes in drug treatment policy occurred. At the time of the Rolleston Report in 1926 there were 500 known addicts in Britain. During the 1950s the number of addicts known to the Home Office was between 300 and 400, increasing from 454 to 753 between 1960 and 1964. This trend, although relatively small, began to cause concern, and thus began widespread medical, official and popular concern about the 'irresponsible' prescribing of opiate drugs by a small minority of private practitioners (Ruggerio and South, 1995). The resonance of history is shown by a recent report that there has been a sustained campaign by Home Office officials to charge doctors, at a leading private drug clinic, with professional misconduct. The report claimed that methadone was being prescribed to 'maintain' rather than achieve abstinence of opiate use in patients (*The Guardian*, 16 February 2004). Responding to the earlier claims, the 1965 Brain Committee's recommendations signalled the beginnings of a major change in the British response to serious drug use (Pearson, 1991). By the 1970s, although 4607 new addicts came to official notice, the 'addict' population was still considered 'stable', contained and locally concentrated in London. Nevertheless, changes in treatment policy responded to evidence of new patterns and prevalence of drug availability. Although allowing continued medical prescribing of opiates (and similar drugs) the 1967 *Dangerous Drugs Act* tightened regulation and control of who could prescribe, where and on what conditions. From now on the explicit aim of treatment policy was to break dependency on street drugs by prescribing methadone as a 'substitute' drug through detoxification or 'maintenance', at designated specialist Drug Dependency Units or clinics (Pearson, 1991). This 'medical management' of users was to exist alongside harsh penal sanctions against drug dealers, reflected in the 1971 *Misuse of Drugs Act*'s distinction between offences of possession and supply, users needing treatment and counselling, and dealers deserving the harshest punishment.

Although many of these changes in treatment policy could be ascribed to a more or less proportionate response to the perceived size of the drug problem, by the 1980s a watershed in British treatment policy would be reached, by which time the opening of new supply routes, and new forms of international trafficking, would have long-term implications for global and local heroin markets. From now on an exponential increase in the heroin, and later, cocaine-using population occurred which had, and continues to have, profound implications for treatment policy and practice. The vastly increased availability of cheap, high purity heroin, a tighter prescribing policy, and the overcoming of psychological barriers to injecting through the availability of heroin that could be smoked, all combined to stimulate the market. The rapid spread of heroin use to places and populations hitherto having no significant heroin using history led many commentators to speak of a heroin 'epidemic' (Parker, Bakx and Newcombe, 1988; Pearson, Gilman and McIver, 1986). From there being 4607 new addicts in the 1970s, 1989 estimates put the opiate dependent population as between 74,000 and 112,000, although cocaine was still of relatively minor importance. By the 1990s a very large 'polydrug' culture was firmly established, a very significant, although relatively small aspect of which was heavy, dependent heroin use, and increasingly, crack cocaine use (Parker, Bury and Egginton, 1998a). Recent estimates suggests that there could be around 266,000 problem drug users in Britain, and of these 161,000 to 169,000 are estimated to have injected drugs (Audit Commission, 2002). Quite simply, the drug treatment system cannot cope. Some medical and other commentators have argued that this rise in prevalence, is at least in part a result of seepage from generous prescribing of opiates and opiate substitutes onto the illegal market (a comment also made in the 1970s). Apart from the fact that opiate prescribing, where it is available, has been far from generous (see below), most evidence points to the opposite conclusion, a very large increase in the supply and availability of cheap heroin. The next section reviews evidence and debates about the key question of voluntary versus coercive approaches to drug treatment.

Voluntary Versus Coercive Approaches to Drug Treatment

The protagonists in this debate are those who advocate early compulsory or coercive treatment aimed at reducing drug-associated crime, and those who emphasise the importance of voluntary motivation on entering treatment, for treatment to be successful (Edmunds, Hough and May, 1999; Gostin, 1993; Hiller *et al.*, 2002). Clearly a non-coercive, harm reduction, rather than crime reduction approach, would seem to be in conflict with criminal justice responses to offending behaviour, which by theie very nature are coercive (Hough, 2002). Those who advocate a criminal justice approach point to evidence that drug users within the criminal justice system who are coerced into treatment achieve the same outcomes as those seeking treatment on a voluntary basis (Audit Commission, 2002; Anglin, Brecht and Maddahian, 1989).

In the British context, Bean (2002), as one of the main advocates of enforced treatment, argues that there is a false dichotomy among practitioners between the benefits of voluntary treatment and criminal justice responses. An insistence on the need for 'voluntary' treatment is based on muddled thinking, while an insistence on 'coercive' treatment and mandatory drug testing is not as coercive as it seems. In any case, successful treatment outcomes are not influenced by whether treatment is voluntary or coercive, but by length of treatment. Bean concludes that the problem isn't that treatment is coercive, but that criminal justice-based routes to treatment such as DTTOs have been poorly implemented, and compare unfavourably with comprehensive and integrated criminal justice-based approaches, such as the Drug Courts in the US.

It is easy to see how such controversies can easily reduce to simplistic notions of coercion versus voluntarism, crime reduction versus harm reduction, and abstinence versus maintenance. Much of this debate also involves entrenched institutional interests, where harm reduction and counselling approaches are located in voluntary and health agencies and coercive approaches in criminal justice agencies. The shift towards criminal justice-based drug treatment cannot be understood simply in terms of a shift from voluntarism towards coercion. For a start, coercion has been a strong feature of medical, harm reduction and counselling approaches, outside the criminal justice system. Clients or patients attending treatment programmes outside the criminal justice system are routinely subjected to enforced drug testing and compliance agreements, as a condition of their treatment. The perceived short-termism and coercion inherent in court led drug treatment orders (that are said to ignore motivation, and impose drug treatment programmes over the course of a sentence, rather than according to clinical and social need) can be matched by similar shortcomings of short-term and inappropriate treatment in non-criminal justice approaches and agencies (Bennett, 1998). After all, the highly respected NTORS – the biggest study of drug treatment ever conducted in Britain – concluded that drug abuse was a chronic relapsing condition that required treatment to fit the client's needs, that drug treatment embrace social care and support as well as clinical intervention, and that most substance misusers require several attempts at treatment before noticeable success occurs (Bean, 2002; Glossop *et al.*, 1997). Although in the 1990s, various reports and research findings emphasised that 'treatment works', and that there were considerable benefits in bringing drug users into treatment, this research tended to be carried out on best practice, and very little evaluative research was carried out on the generality of drug treatment practice. Nevertheless, on the basis of this research, a consensus developed in government drugs policy that treatment approaches become the main platform in the government's aims to reduce substance misuse (Home Office, 1998; Gossop *et al.*, 1997; Gossop, Marsden and Stewart, 1998).

From the late 1990s to the present, there was a clear attempt to link the treatment services with the criminal justice system through the DTTO, provided under the *Crime and Disorder Act* 1998. DTTOs can be a partial or whole element of a sentence handed down by a court. This requires treatment services to work according to criminal justice requirements, and is currently the main bone of contention between approaches and agencies that emphasise the goal of harm reduction (e.g. Health Trusts, Primary Care Practices, Addictive behaviour and Counselling/ Therapeutic Services, Psychiatric Services, etc.), and those that emphasise the goal of crime reduction (The police and courts, Probation, Youth offender Teams, Home Office, etc.). In addition, a further coercive element has been introduced into the treatment system through mandatory drug testing under the *Criminal Justice Act* 2001, the purpose of which is to identify 'drug misusing offenders at every stage in the criminal justice system'. DTTOs, mandatory drug testing (of offenders and alleged offenders), and more recently the Drug Abstinence Order, which requires the offender to refrain from misusing Class A drugs, all mark a shift towards more coercive forms of treatment, and away from earlier voluntary approaches. It should be noted that coercive approaches have been tried before (there have long been facilities to treat offenders under a probation order), but were rarely used because of a belief among probation officers that coercive systems were ineffective (Bean, 2002).

As Bean (2002) concedes, the case for voluntary treatment rests on evidence that there are no 'magic bullets' to cure drug problems, that the best predictor of successful treatment is to keep people in treatment as long as possible, that chronic relapse is ubiquitous in drug treatment, that reduction and detoxification require high levels of motivation to succeed, and that a 'compliance culture' in which treatment 'failure' is 'punished' (the user is returned to court for sentence) is counter-productive. His discussion and endorsement of American neo-conservative approaches to drug treatment are, however, revealing. In this, as in so many other areas of social and public policy (e.g. 'New Deal' as a means of 'getting people back to work'), government support for the introduction of coercive approaches has been influenced by American research, which purports to show that coercive approaches are as successful, if not more successful, than voluntary approaches (Anglin and Hser, 1990; see Bean, 2002:58–73; Bean and Nemitz ,2004). Bean also concedes that the belief that 'treatment works' – whether in a coercive or voluntary context – can be little more than a slogan, given that 'Research has not always made clear how treatment works, with whom it works or whether some treatment modalities work better than others ...' However, for Bean, the justification for coercive or enforced treatment approaches in the British context does not rest primarily on research findings, but on the 'relentless rise in drug use', and associated criminality. It is this fact, rather than evidence about what works, that justifies increasing the range and numbers of coercive treatment programmes 'whether the treatment services like it or not'.

The problem then, for Bean and others, is that British drug treatment policy is not coercive enough compared to the American system. Coercive drug treatment devices such as DTTOs will mean that treatment agencies will become subcontracted to the criminal justice system. British evidence (Turnbull, *et al.* 2000) suggests that DTTOs are failing due to poor implementation, offenders failing to meet the conditions of the order, particularly failure to attend drug treatment, poor and unreliable drug testing procedures, and failure in training and planning. Accordingly, Bean argues that better-designed and more effective DTTOs in Britain should emulate the American drug court as the best model for integrating drug treatment with the criminal justice system. As a 'humane' response to punitive 'three strikes' policy, in which people possessing relatively small amounts of drugs could previously receive very long prison sentences, rather than treatment, drug courts operate according to neo-liberal principles that include an abstinence model, and a 'free market' approach, where the offender is expected to pay towards his or her treatment. According to Bean 'drug courts have produced the largest number of clean addicts to be found anywhere'. In the American context, drug courts are popular, and if they were to have a British equivalent, in a putative, more coherent and integrated criminal justice approach, based on upgraded DTTOs and mandatory drug testing, then such an approach might be popular here. There is little doubt that the 'coercive movement' in the US was born more from Evangelic belief in the efficacy of this approach than any solid evidence about its effectiveness (Gostin, 1993). The appeal of coercive drug treatment is that the immediate aim of abstinence is clear, popular, and lacks the alleged 'muddle' of harm reduction approaches, which often require potentially long-term, costly and complicated programmes of treatment and support.

The debate about coercive versus voluntary approaches leaves unanswered questions about the purposes and philosophy of drug treatment. If initial motivation – whether voluntary or coerced – seems less important when entering programmes, or seems less important than once thought, it continues to be crucial to subsequent treatment outcomes. That is, users must be motivated to stay in programmes. Entering and staying are quite different issues. To stay in, or to leave a treatment programme, will surely, in part, depend on the quality of treatment received, whether or not the condition under which treatment is entered was coercive or voluntary (Glossop *et al.*, 1997; Lockley, 1995). The criminal justice system cannot easily influence the quality, and therefore the effectiveness, of treatment programmes. Above all, it is difficult to see how harm reduction (often requiring maintenance prescriptions, intensive support and counselling, and marked by chronic relapse) can be achieved within the criminal justice system. A harm reduction philosophy would require the criminal justice system 'to turn a blind eye to continued use and use that is unlawful.' (Bean, 2002:72). On the other hand, as O'Malley (2004) argues, harm reduction strategies can be criticised from the point of view that they extend the governance of drug consumption, and draw more and more users into government-based forms of 'normalisation', not because they are 'humane' but because they 'work' or are 'effective', in the sense of preventing initial drug use, and in drawing into treatment the maximum number of illicit drug users.

The debate and evidence about compulsory/coercive versus voluntary treatment isn't really about effectiveness at all, not least because the international evidence is mixed and inconclusive, or simply unavailable, although American research is more unequivocal about, and supportive of, a coercive approach (Stevens, 2003; Luigio, 2000). Recent research has brought more subtlety to the debate by questioning what 'coercion' and 'motivation' mean in the context of drug treatment, rather than these categories being reduced to the issue of whether legal pressure should be brought to bear or not in treatment contexts (Hiller *et al.*, 2002; Young, 2002). Opinion is as much to do with the longevity of – and cultural bias towards – coercive approaches in the US compared to Australasian, Canadian, European and British drug treatment policy. In this debate, more than any other in drug treatment policy, ideological and moral considerations come into play, as well as research findings. Contributions to the debate are better understood in terms of the moral view they hold of drug addiction and drug 'addicts', and whether the latter are to be treated humanely as victims of forces and conditions (e.g. the insertion of an international criminal trade among poor and vulnerable localities and individuals) outside their control, or whether they are seen as culpable and held to account for their addiction (they could have said 'No!').

To conclude this key section, there are two indelible problems with criminal justice-based treatment programmes. Firstly, the criminal justice system currently tends to administer punishments to drug-related offenders, and is not primarily concerned with rehabilitating the offender beyond the duration of a sentence. This is anathema to the logic and practice of drug treatment philosophy (see Kothari, Marsden and Strang, 2002). Secondly, as Gossop and Mitcheson (2003 cited in NACRO, 2003) have recently asserted 'in contrast to the substantial literature on treatment effectiveness, there is little or no evidence to indicate the effectiveness of responses that punish and further criminalise drug users'.

Evidence on Treatment Effectiveness

Research about treatment effectiveness should be interpreted cautiously. The most reliable research is longitudinal, that is, individuals who have undergone treatment are followed up over one, three-and five-year periods after treatment has occurred to see if treatment effects are sustained over time. There are four main problems with effectiveness research. Firstly, most of the research is of adults and little is known about the effectiveness of treatment on young people (Burniston *et al.*, 2002; Elliot *et al.*, 2002). Secondly, few studies use a control group of patients randomly assigned to receive no treatment.[2] In other words, we can't be sure that individuals who reduce or stop using after treatment, might not have done so anyway for 'natural' (e.g. they grow out of using drugs), or for other reasons, regardless of whether or not they underwent treatment (Audit Commission, 2002). Thirdly, we still need to know much more about the mechanisms and contexts through which different treatment approaches operate, and succeed or fail (Pawson and Tilley, 1998). Finally, not all drug users are dependent and the severity and nature of an individual's problems often change over time. Some users are more resilient for a variety of reasons than others (Audit Commission, 2002; HAS, 2001).

Notwithstanding these limitations, the overwhelming finding of studies of drug treatment is that it is effective in reducing drug use, has a significant though smaller effect on reducing crime, and increases health and employment among users who go through treatment. This finding is supported in reviews of the international evidence (Lurigio, 2000; Prendergast *et al.*, 2002), in large national studies in America (Farabee *et al.*, 2001; Simpson, Joe and Bracy, 2002) and Britain (Gossop *et al.*, 2000, 2001, 2002). Although national studies have shown little difference in outcome between different types of treatment, other more focused studies looking at the specific effects of different programmes are contradictory about the success of opiate substitution in reducing crime unless supported by psychological and social assistance, and that substitution programmes have a greater risk of relapse compared to other treatment types (Stevens *et al.*, 2003). All studies seem to agree that the most important influence on positive outcome of drug treatment is retention and length of time in treatment (Stevens *et al.*, 2003). Certain user characteristics such as better education, more employment opportunities, high initial motivation, good relationships with treatment staff, good health, older age and higher socio-economic status, all correlate positively with successful treatment outcomes, according to a range of national and international studies (Stevens *et al.*, 2003). Finally, as would be expected, various studies have suggested that the content and context (and quality) of treatment influence outcome, particularly that there is a provision of aftercare (see, for example, Pearson and Lipton, 1999; Hough, 2002 in the British context). Of particular importance given current controversies about voluntary versus coercive approaches to treatment, research findings in this respect have proved inconclusive. One study suggested that motivation (by implication stronger if it is voluntary) is the most important predictor of both retention and engagement in drug treatment programmes (Simpson, Joe and Brown, 1997). Another study suggests that motivation is a less important predictor of treatment outcomes than the characteristics of treatment undergone (Florentine *et al.*, 1999).

Describing the range of treatment approaches (HAS, 2001), Inpatient programmes rest on detoxification as the first phase of treatment aimed at abstinence. For heroin there is a choice from several medications, although methadone remains the most commonly used withdrawal medication. Community prescribing and detoxification involves community substitution prescribing on either maintenance or reduction programmes (usually oral methadone). Evidence suggests that methadone maintenance treatment (MMT) substantially reduces heroin use, and in the long term can lead to abstinence from heroin, providing that patients are retained in treatment. Successful completion rates for inpatient treatment programmes are more impressive than community-based treatment. It is much more difficult for heroin dependent patients to endure withdrawal symptoms, or maintain their resolve to continue with detoxification, in community settings. Care planned counselling with drug users follows a client-centred, cognitive behavioural framework in which treatment goals tend to be individually determined, and the client is helped to increase understanding of their drug use behaviour, and encourage changes in harmful drug taking behaviour. Evidence suggests that such abstinence-based counselling reduces drug use and crime and improves health. Residential rehabilitation, although having early drop out rates, has very good outcomes for those who remain. Drug treatment generally, and substitute prescribing in particular, have been shown to be highly effective in encouraging patients to change their injecting behaviour and avoid or cease sharing injecting equipment. Although a wide range of treatments can be effective there is substantial variation in the outcomes achieved by different patients, and different treatment agencies. Factors influencing treatment effectiveness (Audit Commission, 2002) range from the availability of specialist care, that there is a high degree of motivation and early engagement in treatment, to the importance of the availability of longer-term maintenance, rehabilitation and counselling.

The question of 'what works' in drug treatment remains abstract without the addition of the supplementary question of 'for whom, under what conditions, and in which context?' A central problem in drug treatment has been reliance on a very narrow range of treatments and approaches, particularly the dominance of community methadone prescribing and a reluctance to try alternatives to methadone (Seivewright, 2000). In this context there is a need to expand the 'toolbox' of treatment approaches. Another important issue are the attitudes that treatment services display towards their clients. These can be stigmatising, unsympathetic, patronising and punitive (Webster and Robson, 2001). The NTA argues that medicine in itself cannot solve the problem. It has to be accompanied by models of care that are integrated and consistent so that the user is helped stay off use, and that users are not passed from one agency to another and end up not being given a service as they fall between services. Nevertheless, prescribing options need to be broadened in terms of what they offer, their effectiveness, how they are delivered, and in what context. For example, both the NTA and the Home Office have consistently resisted allowing the prescribing of pharmaceutical heroin (diamorphine) to those who might benefit. There is not space to discuss the complex arguments for and against heroin prescription here (see the important study by Stimson and Metrebian, 2003). There is however evidence from Swiss and Dutch studies of controlled heroin prescription that heroin can be an effective and safe maintenance or detoxification prescription, particularly for longer-term users (see for example, Swiss Federal Office of Public Health, *Status Report in the Medical Prescription of Narcotics*, January 1995). Suffice to say that the Swiss trials of controlled heroin prescription have reported high levels of programme compliance and retention, and improving health and social integration among users.

Finally, Rumgay (2003:42) has challenged the ways in which scientific evidence about 'what works' in drug treatment becomes selectively used to justify and legitimate either already existing practice, or changes in government policy. She suggests that 'scientific research may be converted to policy less often on the basis of its persuasive evidence than for its instrumental value in promoting achievement of pre-determined goals.'

Conclusion

The history of drug treatment is one of conflict, contradiction and, occasionally, consensus. Conflict is inevitable in a system that traditionally both treats and punishes dependent drug use, according to the interminably confused twin goals of welfare and justice. British drug treatment practice although improving, is still marked by long waiting lists for treatment, under prescribing, a lack of support and after care, coercion rather than co-operation, an inflexible and too narrow approach, a lack of realism based on short-term aims such as abstinence (although not necessarily in practice), and a reluctance to offer users and their families the right to choose their treatment. Across the range of drug treatment agencies there appears to be difficulty in recruiting and retaining face-to-face drug workers, there is poor or non-existent drug awareness training and drug screening and testing skills, and there is a marked reluctance among general practitioner (GPs) to treat drug users (Carnwath *et al.*, 2000). NACRO (2003) argue that the quality of treatment and its suitability given the particular needs of individuals and communities is as important as the quantity of treatment, and suggest that the government's concern with numerical target-setting in respect of getting people into treatment sits uneasily alongside concerns about whether this treatment is effective or not, and wider concerns about the social context that encourages problematic drug use.

Nevertheless, and in contrast to criminal justice approaches to offender populations, a strengthening policy consensus emerged in the British drug treatment field during the 1990s. However poorly this was translated into practice, this consensus benefited from it being based on multi-disciplinary and multi-agency collaborative approaches, a creative relationship between statutory, voluntary and research sectors, and a growing appreciation of the full complexity of the research findings to which policy has appealed for its authority (Rumgay, 2003). The emerging consensus rests on the comparative success and dominance of the harm minimisation approach, and the longstanding tradition of such ideas in British drug treatment. This emerging consensus is currently under threat from American influenced neo-conservative and neo-liberal ideologies that on the one hand emphasise coercive criminal justice-based treatment, and on the other, betray an obsession with target setting. Such approaches ignore the social basis of addiction in deprivation and vulnerability (Foster, 2000). The choice might become one of either incarcerating those who breach DTTOs (the majority do) or, as some commentators argue (Klee, McLean and Yavorsky, 2002; Young, 2002), stabilising users and ex-users by providing them with gainful employment. The choice in drug treatment, as it always was, is between punishment and rehabilitation. Finally, the signs are that the British system of drug treatment may end up with the worst of both neo-conservative and neo-liberal worlds – coercion *and* target setting – neither of which get to the roots of what might cause dependent drug use, or reduce or eradicate it.

Notes

1. In practice, the ad hoc, incremental, and haphazard devolving of drug treatment policy and approach to different agencies produces the opposite to a 'joined up' approach. As agencies proliferate and become located in different voluntary and mandatory sectors, any co-ordination of effort will tend to be compromised by conflicting aims and philosophies, structured by a wider conflict between coercive and voluntary approaches. Just as national policy bodies such as the Home Office, Department of Health and the NTA compete and conflict in their policy aims and approaches towards heroin and cocaine addiction, so do agencies as they attempt to implement policy at the local level. In any given area one is likely to find a confusing and conflicting array of schemes and agencies that range from criminal justice-based approaches such as: Enhanced Arrest Referral (EAR), Mandatory Drug Testing (MDT), Drug testing and Treatment Orders (DTTOs), Counselling, Assessment, Referral, Advice and Throughcare (CARAT), Young People Arrest Referral, Intensive Support and Monitoring (ISM), Intensive Supervision and Surveillance Programme (ISSP) and Criminal Justice Intervention Programme (CJIP), to health, housing and education-based initiatives and agencies such as: Drug Education Teams, Needle Provision, Addiction Behaviour Service (ABS), Specialist GP Practices, Psychiatric Services, and other voluntary sector or grassroots organisations.
2. Randomised controlled trial studies of treatment offer the most convincing evidence on treatment efficacy because other types of 'observational' studies do not allow unequivocal attribution of improvements to treatment in the absence of a control group of patients

randomly assigned to receive no treatment. For example it is possible that patients would have changed significantly over the same period without treatment.

Further Reading

1. Audit Commission (2002). Changing Habits: The commissioning and management of community drug treatment services for adults. London: The Audit Commission.
2. Bean, P., and Nemitz, T. (eds) (2004). *Drug Treatment: What Works?* Abingdon: Routledge.
3. Hough, M. (2002). 'Drug user treatment within a criminal justice context', *Substance Use and Misuse*, 37: 985–96.
4. NACRO (2003). Drugs and Crime: From Warfare to Welfare, London: NACRO.
5. Seivewright, N. (2000). *Community Treatment of DrugMmisuse: More Than Methadone*, Cambridge: Cambridge University Press.
6. Stimson, G. V., and Metrebian, N. (2003) *Prescribing heroin: What is the evidence?* York: Joseph Rowntree Foundation.
7. Young, R. (2002). From War to Work: Drug treatment, social inclusion and enterprise, London: The Foreign Policy Centre.

Study Questions

1. Critically assess, and compare, the arguments of those who advocate coercive and those who advocate voluntary approaches to drug treatment.
2. What is effective in the treatment of dependent drug use?
3. Consider the arguments for and against the controlled prescription of pharmaceutical heroin.

10

Drugs in Britain: Discussion and Conclusions

Robert MacDonald, Tracy Shildrick and Mark Simpson

As we noted in our introduction, a volume like this cannot hope to cover *all* the themes, issues and questions that could be listed as relevant to the study of drugs in Britain. That said, we think the preceding chapters provide a comprehensive discussion of many of the central topics that will be of interest to students of this area. These topic-focused chapters stand as self-contained pieces that require no further summarising here. Rather, our intention is to draw out some of their main conclusions, to point up some of the overall contradictions and controversies to which they refer and, with brief discussion, note some questions and issues which have not been fully addressed in the book.

To facilitate this review and discussion, we adopt a case-study approach. We take the editorial liberty of drawing upon some of our own qualitative research and present an account of the story of Barney, a young man who participated in one of several, recent Teesside-based studies of young people and youth transitions .[1] Obviously with one case we cannot hope to exemplify all of the arguments and conclusions of the preceding chapters but we can highlight at least some of the most interesting ones. We also reflect on the extent to which Barney's story does and does not help us appreciate wider questions about drugs in Britain. One of the most obvious benefits, for us, of this sort of biographical account is that it can help elucidate the changing, *lived experience* of the separate, substantive drug topics raised in earlier chapters and, therefore, the connections between issues of drug consumption, supply and control that have been separated out in preceding chapters.

Barney's Story

Barney was 20 years old when first interviewed. He had grown up in the peripheral council housing estates of Orchard Bank – in Teesside, North East England – one of the most deprived wards in the country.

At this interview, and the second a year later, he was serving a sentence in a Young Offenders Institute (YOI). Although his interviews, as with the research fieldwork as a whole, ranged over broad, interconnected experiences of youth transition, here we concentrate on Barney's experience of drugs and crime.

Typical of others in the Teesside studies with longer-term criminal involvement, Barney's criminal career commenced in his early teenage with shoplifting excursions in the town-centre, often while truanting from school. This was as much leisure-time crime as anything else; a way of spicing up dull truant time: 'I used to just get a buzz out of it. It was daft stuff, sweets, posters, things like that ... nicking off school' (Stephen and Squires, 2003). With others – and again typical – the street corner socialising of early to mid-teenage was enlivened by occasional under-age drinking and, less often, cannabis use. He first smoked cannabis at age 13. He would trade ten cigarettes for a joint 'from lads at school' and would 'just nick out and go into the woods or around the streets and smoke it'. Playing amusement-arcade fruit machines also helped pass the time but became addictive. Shoplifting became more regular and directed to raising funds:

> I was nicking nearly every day, when I was on the fruit machines ... I'd sell around the doors, pulling people over [in the street] and in The Rose Tree [a pub notorious for criminal trading] ... all half price, all the way down the middle: CDs for £6 – Oh aye! They knew it was knock off. Flog it off and spend me money on the fruit machines. Then back into the town [to steal], when I'd spent up.

For Barney and others, social networks of friends (and sometimes siblings) had been the forum in which delinquent identities and activities had first taken hold. Such networks could also provide the context in which to gain new techniques and knowledge about crime and through which to progress to higher-level offending. At 15, Barney's elder brother taught him how to thieve from cars (on the way to school one day) and introduced him to outlets for the selling on of stolen goods (such as certain second-hand shops). At this point he also developed a sideline in the dealing of cannabis, for his Uncle:

> *Barney*: He used to sell it ... I used to just sit in his house all the time and, like, as I got older, I knew a lot about drugs, all kind of drugs, how much they sell for and all that, how much they weigh ... insider stuff.
>
> *RM*: Just from being around your Uncle?
>
> *Barney*: Yeah and on the street and that. He wouldn't let me do it at first but eventually I started doing it cos me older brother was doing it first.

Barney gradually became more alert to criminal possibilities in his neighbourhood and better connected to a growing network of others engaged in offending of one sort or another. His drug-using repertoire also expanded during this period:

> It was tack [cannabis] to acid [LSD] to speed [amphetamine] and from speed to E [ecstasy] … I was smoking tack, just like with the lads in the house. Have a sesh [session], a few of us, on the ganga [cannabis] and like the acid and that and we were going to, like, the under-18s little dances. You know, the clubs, taking acid in there, and like it got to speed and then I started taking E when I started going to the Palms [a local night club], like a rave.

To this point, then, Barney's drug-taking was not wholly different to the recreational, polydrug use now said to be normalised among British youth. His criminal career had consisted of persistent but relatively minor transgressions (i.e. shoplifting, theft from cars and cannabis dealing). He was asked how and why he had made the transition to the more serious crime of burglary:

> *Barney*: Drugs.
>
> *RM*: Heroin?
>
> *Barney*: Yeah…//…Prior to 16 I'd had a few cautions. It just got worse as I was getting older, you know what I mean?
>
> *RM*: But then at 16 you had your first experience of heroin?
>
> *Barney*: Yeah, things changed a lot. I went from E to heroin. I started doing it daily and I had to feed my habit so I was robbing everything in sight…//…everything, from cars, whatever I could sell, I'd rob. Not stealing cars, too dangerous. It's not worth it, cos you don't get money out of it. You get chased, you get killed, you know what I mean? I burgled around then but never got caught…it gets worse every time you come in [prison]. It did for me, heroin. Shoplifting, thefts, then burglary and robbery.

At 16, Barney made the transition from 'recreational' illicit drug use to dependent heroin use. Like others who had done the same, Barney struggled – in the context of a biographical, retrospective interview – to explain, rationally and exactly, a process he now wished 'had never happened': 'it's one of them things. If I never had that go [first use of heroin] I probably wouldn't have been here today [in YOI]'. Interviewees typically referred, *inter alia*, to several explanations. First, some mentioned their lack of preparedness in the face of heroin offers (with some claiming to know little of its potential pharmacological or health effects or even that the drug they used had been heroin). Second, at the time of first use, heroin was comparatively easily available from dealers from whom they had previously purchased cannabis. Third, given the above, informants perceived the step from smoking cannabis to 'smoking' or 'tooting' heroin to be a small one.[2] Fourth, interviews contained implicit costs-benefits analyses in which heroin was deemed cheaper, or as cheap, as cannabis yet gave a greater 'hit'. Fifth, drug decisions were often made in the company of friends who could reinforce pro-drug choices (Pilkington, 2003). Sixth, informants presented equivocal assessments of heroin in which regrets about the negative, later consequences of dependence were contrasted with the pleasures of heroin use. Barney said: 'I enjoy drugs. In my eyes, they're all bad, full stop. Why are they bad? Because they ruin your life … but I still like them though.'

As others have pointed out (Gossop, 2000; Newcombe, Chapter 2), social scientific accounts of drug use sometimes forget that a main reason for using drugs is the pleasures they can bring. Barney described the appeal of heroin in a way that was typical of others in the study:[3]

RM: So what was it like, that first experience of heroin?

Barney: It was wicked, really good.

RM: How did it compare to other drug experiences you'd had?

AB: Same as all when you first have a drug. You think, first go, 'well aye, it's good'. But with heroin, it just gets a grip of you and once it's got a grip of you, that's it man. It's got your life. You've got no care in the world.

RM: In terms of the effect, does it compare with ecstasy or, say, Acid?

AB: No, cause it, like, just takes all your problems away, you know what I mean?

RM: No I don't 'cause I've never done it and it's difficult for me to imagine…

AB: It takes all your problems away. Like, say, for instance I'd just robbed off me mother and if I'd had some heroin I'd forget about it…it just takes the guilt away, you know what I mean? It just wipes everything out. Wipes away bad experiences, just blanks it out.

Barney's criminality subsequent to heroin dependency increased in seriousness and scale. The earnings to be gained by the sale of burgled goods – 'TVs, hi-fis, videos, CDs, videotapes, the lot' – exceeded those from shoplifting. Offending became more intense, driven eventually by daily, habitual heroin use:

Hand to mouth. Burgle on a night, score some money, buy some heroin and always keep £20 for the next morning. £20 would get you over the daytime [i.e. fund the day's heroin use] and on a night we'd go out burgling again [with his brother and friend]. Always the three of us, a regular crew … in the end we all got caught.

When interviewed a second time, Barney was 21 and on remand in a Youth Organizing Institute (YOI), his seventh period of incarceration, awaiting trial for robbery. He described how he had been persuaded by an acquaintance (another heroin addict) to assist in a domestic burglary ('for the money, for the drugs, yeah. For the heroin, for the crack [cocaine]'). This descended into what he claimed was an unplanned, 'knifepoint robbery' of a young man. CCTV and fingerprint evidence was sufficient to lead to Barney's arrest (but he refused to name his accomplice). He intended to plead guilty and expected a long custodial sentence (which he subsequently received):

After this one, that's it for me. I'm 21. I should be about 22, 23 when I get out. I don't wanna keep going back to prison. I wanna try and do summat. I don't know … if I'm good, if it will happen to me. I'm really gonna try to go straight...//...I know it'll be hard for me to get a straight job. Even if I don't go straight as long as I stay out or prison, you know what I mean? I don't think I'll rob … maybe sell drugs. Maybe less risky if you do it right.

The last we heard of Barney was from the local press. He received a three-year prison sentence for this offence. In his second interview, he had told us how he felt about prison. The main problems were separation from his family – 'when the family come [to visit], when they're going, you're going back in there … like you're a bit gutted, getting letters everyday, telling me what's happening and stuff' – and boredom. He said 'the worst thing is it's the same routine everyday, being on the same wing every day, banged up all the time. Boring'. He had recently lost work 'privileges' because he had failed a drugs test and the fact that he had 'turkeyed four or five times' *while serving* custodial sentences reminds us that prisons are far from drug-free environments. Indeed, one of Barney's convictions had been for an attempt to smuggle heroin into prison for his brother who had also been imprisoned for heroin-related crimes (some committed with Barney). Although Barney expressed a desire not to return to prison after his forthcoming stretch, he clearly was not wholly committed – at this point – to desistance from crime and drug use, preferring less risky forms of criminality if 'a straight job' proved unachievable. The only formal drugs treatment that Barney had received came in prison with the offer of two paracetamol tablets to ease the effects of forced heroin withdrawal.

What can we learn from Barney's story? In what ways does it confirm, contradict or add to the main arguments and conclusions from the preceding chapters?

Drugs, Crime and Risk: Some Words of Caution

No doubt Barney's story will be depressingly familiar to those with even passing engagement with the youth justice and drugs fields. The familiarity of his story – and the sense of predictability that it conveys *in retrospect* – should not, though, be mis-read as inevitability.

Our first note of caution applies to the connection between drug use and crime evident in Barney's account. It is important to stress, as Chapter 6 by McSweeney, Hough and Turnbull makes clear, that there are several relationships possible between crime and drug use, including the absence of any causal link. The majority of drug users in Britain do *not* engage in problematic and/ or dependent drug use and nor do they commit crimes that are caused by their drug use (ibid.). If his story is representative at all it is only so in respect of the small minority of drug users in Britain, as in our studies, that have some of the most damaging, chaotic, entwined drug-crime careers.[4] Even where people offend and use heroin, McSweeney *et al.* warn us to avoid a presumption that heroin inexorably *causes* escalating criminality. Barney was a committed shoplifter *prior* to any contact with heroin.

Our second word of caution is in respect of the social causation of the sort of drug-crime career that Barney describes. One of the key, general findings of our research is that shared conditions of existence – uniform starting points among the dispossessed, white working class in the same streets and neighbourhoods and collective, persistent economic marginality and poverty in youth and young adulthood – do *not* generate one, unchanging form of youth transition (Webster *et al.*, 2004; MacDonald and Marsh, 2005). In this sense, it was not inevitable that Barney's life to date should turn out as it has; other biographies had been possible.[5] Many research participants might have been predicted to pursue 'heavy end' careers of crime and drug use given the burden of criminogenic 'risk factors' they carried (Farrington, 1994, 1996). Only some – like Barney – did (see Webster, MacDonald and Simpson, 2006, for a critique of the risk factor paradigm in research on criminal and drug careers). In line with national prevalence trends (see Chapter 2), many young people in these studies had used drugs of one sort or another at some point. For only a few, however, was drug use directly, causally related to offending and for most informants offending never progressed beyond petty crimes in early teenage. Thus, just as the general shape and nature of youth transitions varied, so did the nature of the drug and criminal careers exhibited by research subjects. Simpson (2003), for instance, carefully unravels the complex, differentiated and changing forms of *subcultural* relationships between illegal drug use and crime that existed among his sample of white, working-class young people in a north-east town.

Although the significance of gender in patterns of drug consumption, control and supply might have been made more explicit in this volume, Newcombe (Chapter 2) and Seddon (Chapter 4) do, for instance, point to continuing, substantial gender differences in patterns of drug use. In terms of past-month consumption of the most popular drug (cannabis), for example, male users outnumber female ones by two to one (Newcombe, Chapter 2). The persistence of this gender difference poses an interesting question for Parker and colleagues' theory of drug normalisation (see Chapters 1, 2 and 3), based as it is on claims about the post-modern collapse of social divisions in respect of drug use. Studies have also pointed to the disproportionate involvement of young men, as opposed to young women, in problematic, crime-related drug use (e.g. Campbell, 1983; Bean, 2002). Certainly proportionately far fewer women than men in our studies engaged in the *sort* of heroin-related crime typified by Barney. Collison (1996) describes the significance of a form of young, working-class masculinity for the evolution of stories like his. That is not to say that young women do not become embroiled in destructive, socially excluded, risky transitions in which heroin and offending play a part. However, the nature of these transitions – as reported in other studies (e.g. Cusick and Martin, 2003; Pearce, 2003) and by our research informants – is different and typically involves malign constellations of abusive partners/pimps, failures of the care system and coercion into street prostitution.

Drug Transitions, Careers and Categories

A key benefit of a biographical, case-study method – of close scrutiny of stories like Barney's – is that it can illustrate and investigate individual drug *careers* and *transitions*.[6] Typically, an individual's drug-using behaviour changes over time, as the debate about the most appropriate time measure – 'past month', 'past year', 'life-time' – for prevalence studies attests (see Chapter 2). As Newcombe points out in that chapter, more refined measures are needed in the future to help us capture more accurately differences in forms of drug-using behaviour by individuals and how these change.

Categorisations of drug-using behaviour based on social surveying have been enormously valuable in describing empirical associations between the use of different types of drug (and styles of administration), the social characteristics of predominant user groups and drugs service provision (e.g. Gilman, 1991, 1992; Simpson, 2003; Barton, 2004; Newcombe, this volume). Necessarily, though, they present a static, freeze-frame picture of drug use. They do not really help us understand how individuals might move through the categories they propose, even if – as with Newcombe's discussion – they do point up possible overlaps between drug-using groups and, therefore, possible routes of transition between them. Biographical (or other longitudinal or quasi-longitudinal) methods are more able to delineate patterns of drug career.

While other divisions are possible, for analytic purposes we can sketch how Barney, for instance, moved through six forms of drug-using behaviour in the space of less than 10 years: (i) non-use of any illegal substance in late childhood; (ii) occasional, leisure-based, illegal use of alcohol and cannabis, plus less frequent use of ecstasy and speed in early teenage; (iii) at 16, this recreational, polydrug use combined with early heroin experimentation; (iv) daily, dependent use of heroin; (v) daily dependent use of heroin and crack cocaine and (vi) less regular use of heroin and sporadic, failed attempts at desistance during incarceration.

In his mind, the key transition was from recreational drug use to dependent use of heroin: 'it did for me, heroin'. To be clear, we are not lending support to 'gate-way theories' of drug use, wherein early use of 'soft' drugs opens the door to 'hard' drugs and all step through (see Blackman, Chapter 3). No one claims that *dependent* drug use may become normalised as a mass phenomenon in Britain but it is at least a serious possibility that (some) *recreational* drug use has. As with the national picture, our studies would appear to confirm that a substantial proportion of young people and young adults increasingly use and/or tolerate the use by others and/or receive offers of illicit drugs.[7] Although not based on a statistically random sample, MacDonald and Marsh (2002) identified a three-fold typology of drug-using behaviour in which 'recreational drug users' (as opposed to 'abstainers' and 'dependent users') were the largest sub-sample. Here the typical picture was of individuals who had consumed two or three different substances (usually cannabis, ecstasy and amphetamines) often over a period of years, starting in their early to mid-teens. Drug use was recreational and occasional (in both senses of the word): it was restricted to particular leisure events or occasions and used regularly but intermittently, rather than on a daily basis, as one element in the repertoire of young people's consumer, 'leisure-centred lifestyles' (Perri 6 *et al.*, 1997:7). Reminiscent of Barney's description of this phase of his drug career, recreational drug use became an established element of the youth cultural routines of 'going out' to pubs and clubs at weekends; 'a normal part of the leisure-pleasure landscape' (Parker, Measham and Aldridge, 1995:25). Interviews emphasised the fun, the pleasures and the joys that came from the use of these drugs in these contexts (in contrast to the 'blanking out' of worry and guilt stressed by users of heroin).

Nationally – and in Teesside – most young people do not progress from this form of drug use to dependent opiate use. But some do. It is virtually unknown for heroin users to commence their drug careers with heroin (Prime Minister's Strategy Unit, 2005). As such, we question the hardness of the divide implied in some expert commentaries to separate recreational use of non-addictive drugs (such as cannabis and ecstasy) from dependent use of opiates (Gilman, 1992). Indeed, the received wisdom in the UK drugs research literature has been that recreational and dependent users are distinct, separate groups. The former are 'sociable, sensible, and morally aware as non-users' (Perri 6 *et al.*, 1997:45); like most young people, they view 'taking hard drugs and actually injecting as anathema: a Rubicon they will never cross' (Parker, Aldridge and Measham, 1998b:132). Dependent users of heroin, on the other hand, are 'from the edges' (Parker, Bury and Egginton, 1998a). The 'basic identi-kit of the most likely heroin user' would list 'poor school performance and attendance, light parental supervision' and having grown up 'at the wrong end of town' on 'the poorest estates'. Parker *et al.*, 1998b conclude that:

> the least worst scenario is that heroin trying does not become accommodated within the far larger 'recreational' drugs scene but remains predominantly associated with degrees of social exclusion. (1998a:45–46)

If we had interviewed him before the age of 16 we guess that Barney would have concurred with this statement from Parker and colleagues and viewed the transition to heroin use as impossible. Those interviewees with longer-term careers of dependent drug use uniformly expressed a sense of bemusement at how they had come to this situation, especially given their earlier antipathy towards heroin use and, even more emphatically, heroin users (Gilman, 1992). As Rebecca, a local drugs worker, told us:

> They say 'I can't believe I'm here [attending the drugs service], I'm so ashamed of being here because, you know, I used to call them [verbally abuse heroin users] and now I am one'. If I had a pound for every time they say that! They really honestly think that they can [just] try it; it's the trying, the trying.

In a prescient statement in the early 1990s, Gilman warned that 'it would be disastrous if they [Group B, recreational drug users] were to be attracted to group A-style drug use by a return of the conditions which attracted the streetwise to heroin in the early 1980s' (1992:16). A number of recent studies have pointed out that, later in that decade, this is exactly what happened (Foster, 2000; Johnston *et al.*, 2000; Simpson, 2003; Webster *et al.*, 2004; MacDonald and Marsh, 2005).

Putting aside the question of drug careers and transitions between categories of drug-using behaviour, cases like Barney's also raise questions about exactly how accurate and sensitive such categorisations are (see Newcombe's discussion of this in Chapter 2). As noted, Gilman (1992) has very usefully differentiated Group A (dependent opiate users) from Group B (recreational, non-opiate) users. Parker and colleagues, in particular, have advanced our understanding of contemporary forms of recreational drug use in Britain (Parker, Measham, and Aldridge, 1995; Parker, Aldridge, and Measham, 1998b; Parker *et al.*, 2001). Yet we wonder whether descriptions of the latter – as an exciting aspect of the postmodern, consumer cultures and club-cultural, night-life of metropolitan centres – really accords with the meaning of cannabis use in the bored, out-of-school, street corner socialising of young men in Britain's peripheral housing estates (Pavis and Cunnigham-Burley, 1999; MacDonald and Shildrick, 2004)? Similarly, on the basis of his own north-east research, Simpson (2003) has argued that drugs typically categorised as 'recreational' can be used in ways which do not appear to fit popular assumptions. Some of his informants described heavy, daily, habituated, solo use of cannabis and amphetamine in the context of the endless days of unstructured unemployment. This was not the addicted use of opiates classified as Group A, nor the pleasurable, sociable fun of Group B but something in-between – what he calls persistent, Group C drug-using behaviour.[8] Simpson's model is based on closely focused, ethnographic research that attempted to differentiate the drug and criminal careers of his sample. As such, it was attuned to the subtleties of less obvious forms of drug use and how these came together in a longer-term, drug-using biography. Identifying this category of drug-using behaviour also helps us understand that some may drift through it to dependent use of opiates (from Group C to A). The four-fold typology of drug users presented by Newcombe in Chapter 2 is based on their access to services, demographic characteristics and types of drugs used and is another example of an attempt to classify drug use in Britain. His model is more interested in describing the larger, national picture and is less sensitive to, or focused on, individuals' movement between these categories.

The Contexts of Drug Use and Changing Drug Markets

Implicit in Barney's story is the significance of geographic and historical context and, within this, drug supply. MacDonald and Marsh (2005) note the temptation provided by close-up, ethnographic interrogation of young people's lives to seek explanations of drug careers (and youth transitions more generally) at the level of individual agency and decision-making. This is all the more so when informants, such as Barney, insisted as they did that they were the authors of their own destinies and claimed that no one or nothing else should be implicated as influences on their transitions and outcomes: 'I've done everything meself, so I can't blame no-one'. As Melrose puts it (2004:332), 'their exclusion is (mis)recognised as almost purely volitional'. Incidental to our main point here, in Chapter 8 McInnes and Barrett mention the problems with popular, 'inadequacy theories of peer pressure' in explaining individual's drug choices. Barney would obviously disagree with them too (even if he did, in our view, choose to downplay the influence of his brother, Uncle and friends on his drug career). Coggans and McKellar (1994) offer instead the idea of 'peer preference' (see Chapter 8), wherein individuals 'gravitate toward like-minded people' (Warburton, Turnbull and Hough, 2005:3), which can include becoming involved in social networks that facilitate drug use.

MacDonald and Marsh (2005) go on to argue that proper explanation of the life stories interviewees reported requires, as well as attention to individual choice-making, proper understanding of the social and economic conditions through which those lives were made. Roberts (1995) refers to the 'the structure of opportunities' presented to young people and how individual transitions emerge out of the interplay between individual agency and the opportunities presented as possible to a young person growing up in a particular place and time. Most discussions of the structures of opportunity that shape youth transitions refer to the opportunities, or lack of them, provided by formal, legitimate markets in employment, education and training. To understand the most socially excluded transitions they uncovered, MacDonald and Marsh added in consideration of the opportunities offered in local criminal and drug markets (see also Johnston *et al.*, 2000).

The influx of cheap heroin into the estates of Teesside happened just as informants were making impoverished, economically marginal transitions from school into a collapsed local labour market. As we have noted, some described being unprepared for its temptations and rapidly progressed to dependent use of heroin, funded by increasingly serious criminal careers. Seddon (in Chapter 4) and Parker, Bury, and Egginton (1998a) identify the advent of the second wave of heroin outbreaks in the UK in the mid-1990s. Heroin markets spread to parts of England (particularly east of the Pennines) that until then had had a negligible history of heroin. Teesside was one of the urban areas affected. Thus, prior to then, the *opportunity* to embark on the sort of drug career described by Barney was virtually absent here. In short, a particular change to this local drug market had enormous repercussions for the sorts of transitions possible for local youth and for the conditions of community life.

In Chapter 9, when Webster identifies that morality and politics lie behind much debate and research in the drugs treatment field, he neatly captures the point that we are trying to make here about individual choice and the social conditions of choice. He sees debates as hinging on whether:

> drug 'addicts' ... are to be treated humanely as victims of forces and conditions (e.g. the insertion of an international criminal trade among poor and

vulnerable localities and individuals) outside their control, or whether they are seen as culpable and held to account for their addiction (they could have said 'No!').

Of course Barney could have said 'no' to heroin. But he would not have *been able* to say 'yes' without the unpredicted, dramatic arrival of this 'criminal trade' in Teesside. As Pearson notes in Chapter 5, 'drugs markets...are always mutating' and, since the late 1990s, use of crack cocaine now often features alongside heroin in the profiles of 'heavy end', criminally involved drug users in Teesside as elsewhere (see Chapters 2, 4 and 9). Barney, again, reflected this development in his own drug career.

In Chapter 4, Seddon characterises the connections between poverty, deprivation, unemployment and the social decline of heroin-blighted towns and cities in Britain in the 1980s and 1990s. This description was exactly replicated in the way that our research informants described the changed conditions of life in their neighbourhoods post-heroin. In these *places* during these *periods* for these *users* and these *communities*, heroin had dire consequences. Yet Seddon is absolutely correct to warn against unreflectively adding to the demonisation of heroin and its users. As he says, there is not an 'inevitable or natural association of heroin with urban deprivation and crime'. In a similar vein, new research by May *et al.* (2005) examines the complex and varied relationships that can exist between local communities and drug markets. As well as more socially fragmented ones, deprived but relatively cohesive neighbourhoods – like those we studied in Teesside – can, in subtle ways, provide fertile ground for the imbedding of drug markets. Context is critical and Seddon is, in our view, correct again to argue that 'the most vital contextual factor is economic'. Although MacDonald and Marsh's (2002) characterisation of the appeal of heroin as a 'poverty drug' might have descriptive purchase for the bulk of Teesside users in the 1990s, clearly heroin use had a different meaning in the context of what Webster in Chapter 9 describes as the 'middle-class, middle-aged, small and receding' heroin-using population of Britain in the 1930s and 1940s (Barton, 2003).

Intriguing recent research by Warburton, Turnbull and Hough (2005) has investigated the *non*-dependent and *controlled* use of heroin, contrasting the drug-using behaviour of this 'hidden population' with the stereotypical images of the contemporary British heroin user (and, we would add, with that of individuals like Barney). They found that 'some people in some circumstances can effectively manage their heroin use so it causes few problems' (ibid.:3): context again. The description of Warburton *et al.*'s respondents contrasted sharply with that of interviewees in the Teesside studies. For Barney, the chaos and drama of his drug-crime career matched the turbulence and problems of his wider life. Warburton *et al.*'s sample appeared to be living much more socially included, stable lives. For them, controlling the amount and frequency of use was a key strategy as was hiding their consumption and avoiding association with the heroin-using 'scene' and related personal identities. Some informants had maintained non-dependent use for up to 10 years and, equally interestingly, some others now reported dependent but controlled, stable use after earlier periods of problematic, uncontrolled heroin taking. One of the researchers' conclusions is, therefore, that controlled use ought to be considered as an acceptable short- to mid-term goal for clients of drugs treatment agencies.

Care or Control (or Neither)?

On the face of it, Barney's account is one of unequivocal failure in terms of systems of drugs education, treatment and care. His interview did not dwell on the details of school-based drugs education programmes that he may have been party to. McInnes and Barrett (in Chapter 8) describe how these have become more extensive in Britain since the late 1990s, *after* Barney left school. He might not, then, have had the chance to learn from such programmes (but even if they were present in his school, he was often not). It might also be the case that education and mass media campaigns had positive impacts that are not obvious given his speedy transition into one of the most damaging, problematic forms of drugs 'lifestyle'. For instance, Barney *did* attempt to reduce the health risks of heroin use by refusing to inject the drug. McInnes and Barrett demonstrate the difficulties in evaluating the effects of drugs education. We need, therefore, to be hesitant – even with cases such as this – about unequivocally declaring its failures.

Similarly, systems of drugs treatment do not seem to have served Barney well. He reported no contact with official drug services. Even if he had it is debatable whether his outcomes would have been much better. Several other interviewees did report unsuccessful engagement with treatment. There are *general* difficulties in successfully treating this 'chronic, relapsing condition' with socially marginalised, chaotic heroin users under current policy and practice arrangements – and even greater challenges in respect of crack cocaine use (see Webster, Chapter 9). Furthermore, just as markets in drug supply are localised and rapidly changing, so are markets in drugs treatment. For instance, Webster and Robson (2001) provide a critical review of drug service provision in one part of Teesside. Systematic under-prescribing of methadone substitutes coupled with a punitive approach to breaches of treatment regimes (in part caused by this under-prescription) led many clients to 'fail' programmes and go back to criminally-funded use of street heroin. Yet, in a neighbouring town, dependent heroin users benefited from the more therapeutic, humane treatment regime offered by a specialist drugs treatment general practice surgery that has been nationally recognised for its good practice. Partly as a result of Webster and Robson's review, at least some elements of the good practice of the latter has now been extended across Teesside.

As Webster points out in Chapter 9, British systems of drugs treatment have shuttled between the 'interminably confused twin goals of welfare and justice' and, at core, continue to be torn between the impulse to reha-bilitate and the impulse to punish. Essentially the same moral/political conflict is revealed in McInnes and Barrett's discussion about abstinence versus harm reduction approaches in drugs education. In conclusion, that chapter quotes Barton's idea (2003:147) that we may see 'a more liberal future' in drugs policy, with harm minimisation approaches taking hold, as the trend towards the normalisation of illicit drug use continues and a growing proportion of adult society becomes (at least one-time) drug users. Webster, on the other hand, appears more pessimistic noting that the 'harm reduction response to drug misuse seems to be on the wane' in Britain under the influence of neo-conservative ideology. Another viewpoint is that neither 'care' not 'control' is now or will be the organising principle of British drugs policy. The government's *Tackling Drugs to Build a Better Britain* (Home Office, 1998a) reflects a more general move in the criminal justice field towards 'managerialism' (Muncie and Hughes, 2002). The emphasis here is neither directly upon the punishment of drug users nor their social care (both of which *may* be by-products of interventions) but upon the risks that they pose. Drug testing of offenders has been used as a mechanism for the imposition of treatment orders and further testing, monitoring and surveillance so as to 'manage' risk (see Chapters 7 and 9).

It would certainly seem foolish to unequivocally predict the future nature and arrangements of drugs policy in Britain (in respect of treatment and education and more generally). What is perhaps most likely is that the correct stance the state should take towards illicit drug use will continue to be mired in uncertainty and contradiction. One small but telling instance can be found in the continuing controversy and confusion surrounding the status of cannabis in Britain. As Newcombe in Chapter 2 notes, this is by far the most commonly used illicit drug in Britain. Crowther-Dowey, in Chap-ter 7, describes how, partly as a result of its normalisation, the government came to 'decriminalise' cannabis in 2004, reclassifying it as a Class C, rather than Class B, drug with the support of most if not all drugs campaigners and researchers. At the time of writing this chapter, less than two years later, the British press has been reporting a potential government U-turn (because of its confusing legal status and some limited medical evidence linking the use of cannabis to mental illness in a small number of cases). Such a move would have been in direct opposition to the recommendations of its expert scientific panel, the ACMD. *The Guardian* (14 January 2006) reported that several members of ACMD were considering resigning as a consequence and one publicly complained about the government's 'politicisation' of the cannabis issue. Perhaps as a consequence, the government announced that it would not, after all, change the legal status of the drug (*The Guardian*, 19 January 2006).

We have commented on the apparently limited success of drugs education and treatment in respect of Barney's case. It is less easy to say whether policing – and the criminal justice system more generally – has been more successful in respect of his drugs-crime career and that of others like him in the study. As Crowther-Dowey notes in Chapter 7, 'the policing of drugs is fraught with the difficulties of balancing justice, economic and health priorities'. With Barney's case we perhaps have a good example of 'neither care nor control being achieved' (ibid.).[9] If one interprets the goals of policing as the detection of crime and those of the criminal justice system as being to mete out punishment and to contain offenders, then they have been reasonably successful in Barney's case. He had been apprehended frequently and spent much of his youth behind bars. More generally, during the 2000s, policing in Teesside has had a key target of disrupting drug markets with high profile campaigns to arrest 'a dealer a day'. Unsurprisingly, it would seem that most success has been had at the lower rungs of drug supply and dealer chains (see Pearson, Chapter 5; see Prime Minister's Strategy Unit, 2005). Such strategies face real challenges. In comparison with national figures Teesside has been identified as having the one of the highest rates of problem drug use (Prime Minister's Strategy Unit, 2005) and some of the worst problems of drug-related crime (Home Office, 2003).

In Chapter 7, Crowther-Dowey goes on to comment on the issue of the policing of drugs with and without community consent, noting the turbulent history of drug policing in Brixton, London. This provides another example of the importance of social context. In contrast, authoritarian crackdowns by police on drug dealing and drug crime seem to have popular support on Teesside. Indeed, non-heroin using young interviewees in MacDonald and Marsh's study (and some local professional workers) often cited the local heroin trade, and its associated criminality, as *the* main problem affecting their poor neighbourhoods. Draconian policy responses found favour, such as 'shoot the dealers!' in the words of one young woman. There was no shortage of interview material that would support Seddon's claim in Chapter 4 that heroin is the most 'mythologized and demonised drug in Britain'. Numerous interviewees sought to blame community decline – not on processes of massive local de-industrialisation and associated mass unemployment – but squarely on heroin and its users and dealers.

There is little indication, however, that the criminal justice goals of deterrence and rehabilitation are working in Barney's case (bar potentially being 'deterred' towards a type of offending with a perceived lesser risk of apprehension). In contrast, a good proportion of those young men with long-standing careers of drug-related crime in MacDonald and Marsh's study, and even more in a later follow up of some of the same individuals (Webster *et al.*, 2004), *were* making genuine, progressive steps towards desistance.

Social Inclusion: Desistance from Drug Use and Crime

Desistance is another issue that warrants greater discussion than has been allowed for in this volume. In Webster *et al.* (2004), some of the most socially excluded of interviewees were making difficult and what seemed to us to be both surprising and successful attempts to turn away from crime and drugs. That said, the criminal justice system was playing little more than a marginal – and sometimes obstructive – role in this process. Webster *et al.* (2004) coin the term 'corkscrew heroin careers' to capture how cumulative, long-term, enmeshed careers of crime and dependent heroin use progressively marginalised people from their friends, families and prospects for social inclusion and immersed them deeper and deeper in destructive lifestyles. Having plumbed the social and psychological depths of corkscrew heroin careers, these individuals were catalysed into making the long, arduous, risk-laden journey back to 'normal life' (as one interviewee put it).

Physical separation from the neighbourhoods in which they had grown up and social distancing from the networks that had encouraged and reinforced drug-using behaviour were universally cited as positive aids to 'going straight'. Ready, repeat access to non-punitive, therapeutic drugs treatment was also for many a significant factor in desistance. In addition, some of the common resolutions of youth transitions helped in completing this journey and warded against relapse to heroin. As in other criminological research (e.g. Rutherford, 1992; Barrow Cadbury Trust, 2005), becoming a parent, forming new, stable partnerships and gaining regular employment were all identified as factors that aided desistance.

Of course, recurrent imprisonment made these sorts of resolution all the harder. Individuals like Barney are perhaps unlikely to be perceived as attractive potential fathers, partners and employees. The Barrow Cadbury Trust's *Lost in Transition* report (2005) makes a compelling case for reform of the criminal justice system for young adults over the age of 18 years. It argues for a re-balancing in favour of social rather than criminal justice priorities for young adults in transition, claiming that:

> Criminal justice policies … do unnecessary damage to the life chances of young adult offenders and often make them more, not less, likely to re-offend.

They make it harder for young adults to lead crime-free lives and exacerbate the widespread problems of social exclusion. (Barrow Cadbury Trust, 2005:9)

One of the arguments of the report is the same as that here: 'spending time in custody disrupts the ability of young adults to complete the transition to adulthood that growing out of crime requires' (ibid.:25). It goes on to document the numerous problems of current criminal justice arrangements for this age group and in particular argues for improvements in respect of treatment for young adults with drug and alcohol problems; health, specifically mental health, care; and access to decent education, employment, training and housing. In other words, it recognises the need for the sort of joined-up, holistic approach to desistance from crime and problematic drug use that Webster in Chapter 9 identifies as crucial. He sums up the central question underpinning shifting, national drugs treatment regimes: 'whether drug addiction, its control and treatment should primarily be understood as a moral, medical or criminal problem?' What Webster is really advocating is a *social* understanding of drug dependency and its treatment and one that, therefore, assists in addressing the multiple, social needs of (ex)-users. For our research participants, desistance depended upon incremental steps towards social inclusion.

On the basis of her study of socially excluded young people (2004:327), Melrose argues that while 'drug use may be understood as a consequence of, or response to, the disadvantages these young people have experienced in their lives, it can be at the same time be seen to further entrench those disadvantages'. In the same vein, it would be too much for us to claim that social exclusion *caused* Barney's 'corkscrew heroin career' (as we've noted the majority started out similarly disadvantaged but did not seriously engage with crime and drugs). The opposite is also not correct: the hardships borne by Barney and those like him were not reducible to heroin. Nevertheless, of all interviewees in these Teesside studies, 'social exclusion' was a term that best fitted those individuals with long-term careers of dependent drug use and crime.

In this chapter, we have in effect been suggesting the value of a careful, *sociological* approach to understanding issues of drug consumption, supply and control. In the introductory chapter, we argued for a more differentiated understanding of how *some* drug use has become normalised in *some* ways for *some* people (Shildrick, 2002). Our conclusion has stressed a similar approach in respect of discussions of the social distribution and nature of drug careers and transitions, categorisations of drug using behaviour, drug markets and the contexts of drug use, the care and control of drug users and processes of desistance. Here we have underlined the importance of social and economic context, of social change, of history and place and of the socially conditioned choices and agency of human actors.

In re-reading the volume's substantive chapters and attempting to discuss these in relation to our own, particular Teesside studies, we have been forced to think more carefully about the limitations of the latter and to be more measured in what we can claim to know from them. Barney's is a useful story but it cannot hope to tell us the whole story. That said, we are convinced of the value of an approach that attempts to reveal the human experience that lies behind the bare statistics of drug prevalence and the rhetoric of drugs policy pronouncements.

This sometimes gets lost, particularly when we are fighting 'a war on drugs'. In this chapter, we have resisted dealing directly with an assessment of drugs policy in Britain. Nevertheless, the evidence of this chapter and the preceding ones makes it easy to agree with Newcombe's position that 'trends in drug prevalence in Britain strongly supports the conclusion that prohibition is ineffective and should be replaced with an alternative drug policy'. It is much less easy to say exactly what that 'alternative policy' should be. Given the difficulty and complexity of this question, it would not be possible to declare, as editors, a set of policy pronouncements with which all contributing authors would agree. What we can do, though, is sketch out some of the most obvious failings of the current 'war on drugs' and draw from this some implications for policy directions. We do this by referring directly and in some detail to the government's own evidence.

In July 2005, on the eve of the Live 8 concert and G8 meeting, the Prime Minister's Strategy Unit partly released its phase one report on drug issues. As one commentator said at the time, this seemed a pretty clear attempt at 'burying bad news' (*The Guardian*, 5 July 2005), especially given that the government refused to publish the second half of the report. This was, though, leaked to the same newspaper, which posted the full report on its web site. The report presents an extraordinarily candid, serious, expert and depressing account of the deeply entrenched problems of the policy status quo. In relation to the connections between drug use, crime and treatment it concluded that, while non-drug-motivated crime has fallen or remained stable, since 1995 drug-motivated crime had risen and now accounts for 56 per cent of all crime. For some offences, such as shoplifting (85 per cent) and domestic burglary (80 per cent), the proportion is far higher. Ten per cent of those who use heroin and/or crack cocaine commit around a third of all drug-related crime in Britain.

The report is frank about the problems facing drugs treatment policy and provision, noting that current and planned treatment capacity 'may be insufficient to deal with the scale of high harm causing use' (Prime Minister's Strategy Unit, 2005:22). At any one time in Britain 220,000 'high harm causing drug users' are not in treatment. Less than half of 'high harm causing drug users' enter treatment each year yet nearly half are arrested each year. Of those arrested, less than 1 in 5 are referred to treatment and less than 1 in 25 of these attend.

The section of the report that deals with the policing of drug trading and markets is particularly candid and has about it the strongest air of policy desperation (this was the part that was not intended for publication). It demonstrates that the drugs trade is *highly* lucrative and that 'profit margins for traffickers can be even higher than those of luxury goods companies' (Prime Minister's Strategy Unit, 2005:69). It documents how traffickers have adapted effectively to government interventions and that UK importers and suppliers make enough profit to absorb the modest cost of drug seizures. These are 'a cost of business rather than a substantive threat to the industry's viability' (94). Declining drug prices and rising consumption indicate that an ample supply of heroin and cocaine reaches the UK market. The report concludes with a clear, bald statement of the state of play:

> The drugs supply market is highly sophisticated, and attempts to intervene have not resulted in sustainable disruption to the market at any level. As a result, the supply of drugs has increased, prices are low enough not to deter initiation, but prices are high enough to cause heavy users to commit high levels of crime to fund their habits. (104)

To finish, we note what to us seem to be three, pretty clear implications of this report. First, the British government's strategies to control the supply and consumption of those drugs that it identifies as causing the most harm to users and others (i.e. heroin and crack cocaine) have failed. Second, in respect of eliminating or even substantially reducing supply, the 'war on drugs' cannot be won; the profits to be gained from their sale and the difficulties of seriously combating complex drug markets are too great. Finally, therefore, drugs policy in Britain might be better targeted at firstly, tackling the adverse social and economic conditions that seem to provide the demand and context for some of the most damaging forms of illicit drug use and secondly, responding to the flaws in current drugs treatment provision that the government itself identifies.

Notes

1. He was one of 88 young people interviewed for *Disconnected Youth? Growing up in Britain's Poor Neighbourhoods* conducted and authored by MacDonald and Marsh (2005). Funded by the ESRC, primarily this was initiated as a critique of theories of the underclass and social exclusion that investigated young people's school to work, housing, family, leisure, criminal and drug-using 'careers'. Shildrick (2002, 2003) and Simpson (2003, 2004) have separately undertaken related studies of young people, youth culture, drug use and crime and, with MacDonald and others, were authors of a related, follow-up study, *Poor Transitions* (Webster *et al.*, 2004). Although each of these studies had unique methodological and theoretical features, they shared common findings in respect of the topics dealt within this chapter.

2. Barney – and his peer group - had never injected heroin. Others in our study had.
3. He also described the appeal of crack cocaine, which he first used in his late teens: 'a lovely drug, crack, a lovely drug … just a feeling like your on top of the world. Just, like, dead hyperactive. You get a big rush, you know what I mean? When that's gone, like woooah, you need some more and it only lasts two, three minutes … and then you've got the heroin to bring you down. People have the crack and then the heroin to bring em down. And when you've ran out, out to rob again.'
4. Barney's story was generally characteristic of the other young men in these studies who had longer-term experience of heroin use. There are, though, elements to it which were not common (e.g. he was one of the few that described any earlier, serious family involvement in crime or drug use).
5. There is also nothing inevitable about the conditions of existence through which young people like him carved out transitions. Over the past 30 years, rapid de-industrialisation in Teesside has dramatically restructured the sorts of transitions made by working-class youth. And of particular significance for our discussion, as we shall see, has been the new arrival of a particular form of drug market in Teesside at a point in history that coincided with key moments in Barney's transition to adulthood.
6. Chamberlayne, Rustin and Wengraf (2002) and Roberts (2002) provide excellent discussions of the promise of biographical methods. Coles (2000) and MacDonald and Marsh (2005) give detailed descriptions of the aims and value of research on youth transitions and careers.
7. This does not imply that this process of normalisation was universal or straightforward (Shildrick, 2002). Compare these comments from two young women interviewees:
'I'd say that everyone gets offered drugs when they're growing up but some people take it and others don't. It's normal to be offered but not normal to use it' (Clare).
'It's just the norm, it's so easy. I mean, you're out of it if you're not on 'em or don't try 'em' (Annie).
8. Interestingly, Barton (2003:96–104) also conjures with Groups A, B and C but these have different meanings and his purpose is to create a typology of relationships between drugs and crime rather than drug using behaviour *per se*.
9. It should be noted that, because of the timing of his criminal career, Barney had not been subjected to the ARS and DTTOs designed to provide a more rounded response to drug crime.

Further Reading

MacDonald, R., and Marsh, J. (2005). 'Disconnected Youth? Growing up in Britain's Poor Neighbourhoods', Basingtoke, Palgrave.

Shildrick, T. (2002). 'Young people, illicit drugs and the question of nomalisation', Journal of Youth Studies, 5, 35–48.

Simpson, M. (2003). 'The relationship between drug use and crime: a puzzle inside an enigma', International Journal of Drug Policy, 14, 307–19.

Study Questions

1. What are the main lessons to be learned from Barney's story about the supply, consumption and control of drugs in Britain?
2. What are the key factors that might lead to the onset of and desistance from drug using careers?
3. What lessons about drug policy do you draw from the Prime Minister's Strategy Unit report of 2005?

References

Acker, C. J. (1995). From all purpose anodyne to marker of deviance: physicians' attitudes towards opiates in the US from 1890 to 1940. In R. Porter & M. Teich (Eds), *Drugs and Narcotics in History* (pp. 114–32). Cambridge: Cambridge University Press.

Adler, P. A. (1985). *Wheeling and Dealing: An Ethnography of an Upper-Level Drug Dealing and Smuggling Community.* New York: Columbia University Press.

Adorno, T. (1999). *Sound Figures.* Stanford: Stanford University Press.

Advisory Council on the Misuse of Drugs (ACMD) (1982). *Treatment and Rehabilitation.* London: HMSO.

—— (1984). *Prevention.* London: Home Office.

Agar, M. (1997). Ethnography: an overview. *Substance Use and Misuse,* 32, 1155–73.

Akhtar, S., & South, N. (2000). 'Hidden from heroin's history': heroin use and dealing within an English Asian community. In M. Hough & M. Natarajan (Eds), *Illegal Drug Markets: From Research to Prevention Policy.* Monsey, NY: Criminal Justice Press.

Allen, R. (2002). What does the public think about prison? *Criminal Justice Matters,* 49, 6–7.

Allen, C. (2005). The links between heroin, crack cocaine and crime: where does street crime fit? *British Journal of Criminology,* 45, 355–72.

Andell, P., & McManus, J. (2002). *Delivering Interventions Under the Communities Against Drugs Fund – Some Key Issues.* London: NACRO.

Anger, K. (1975). *Hollywood Babylon.* London: Arrow Books.

Anglin, M. D., Brecht, M., & Maddahian, E. (1989). Pre-treatment characteristics and treatment performance of legally coerced versus voluntary methadone maintenance. *Criminology,* 27(3), 537–549.

Anglin, M. D., & Hser, Y. I. (1990). Treatment of drug abuse. In M. Tonry & J. Q. Wilson (Eds), *Drugs and the Crime.* Chicago: University of Chicago Press.

Anglin, M. D., & Perrochet, B. (1998). Drug use and crime: a historical review of research conducted by the UCLA Drug Abuse Research Center. *Substance Use and Misuse,* 33, 1871–914.

Anglin, M. D., & Speckart, G. (1988). Narcotics and crime: a multi-sample, multi-method analysis. *Criminology,* 26, 197–233.

Anthony, W. (1998). *Class of 88: The True Acid House Experience.* London: Virgin.

Arlacchi, P. (1988). *Mafia Business: The Mafia Ethic and the Spirit of Capitalism.* Oxford: Oxford University Press.

Ashton, M., & Witton, J. (2003). Role reversal. *Drug and Alcohol Findings,* 9, 16–23.

Association of Chief Police Officers of England Wales and Northern Ireland (2002). *A Review of Drugs Policy and Proposals for the Future.* London: ACPO.

Audit Commission (2002). *Changing Habits: The Commissioning and Management of Community Drug Treatment Services for Adults.* London: The Audit Commission.

Audit Commission (2004). *Drug Misuse 2004. Reducing the Local Impact.* London: Audit Commission.

Auld, J., Dorn, N., & South, N. (1984). Heroin now: bringing it all back home. *Youth and Policy,* 9, 1–7.

—— (1986). Irregular work, irregular pleasures: heroin in the 1980s. In R. Matthews & J. Young (Eds), *Confronting Crime.* London: Sage.

Aust, R., & Cordon, J. (2003). *Geographical Variations in Drug Use: Key Findings from the 2001/02 British Crime Survey Research.* London: Home Office.

Aust, R., Sharp, C., & Goulden, C. (2002). *Prevalence of drug use: Key Findings from the 2001/02 British Crime Survey*. London: Home Office.

Aust, R. & Smith, N. (2003). Ethnicity and drug use: key findings from the 2001/02 British Crime Survey. *Home Office Research Findings No.209*. London: Home Office.

Australian Institute of Health and Welfare (2002). *2001 National Drug Strategy Household Survey*. Canberra: AIHW.

Bagnall, G. (1991). *Educating Young Drinkers*. London: Tavistock/Routledge.

Bailey, P. (1978). *Leisure and Class in Victorian Britain*. London: Routledge.

—— (2000). *Young people and Illegal Drugs into 2000*. Exeter: Schools Health Education Unit.

Balding, J. (2000). *Young People and Illegal Drugs into 2000*. Exeter: Schools Health Education Unit.

Ball, J. C., Schaffer, J. W., & Nurgo, D. N. (1983). The day-to-day criminality of heroin addicts in Baltimore – a study in the continuity of offence rates. *Drug and Alcohol Dependence*, 12, 119–42.

Bancroft, A. (1978). *Modern Mystics and Sages*. London: Paladin.

Barnes, R. (1979). *Mods!* London: Eel Pie.

Barnes, T., Elias, R., & Walsh, P. (2000). *Cocky. The Rise and Fall of Curtis Warren Britain's Biggest Drug Baron*. Bury: Milo Books.

Barrow Cadbury Trust (2005). *Lost in Transition: A Report of the Barrow Cadbury Commission on Young Adults and the Criminal Justice System*. London: Barrow Cadbury Trust.

Barton, A. (2003). *Illicit Drugs*. London: Routledge.

Bean, P. (1974). *The Social Control of Drugs*. Basil: Blackwell.

—— (2002). *Drugs and Crime*. Cullompton: Willan.

Bean, P., & Nemitz, T. (2004). *Drug Treatment: What Works?* Abingdon: Routledge.

Beck, U. (1992). *Risk Society*. London: Sage.

Becker, H. S. (1963). *Outsiders*. New York: Free Press.

Becker, H. S. (1964). *The Other Side: Perspective on Deviance*. New York: Free Press.

Bennett, T. (1998). *Drugs and Crime: The Results of Research in Drug Testing and Interviewing Arrestees*. London: Home Office.

—— (2000). *Drugs and Crime: The Results of the Second Development Stage of the NEW-ADAM Programme*. London: Home Office.

Bennett, T., & Holloway, T. (2005). *Understanding Drugs, Alcohol and Crime*, Open University Press.

Bennett, T., Holloway, K., & Williams, T. (2001). *Drug Use and Offending: Summary Results of the First Year of the NEW-ADAM Research Programme*. London: Home Office.

Berridge, V. (1978). War conditions and narcotics control: the passing of Defence of the Realm Act Regulation 40B. *Journal of Social Policy*, 7, 285–304.

—— (1999). *Opium and the People: Opiate Use and Drug Control Policy in Nineteenth and Early Twentieth Century England*. London: Free Association Press.

—— (2005). *Temperance: Its History and Impact on Current and Future Alcohol Policy*. York: Joseph Rowntree Foundation.

Berridge, V., & Edwards, G. (1987). *Opium and the People*. New Haven: Yale University Press.

Best, D., Harris, J., Gossop, M., Farrell, E., & Finch, A. (2001). Use of non-prescribed methadone and other illicit drugs during methadone maintenance treatment. *Drug and Alcohol Review*, 19, 9–16.

Best, D., Man, L., Gossop, M., Harris, J., Sidwell, C., & Strang, J. (2001). Understanding the developmental relationship between drug use and crime: are drug users the best people to ask? *Addiction Research & Theory*, 9, 151–64.

Best, D., Man, L., Rees, S., Witton, J., & Strang, J. (2003). *Evaluating the Effectiveness of Drug Treatment and Testing Orders in London. A report to the London Probation Area*. London: National Addiction Centre.

Best, D., Sidwell, C., Gossop, M., Harris, J., & Strang, J. (2001). Crime and expenditure amongst polydrug users seeking treatment: the connection between prescribed methadone and crack use and criminal involvement. *British Journal of Criminology*, 41, 119–26.

Bewley, T. (1996). Recent changes in the pattern of drug abuse in the United Kingdom. *Bulletin on Narcotics*, 18, 1–9.

Bez (1998). *Freaky Dancing*. London: Pan.

Biehal, N., Clayden, J., Stein, M., & Wade, J. (1995). *Moving On. Young People and Leaving Care Schemes*. London: HMSO.

Blackman, S. J. (1995). *Youth: Positions and Oppositions – Style, Sexuality and Schooling*. Aldershot: Avebury Press.

—— (1996). Has drug culture become an inevitable part of youth culture? A critical assessment of drug education. *Educational Review*, 48, 131–42.

—— (2004). *Chilling Out: the Cultural Politics of Substance Consumption, Youth and Drug Policy*. Maidenhead/New York Open University Press/McGraw-Hill.

Blackwell, J. (1983). Drifting, controlling and overcoming: opiate users who avoid becoming chronically dependent. *Journal of Drug Issues*, 13, 219–36.

Botvin, G. (1990). Preventing adolescent cigarette smoking: resistance skills in training and the development of life skills. *Special Services in Schools*, 6, 37–61.

Bourdieu, P. (1996). *The Rules of Art*. Oxford: Polity.

Bourgois, P. (1995). *In Search of Respect. Selling Crack in El Barrio*. Cambridge: Cambridge University Press.

Bowling, B., & Phillips, C. (2002). *Racism, Crime and Justice*. Harlow: Longman.

Brain, K., Parker, H., & Bottomley, T. (1998). *Evolving Crack Cocaine Careers: New Users, Quitters and Long Term Combination Drug Users in NW England*. Manchester: University of Manchester.

—— (1998). *Evolving Crack Cocaine Careers: New Users, Quitters and Long Term Combination Drug Users in NW England*. Manchester: University of Manchester.

Brake, M. (1980). *The Sociology of Youth Culture and Youth Subculture*. London: Routledge.

Bramley-Harker, E. (2001). *Sizing the UK market for illicit drugs*. London: Home Office

Branigan, T., & Glover, J. (2005). "The drug question that won't go away." *The Guardian* 15th October 2005.

Bridgwood, A., Rainford, L., Walker, A., Hickman, M., & Morgan, A. (1998). *All Change? The Health Education Monitoring Survey One Year On*. London: HEA & ONS.

Burniston, S., Dodd, M., Elliott, L., Orr, L., & Watson, L. (2002). *Drug Treatment Services for Young People: A Research Review*. Scotland: Effective Interventions Unit, Scottish Executive.

Burr, A. (1987). Chasing the dragon: heroin misuse, delinquency and crime in the context of South London culture. *British Journal of Criminology*, 27, 333–57.

Burroughs, W., (1967). Cannabis and opiates. In G. Andrews & S. Vinkenoog (Eds), *The Book of Grass*. London: Penguin.

Burroughs, W., & Ginsberg, A. (1963). *The Yage Letters*. San Francisco: City Lights Publishers.

Butler, T. (1997). *Preliminary Findings from the Inmate Health Survey of the Inmate Population in the New South Wales Correctional System*. Sydney: New South Wales Department of Corrective Services.

Campbell, B. (1983). *Goliath: Britain's Dangerous Places*. London: Methuen.

Carnwath, T., & Smith, I. (2002). *Heroin Century*. London: Routledge.

Carnwath, T., Gabbay, M., & Barnard, J. (2000). A Share of the Action: General Practitioner involvement in drug misuse treatment in Greater Manchester. *Drugs: Education, Prevention and Policy*, 7, 235–50.

—— (2000). A share of the action: general practitioner involvement in drug misuse treatment in greater Manchester. *Drugs: Education, Prevention and Policy*, 7, 235–250.

Carr, R., Case, B., & Dellar, F. (1986). *The Hip*. London: Faber and Faber.

Castaneda, C. (1968). *The Teachings of Don Juan: a Yaqui Way of Knowledge*. Berkeley: University of California Press.

Castells, M. (2000). *End of Millenium*. Oxford: Blackwell.

Centre on Addiction and Substance Abuse (1998). *Behind bars: Substance abuse and America's Prison Population*. New York: Columbia University.

Chamberlayne, P., Rustin, M., & Wengraf, T. (2002). *Biography and Social Exclusion in Europe*. Bristol: Policy Press.

Chambers, I. (1981). Pop Music: a teaching perspective. *Screen Education*, 39, 35–46.

Chatterton, M., Varley, M., & Langmead-Jones, P. (1998). *Testing Performance Indicators for Local Anti-Drugs Strategies*. London: Home Office.

Chatwin, C. (2003). Drug policy developments within the European Union: the destabilizing effects of Dutch and Swedish policies. *British Journal of Criminology*, 43, 567–82.

Chein, I., Ferard, D., Lee, R., & Rosenfeld, F. (1964). *The Road to H: Narcotics, Delinquency and Social Policy*. London: Tavistock.

Chivite-Matthews, N., et al. (2005). *Drug use Declared: Findings from the 2003/04 British Crime Survey*. London: Home Office.

Choongh, S. (1999). *Policing as Social Discipline*. Oxford: Oxford University Press.

Clark, N. H. (1976). *Deliver us from Evil*. New York: Norton and Company.

Coggans, N., & McKellar, S. (1994). Drug use among peers: peer pressure or peer preference? *Drugs: Education, Prevention and Policy*, 1, 15–26.

Coggans, N., Shewan, D., Henderson, M., & Davies, J. B. (1991). *National Evaluation of Drug Education in Scotland*. London: ISDD.

Coggans, N., Shewan, D., Henderson, M., Davies, J. B., & O'Hagan, F. J. (1989). *National Evaluation of Drug Education in Scotland*. Centre for Occupational and Health Psychology: University of Strathclyde.

———— (1990). *National Evaluation of Drug Education in Scotland: Final Report*. Coggnas, Edinburgh: Scottish Educational Department.

Cohen, S. (1972/1980). *Moral Panics and Folk Devils*. Oxford: Martin Robertson.

Cohen, J. (2002). Just say – oh no, not again. *D ruglink*, 17, 13–14.

Coid, J., Carvell, A., Kittler, Z., Healey, A., & Henderson, J. (2000). *Opiates, Criminal Behaviour, and Methadone Treatment*. London: Home Office.

Coles, B. (2000). *Joined Up Youth Research, Policy and Practice: An Agenda for Change?* Leicester: Youth Work Press.

Collin, M., & Godfrey, J. (1997). *Altered States: The Story of Ecstasy Culture and Acid House*. London: Serpent's Tail.

Collison, M. (1996). In Search of the Highlife British Journal of Criminology, 36(3), 428–430.

Condon, J., & Smith, N. (2003). *Prevalence of Drug Use: Key Findings from the 2002/03 British Crime Survey*. London: Home Office (Findings 229).

Connell, P. H. (1965) Adolescent drug taking. *Proceedings of the Royal Society of Medicine*, 58: 409–12.

Cornish, D., & Clarke, R. V. (1986). *The Reasoning Criminal*. New York: Springer-Verlag.

Costa, E., & Silva, J. (2002). Evidence-based analysis of the worldwide abuse of licit and illicit drugs. *Human Psychopharmacology*, 17, 131–40.

Craver, J. (2004). Drug Testing: a necessary prerequisite for treatment and for crime contro'l. In P. Bean & T. Nemitz (Eds), *Drug Treatment What Works?* London: Routledge.

Crowther, C. (2000). *Policing Urban Poverty*. Basingstoke: Macmillan.

Crowther, C. (2002). The politics and economics of disciplining an inclusive and exclusive society. *Social Policy Review*, 14, 199–224.

———— (2004). Over-policing and under-policing Social Exclusion. In R. Hopkins-Burke (Ed.), *'Hard Cop/Soft Cop': Dilemmas and Debates in Contemporary Policing*. Cullompton: Willan.

Crusick, J. (2005). "The Tory war on drugs." *The Sunday Herald* 16th October 2005.

Currie, C., Roberts, C., Morgan, A., Smith, R., Settertobulte, W., Samdal, O., & Rasmussen, V. (2004). *Young People's Health in Context: Health Behaviour in School-Aged Children (HBSC) Study: International Report from the 2001/02 survey*. Copenhagen: WHO Regional Office for Europe.

Cusick, T. (2005). Tory War on Drugs, *Sunday Herald*, October 16th 2005.

Cusick, L., & Martin, A. (2003). *Vulnerability and involvement in drug use and sex work*. London: Home Office.

Dapp, R. (2002). Fact about the Lambeth cannabis pilot scheme, *Urban 75*.

Davies, J. B. (1992). *The Myth of Addiction: An Application of the Psychological Theory of Attribution to Illicit Drug Use*. Chur, Switzerland: Harwood Academic Publishers.

De Alarcon, R. (1969). The spread of heroin abuse in a community. *Bulletin on Narcotics*, 21, 17–22.

De Angelis, D., Hickman, M., & Yang, S. (2004). Estimating long-term trends in the incidence and prevalence of opiate use/injecting drug use and the number of former users: back-calculation methods and opiate overdose deaths. *American Journal of Epidemiology*, 160, 994–1004.

De Haes, W. F. M. (1994). Looking for effective drug education programmes: fifteen years exploration of the effects of different drug education programmes. In R. Coomber (Ed.), *Drugs and Drug Use in Society. A Critical Reader*. Kent: Greenwich University Press.

De Haes, W. F. M., & Schuurman, J. H. (1975). Results of an evaluation study of three drug education methods. *International Journal of Health Education*, 18, 1–16.

De Li Periu, H., & MacKenzie, D. (2000). Drug involvement, lifestyles and criminal activities among probationers. *Journal of Drug Issues*, 30, 593–620.

Deaton, S. (2004). *On-charge Drug Testing: Evaluation of Drug Testing in the Criminal Justice System*. London: Home Office.

Deehan, A. (1999). *Alcohol and Crime: Taking Stock*. London: Home Office.

Deitch, D., Koutsenok, I., & Ruiz, A. (2000). The relationship between crime and drugs: what we have learned in recent decades. *Journal of Psychoactive Drugs*, 32, 391–97.

Department for Education and Employment (DfEE) (1998). *Protecting Young People: Good Practice in Drug Education in Schools and the Youth Service*. London: DfEE.

—————— (2000). *Connexions: The Best Start in Life for Every Young Person*. London: Department for Education and Employment.

Department for Education and Skills (DfES) (2000). *Sex and Relationship Education Guidance*. London: DfES.

—————— (2004). *Drugs: Guidance for Schools*. London: DfES.

Department for Education and Skills (DfES) and Department of Health (DoH) (2003). *National Healthy Schools Standard: Drug Education*. London: DfES and DoH.

Department of Health (DoH) (1996). *The Task Force to Review Services for Drug Misusers. Report of an Independent Revie w of Drug Treatment Services in England*. London: Department of Health.

—————— (1998). *Welsh Youth Health Survey*. Cardiff: Health Promotion Wales.

—————— (1999). *Drug Misuse and Dependence: Guidelines on Clinical Management*. London: The Stationary Office.

—————— (2002). *Models of Care for Substance Misuse Treatment: PromotingQuality, Efficiency and Effectiveness in Drug Misuse Treatment Services*. London: Department of Health/ National Treatment Agency.

—————— (2003). *Provisional Statistics from the National Drug Treatment Monitoring System in England, 2001/02 and 2002/03*. London: Department of Health.

—————— (2004). *Drug Use, Smoking and Drinking Among Young People in England in 2003*. London: Department of Health.

Dingwall, G. (2005). *Alcohol and Crime*. Cullompton: Willan.

Ditton, J., & Frischer, M. (2001). Computerised projection of future heroin epidemics: a necessity for the 21st century? *Substance Use and Misuse*, 36, 151–66.

Ditton, J., & Speirits, K. (1981). *The Rapid Increase of Heroin Addiction in Glasgow during 1981. Background Paper No 2*. Glasgow: Department of Sociology, University of Glasgow.

Dobinson, I., & Ward, P. (1986). Heroin and property crime: an Australian perspective. *Journal of Drug Issues*, 16, 249–62.

Dorn, N. (1981). Social analyses of drugs in health education and the media. In G. Edwards & C. Busch (Eds), *Drug Problems in Britain*. London: Academic Press. .

—————— (1994). Three faces of police referral: welfare, justice and business perspectives on multi-agency work with drug arrestees. *Policing and Society* 4, 13–34.

Dorn, N., & Murji, K. (1992). *Drug Prevention: A Review of the English Language Literature*. London: ISDD.

Dorn, N., Murji, K., & South, N. (1992). *Traffickers: Drug Markets and Law Enforcement*. London: Routledge.

Dorn, N., Oette, L., & White, S. (1998). Drugs importation and the bifurcation of risk: capitalization, cut outs and organised crime. *British Journal of Criminology*, 38, 537–60.

Dorn, N., Ribbens, J., & South, N. (1987). *Coping with a Nightmare: Family Feelings about Long Term Drug Use*. London: ISDD.

Dorn, N., & South, N. (1987). Reconciling policy and practice. In N. Dorn & N. South (Eds), *A Land Fit for Heroin? Drug Policies, Prevention and Practice*. London: Macmillan.

— (1992). The Power Behind Practice: Drug Control and Harm Minimisation in the Inter-Agency and criminal Law Contexts. In J. Strang & M. Gossop (Eds), *Heroin Addiction and Drug Policy: the British System*. Oxford: Oxford medical Press.

Downes, D. (1977). The drug addict as folk devil. In P. Rock (Ed.), *Drugs and Politics* (pp. 89–97). New Brunswick, New Jersey: Transaction Books.

Druglink (2004). Minister 'misled' over numbers in drug treatment, Nov/Dec 2004.

Drug Prevention Initiative (1996). *Young People, Drugs and Peer Education: An Evaluation of the Youth Awareness Programme*. London: Home Office.

Drugscope (2000). *Drugs: Your Questions Answered*. London: DrugScope.

────── (2002). *Summary of UK Drug Situation 2001*. London: DrugScope.

Drury, N. (1979). *Inner Visions: Explorations in Magical Consciousness*. London: Routledge.

Dunlap, E., Golub, A., Johnson, B., & Wesley, D. (2002). Intergenerational transmission of conduct norms for drugs, sexual exploitation and violence: a case study. *British Journal of Criminology*, 42, 1–20.

Edmunds, M., Hough, M., & May, T. (1999). *Doing Justice to Treatment: Referring Offenders to Drug Services*. London: Home Office.

Edmunds, M., Hough, M., & Urquia, N. (1996). *Tackling Local Drug Markets*. London: Home Office Police Research Group.

Edmunds, M., May, T., Hough, M., & Hearnden, I. (1998). *Arrest Referral: Emerging Lessons from Research*. London: Home Office.

Egginton, R., Bury, C., & Parker, H. (1998). Heroin still screws you up: Responding to new heroin outbreaks. *Druglink*, 13, 17–20.

Egginton, R., & Parker, H. (2000). *Hidden Heroin Users: Young People's Unchallenged Journeys to Problematic Drug Use*. London: DrugScope.

Eley, S., Gallop, K., McIvor, G., Morgan, K., & Yates, R. (2002). *Drug Treatment and Testing Orders: Evaluation of the Scottish Pilots*. Edinburgh: Scottish Executive Central Research Unit.

Elkind, D. (1985). Cognitive development and adolescent disabilities. *Journal of Adolescent Health Care*, 6, 84–89.

Elliot, L., Orr, L., Watson, L., & Jackson, A. (2002). *Drug Treatment Services for Young People: A Systematic Review of Effectiveness and the Legal Framework*. Scotland: Scottish Executive.

Engineer, R., Phillips, A., Thompson, J., & Nicholls, J. (2003). *Drunk and Disorderly:A Qualitative Study of Binge Drinking among 18 to 24-Year-Olds*. London: Home Office.

European Monitoring Centre for Drugs and Drug Addiction (EMCDDA) (2003). *The State of The Drugs Problem in The European Union and Norway*. Luxembourg: EMCDDA.

Farabee, D., Shen, H. K., Hser, Y. I., Grella, C. E., & Anglin, M. D. (2001). The effect of drug treatment on criminal behaviour among adolescents in DATOS-A, *Journal of Adolescent Research*, 16, 679–96.

Farrington, D. (1994). Human development and criminal careers. In M. Maguire, R. Morgan & R. Reiner (Eds), *The Oxford Handbook of Criminology*. Oxford: Oxford University Press.

────── (1996). *Understanding and Preventing Youth Crime*. York: Joseph Rowntree Foundation.

Fazey, C., Brown, P., & Batey, P. (1990). *A socio-demographic analysis of patients attending a drug dependency clinic*. Liverpool: Centre for Urban Studies, University of Liverpool.

Fionda, J. (2000). New managerialism, credibility and the sanitisation of criminal justice. In P. Green & A. Rutherford (Eds), *Criminal Policy in Transition* (pp. 109–27.). Oxford: Hart.

Fitzgerald, J., & Chilvers, M. (2002). *Multiple Drug Use Among Police Detainees. Contemporary Issues in Crime and Justice*. Sydney: New South Wales Bureau of Crime Statistics and Research.

Flood-Page, C., Campbell, S., Harrington, V., & Miller, J. (2000). *Youth Crime: Findings from the 1998/99 Youth Lifestyles Survey*. London: Home Office.

Florentine, R., et al. (1999). Client engagement with drug treatment. *Journal of Substance Abuse*, 17, 199–206.

Fluke, B., & Donato, L. (1959). Some glues are dangerous, *Empire Magazine, (Supplement to Denver Post)*, August 2nd, 1959.

Foster, J. (2000). Social exclusion, crime and drugs. *Drugs: Education, Prevention & Policy*, 7, 317–30.

Foucault, M. (1977). *Discipline and Punish*. London: Allen Lane.

────── (1991). Governmentality. In G. Burchell, C. Gordon & P. Miller (Eds), *The Foucault Effect: Studies in Governmentality*. Hemel Hempstead: Harvester Wheatsheaf.

Fountain, J., Bashford, J., & Winters, M. (2003). *Black and Minority Ethnic Communities in England: A Review of the Literature on Drug Use and Related Service Provision.* . London: National Treatment Agency.

Frischer, M. (1997). Estimating the prevalence of drug abuse using the multiplier method: an overview. In G. Stimson (Ed.), *Estimating the Prevalence of Drug Misuse in Europe*. Luxembourgh: Council for Europe/EMCDDA.

Frischer, M., Goldberg, D., & Green, S. (1993). How many drug injectors are there in the UK? *International Journal on Drug Policy*, 4, 190–93.

Frischer, M., Hickman, M., Kraus, L., Mariani, F., & Wiessing, L. (2001). A comparison of different methods for estimating the prevalence of problematic drug use in Great Britain. *Addiction*, 96, 1465–76.

Frischer, M., Leyland, A., Cormack, R., Goldber, D., Bloor, M., Green, S., Taylor, A., Covell, R., McKeganey, N., & Platt, S. (1993). Estimating population prevalence of injection drug use and HIV infection among injection drug users in Glasgow. *American Journal of Epidemiology*, 138, 170–81.

Frischer, M., & Taylor, A. (1999). Issues in assessing the nature and extent of local drug misuse. In C. Stark, B. Kidd & R. Sykes (Eds), *Illegal Drug Use in the United Kingdom: Prevention, Treatment and Enforcement*. Aldershot: Ashgate.

Frith, S. (1983). *Sound Effects: Youth, Leisure and the Politics of Rock 'n' Roll*. London: Constable.

Galeotti, M. (2001). Afghanistan's narcotics – Drugs fund war, *World Today* 57, 12–13.

Garland, D. (1985). *Punishment and Welfare*. Aldershot: Gower.

——— (2001). *The Culture of Control: Crime and Social Order in Contemporary Society*. Oxford: Oxford University Press.

Garratt, S. (1998). *Adventures in Wonderland*. London: Headline.

Gilman, M. (1991). Beyond opiates... and into the '90's. *Druglink*, November/ December, 16–17.

——— (1992). No more junkie heroes? *Druglink*, May/June, 16.

Gilman, M., & Pearson, G. (1991). Lifestyle and law enforcement. In D. K. Whynes & P. T. Bean (Eds), *Policing and Prescribing. The British System of Drug Control*. Basingstoke: Macmillan.

Goddard, E., & Higgins, V. (1999). *Smoking, Drinking and Drug Use among Young Teenagers in 1998*. London: Stationery Office (Volumes 1 & 2: England and Wales).

Godfrey, C., Eaton, G., McDougall, C., & Culyer, A. (2002). *The Economic and Social Costs of Class A Drug Use in England and Wales, 2000*. London: Home Office.

Goldstein, P. (1985). The Drugs/Violence Nexus: a tripartite conceptual framework. *Journal of Drug Issues*, 15, 493–506.

Goodman, M. (1998). Public enemy number one. *Druglink*, 13, 23–25.

Gossop, M. (2000). 5th edition. *Living with Drugs*, Aldershot: Ashgate.

Gossop, M., & Keaney, F. (2004). Research note – prescribing diamorphine for medical conditions: a very British practice. *Journal of Drug Issues*, 34, 441–50.

Gossop, M., Marsden, J., & Stewart, D. (1998). *NTORS at One Year. The National Treatment Outcome Research Study. Changes in Substance Use, Health and Criminal Behaviour at One Year after Intake*. London: Department of Health.

Gossop, M., Marsden, J., Stewart, D., Edwards, C., Lehmann, P., Wilson, A., & Segar, G. (1997). The National Treatment Outcome Study in the UK: six month follow up outcomes. *Psychology of Addictive Behaviour*, 11, 324–37.

Gossop, M., Marsden, J., Stewart, D. (2000) & Treatment outcomes of stimulant misusers: One year follow-up results from the National Treatment Outcome Research Study (NTORS) *Addictive Behaviors*, 25, 509–22.

Gossop, M., Marsden, J., Stewart, D., & Kidd, T. (2002). Changes in use of crack cocaine after drug misuse treatment: 4–5 year follow-up results from the National Treatment Outcome Research Study. *Drug and Alcohol Dependence*, 66, 21–28.

Gossop, M., Marsden, J., Stewart, D., Lehmann, P., Edwards, C., Wilson, A., & Segar, G. (1998). Substance use, health and social problems of service users at 54 drug treatment agencies. *British Journal of Psychiatry*, 173, 166–71.

Gossop, M., Marsden, J., Stewart, D. & Kidd, T. (2003). The national treatment outcome research study (NTORS): 4–5 year follow-up results. *Addiction*, 98, 291–303.

Gossop, M., Marsden, J., Stewart, D., & Treacy, S. (2001). Outcomes after methadone maintenance and methadone reduction treatment: follow up results from the National Treatment Outcome Research Study. *Drug and Alcohol Dependence*, 62, 255–64.

—— (2002). Change and stability of change after treatment of drug misuse: two-year outcomes from the National Treatment Outcome Research Study (UK). *Addictive Behaviours*, 27, 155–66.

Gossop, M., & Mitcheson, L. (2003). Research Note – Illegal drug problems and their treatment, *The Psychologist*, 16(2), 66–68.

Gossop, N. (2005). *Drug Misuse Treatment and Reduction in Crime Findings from the National Treatment Outcomes Research Survey.* London: NHS and National Treatment Agency for Substance Misuse.

Gostin, L. O. (1993). Compulsory treatment for drug-dependent persons: justifications for a public health approach to drug dependency. In R. Bayer & G. M. Oppenheimer (Eds), *Drug Policy: Illicit Drugs in a Free Society.* Cambridge: Cambridge University Press.

Goulden, C., & Sondhi, A. (2001). *At the Margins: Drug Use by Vulnerable Young People in the 1998/99 Youth Lifestyles Survey.* London: Home Office.

Griffiths, P., Vingoe. I., & Jansen, K. (1997). New trends in synthetic drugs in the European Union. Lisbon: Home Office (2002). *Drug Seizure and Offender Statistics.* London: Home Office.

Gruppo Abele (2003). *Synthetic Drugs Trafficking in Three European Cities: Major Trends and the Involvement of Organised Crime.* Turin: Gruppo Abele.

Hall, S. (1968). *The Hippies: An American Moment.* Birmingham: Centre for Contemporary Cultural Studies, University of Birmingham.

Hall, S., Critcher, C., Jefferson, T., Clarke, J., & Roberts, B. (1978). *Policing the Crisis: Mugging, the State and Law and Order.* London: Macmillan.

Hall, S., & Jefferson, T. (1975). *Resistance Through Rituals.* London: Hutchinson.

Hammersley, R. (2005). Theories of normal drug use. *Addiction, research and theory*, 13(3), 201–03.

Hammersley, R., Khan, F., & Ditton, J. (2002). *Ecstasy.* London: Routledge.

Hammersley, R., Marsland, L., & Reid, M. (2003). *Substance Use by Young Offenders: The Impact of the Normalisation of Drug Use in the Early Years of the 21st Century.* London: Home Office.

Hammersley, R., & Pearl, S. (1997). Show me the way to go home: young homeless people and drugs. *Druglink*, 12, 11–13.

Hammersley, R. H., Forsyth, A., Morrison, V., & Davies, J. B. (1989). The relationship between crime and opioid use. *British Journal of Addiction*, 84, 1029–1043.

Harocopos, A., Dennis, D., Turnbull, P. J., Parsons, J., & Hough, M. (2003). *On the Rocks: A Follow-up Study of Crack Users in London. A Report of an independent study funded by the Community Fund and the National Treatment Agency for Substance Misuse.* London: Criminal Policy Research Unit, South Bank University.

Harris Research Centre (1992). *Young People's Poll. Report to Reportage.* London: BBC.

Harrison, L. D. (1992). The drug-crime nexus in the USA. *Contemporary Drug Problems*, 19, 181–202.

Harrison, L. D., & Backenheimer, M. (1998). Research Careers in unravelling the drug-crime nexus in the U.S. *Substance Use and Misuse*, 33, 1763–2003.

Hartnoll, R. (1997). General introduction. In G. Stimson (Ed.), *Estimating the Prevalence of Problem Drug Use in Europe.* Luxembourg: EMCDDA.

Hartnoll, R., Daviaud, E., Lewis, R., & Mitcheson, M. (1985). *Drug Problems: Assessing local needs. A Practical Manual for Assessing the Nature and Extent of Problematic Drug Use in a Community.* London: Drug Indicators Project.

Haw, S. (1985). *Drug Problems in Greater Glasgow.* London: SCODA.

Hay, G., & McKeganey, N. (1996). Estimating the prevalence of drug misuse in Dundee, Scotland: an application of capture-recapture methods. *Journal of Epidemiology & Community Health*, 50, 469–72.

Hay, G., & Smit, F. (2003). Estimating the number of drug injectors from needle exchange data. *Addiction Research & Theory*, 11, 235–43.

Health Advisory Service (HAS) (2001). *The Substance of Young Needs; Review 2001.* London: Health Advisory Service.

Health Development Agency (1997). *Health Promotion in Younger People for the Prevention of Substance Misuse.* London: Health Development Agency.

Health Education Authority (HEA) (1996). *Drug Realities – National Drug Campaign Survey.* London: HEA.

Health Education Authority (HEA) (1997). *Drug Use in England.* Abingdon: Marston Books.

Health Protection Agency (2003). *Shooting Up: Infections among Injecting Drug Users in the UK 2002 – An Update: December 2003.* London: Health Protection Agency.

Hearnden, I., & Harocopos, A. (2000). *Problem Drug Use and Probation in London.* London: Home Office.

Hearnden, I., & Magill, C. (2004). *Decision-Making by House Burglars: Offenders' Perspectives.* London: Home Office.

Hebdige, D. (1975). The Meaning of Mod. In S. Hall & T. Jefferson (Eds), *Resistance Through Rituals.* London: Hutchinson.

———— (1979). *Subculture: The Meaning of Style.* London: Methuen.

Hewitt, P. (1999). *The Sharper Word: A Mod Anthology.* London: Helter Skelter.

———— (2000). *The Soul Stylists.* Edinburgh: Mainstream.

Hibell, B., Andersson, B., Bjarnason, T., Kokkevi, A., Morgan, M., & Narusk, A. (1997). *The 1995 ESPAD Report.* Stockholm: The Swedish Council for Information on Alcohol and Other Drugs.

Hickman, M., Cox, S., Harvey, J., Howes, S., Farrell, M., Frischer, M., Stimson, G., Taylor, C., & Tilling, K. (1999). Estimating the prevalence of problem drug use in inner London: a discussion of three capture-recapture studies. *Addiction*, 94, 1653–62.

Hiller, M. L., Knight, K., Leukefeld, C., & Simpson, D. D. (2002). Motivation as a predictor of therapeutic engagement in mandated residential substance abuse treatment. *Criminal Justice and Behaviour*, 29, 56–75.

Hobbs, D. (1995). *Bad Business: Professional Crime in Modern Britain.* Oxford: Oxford University Press.

———— (2001). The Firm: Organisational Logic and Criminal Culture on a Shifting Terrain. *British Journal of Criminology*, 41, 549–60.

Hobbs, D., Hadfield, P., Lister, S., & Winlow, S. (2003). *Bouncers. Violence and Governance in the Night-Time Economy.* Oxford: Oxford University Press.

Holloway, K., Bennett, T., & Farrington, D. (2005). *The Effectiveness for Criminal Justice and Treatment Programmes in Reducing Drug-Related Crime: A Systematic Review.* London: Home Office.

Holloway, K., Bennett, T., & Lower, C. (2004). *Trends in drug use and offending: the results of the NEW-ADAM programme 1999–2002.* London: Home Office.

Home Affairs Committee (2002). *The Government's Drugs Policy: Is It Working?: Vol 1 Report and Proceedings of The Committee.* London: The Stationery Office.

Home Office (1980). *Statistics of the Misuse of Drugs in the United Kingdom, 1979.* London: HMSO.

———— (1990). *Statistics of the Misuse of Drugs: Addicts Notified to the Home Office, United Kingdom, 1989.* London: HMSO.

———— (1994). *Tackling Drugs Together: A Consultation Document Strategy for England 1995–1998.* London: HMSO.

———— (1997). *Statistics of Drug Addicts Notified to the Home Office, United Kingdom, 1996.* London: HMSO.

———— (1998a). *Tackling Drugs to Build A Better Britain: The Government's Ten Year Strategy for Tackling Drugs Misuse.* London: HMSO.

———— (1998b). *The Crime and Disorder Act: Community Safety and the Reduction and Prevention of Crime ? A Conceptual Framework for Training and the Development of a Professional Discipline.* London: HMSO.

———— (1999). *UK Anti-Drugs Coordinators Annual Report 1998/99 and National Plan 1999/2000.* London: HMSO.

———— (2000). *A Guide to the Criminal Justice System in England and Wales.* London: HMSO.

———— (2002). *Updated Drug Strategy 2002: Tackling Drugs.* London: HMSO.

———— (2003). 'Government cracking crime in Middlesbrough' press release, www.drugs.gov. uk/news, accessed 1/9/03.

———— (2004). *Drug Seizure and Offender Statistics, UK, 2001 & 2002.* London: HMSO.

—— (2004). *Arrests for Notifiable Offences and the Operation of certain police powers under PACE, England & Wales, 2003/04*. London: HMSO.

—— (2004). *Home Office Probation Statistics for England and Wales 2002*. London: HMSO.

—— (2004). *Tackling Drugs. Changing Lives: Keeping Communities Safe from Drugs*. London: Home Office.

Hore, C. (1993). Jazz-a people's music? *International Socialism*, 61, 91–108.

Hough, M. (1996). *Drug Misusers and the Criminal Justice System: A Review of the Literature*. London: Home Office.

—— (2002). Drug user treatment within a criminal justice context. *Substance Use and Misuse*, 37, 985–96.

Hough, M., McSweeney, T., & Turnbull, P. (2001). *Drugs and Crime: What are the Links? Evidence to the Home Affairs Committee Inquiry into Drug Policy*. London: DrugScope.

Hughes, P. (1977). *Behind the Wall of Respect*. Chicago: University of Chicago Press.

Hughes, P., & Rieche, O. (1995). Heroin epidemics revisited. *Epidemiologic Reviews*, 17, 66.

Hunt, L., & Chambers, C. (1967). *The Heroin Epidemic: A Study of Heroin Use in the United States 1965–75*. New York: Spectrum.

Hunt, N., & Stevens, A. (2004). Whose harm? Harm reduction and the shift to coercion. *UK Drug Policy, Social Policy and Society*, 3, 1–10.

Hunter, G., Donoghoe, M., & Stimson, G. (1995). Crack use and injection on the increase among injecting drug users in London. *Addiction*, 90, 1397–1400.

Hurry, J., & Lloyd, C. (1997). *A Follow-up Evaluation of Project Charlie: A Life Skills Drug Education Programme for Primary Schools*. London: Home Office.

Huxley, A. (1954). *The Doors of Perception*. London: Chatto and Windus.

Information & Statistics Division (2000). *Drug Misuse Scotland 2000*. Edinburgh: Common Services Agency.

Inner London Probation Service (ILPS) (1995). *An Assessment of Housing Need in Hammersmith and Fulham*. London: unpublished ILPS report.

ISDD (1996). *Drug Misuse in Britain 1995*. London: Institute for Study of Drug Dependence.

—— (1999). *Drug Misuse in Britain 1998*. London: Institute for the Study of Drug Dependence.

Jackson, J. (1991). 'Concluding comment'. In C. Lusanne (Ed.), *Pipe Dream Blues*. Boston: South End Press.

Jackson, P. (2004). *Inside Clubbing*. Oxford: Berg.

Jacobs, B. A. (1996). Crack dealers and restrictive deterrence: identifying narcs. *Criminology*, 34, 409–31.

—— (1999). *Dealing Crack. The Social World of Streetcorner Selling*. Boston: Northeastern University Press.

—— (2000). *Robbing Drug Dealers. Violence Beyond the Law*. New York: Aldine de Gruyter.

Jacobson, J. (1999). *Policing Drug Hot-Spots*. London: HMSO.

Jarvis, G., & H., P. (1989). Young heroin users and crime: How do the "new users" finance their habits? *British Journal of Criminology*, 29, 175–85.

Johnson, B. D., Goldstein, P. J., Preble, E., Schmeidler, J., Lipton, D. S., Spunt, B., & Miller, T. (1985). *Taking Care of Business. The Economics of Crime by Heroin Abusers*. Lexington, Mass: Lexington Books.

Johnston, L. (1999). *Policing Britain: Risk, Security and Governance*. Harlow: Longman.

Johnston, L., MacDonald, R., Mason, P., Ridley, L., & Webster, C. (2000). *Snakes & Ladders: Young People, Transitions & Social Exclusion*. Bristol: Policy Press.

Kaplan, J. (1983). *The Hardest Drug: Heroin and Public Policy*. Chicago: University of Chicago Press.

Keith, M. (1993). *Race, Riots and Policing*. London: UCL Press.

Kevin, M. (2000). *Using Drugs in Prison. Research Summary*. Sydney: New South Wales Department of Corrective Services.

Klee, H., McLean, I., & Yavorsky, C. (2002). *Employing Drug Users: Individual and Systematic Barriers to Rehabilitation*. York: Joseph Rowntree Foundation.

Klee, H., & Reid, P. (1998). Drugs and youth homelessness: reducing the risks. *Drugs: Education, Prevention and Policy*, 5, 269–80.

Klein, N. (2000). *No Logo*. London: Flamingo.

Kothari, G., Marsden, J., & Strang, J. (2002). Opportunities and obstacles for effective treatment of drug misusers in the criminal justice system in England and Wales. *British Journal of Criminology*, 42, 412–32.

Kraus, L., Augustin, R., Frischer, M., Kummler, P., Uhl, A., & Wiessing, L. (2003). Estimating prevalence of problem drug use at national level in countries of the European Union and Norway. *Addiction*, 98, 471–85.

Kraus, L., Simon, R., Bauernfeind, R., & Pfeiffer, T. (1999). *Study to Obtain Comparable National Estimates of Problem Drug Use Prevalence for all EU Member States*. Lisbon: EMCDDA.

Labrousse, A., & Laniel, L. (2001). The World Geopolitics of Drugs, 1998/1999. Special issue of *Crime, Law and Social Change*, 36 (1–2), 1–284.

Leary, T. (1970). *The Politics of Ecstasy*. London: MacGibbon and Kee.

Lee, M., & Shlain, B. (1992). *Acid Dreams*. New York: Grove Press.

Lee, M., & South, N. (2003). Drugs policing. In T. Newburn (Ed.), *The Handbook of Policing*. Cullompton: Willan.

Lentz, G. (2002). *The Influential Factor*. Horsham: GEL Publishing.

Lewis, R., Hartnoll, R., Bryer, S., Daviaud, E., & Mithceson, M. (1985). Scoring Smack: The Illicit Heroin Market in London, 1980–1983. *British Journal of Addiction*, 80, 281–90.

Linken, A. (1963). "Young Drug Takers." *Sunday Times* 27th January 1963.

Lloyd, C. (1998). Risk factors for problem drug use: identifying vulnerable groups. *Drugs: Education, Prevention and Policy*, 5, 217–32.

Lloyd, C., Joyce, R., Hurry, J., & Ashton, M. (2000). The effectiveness of Primary school drug education. *Drugs: Education, Prevention and Policy*, 7(2), 109–26.

Lockley, P. (1995). *Counselling: Heroin and Other Drug Users*. London: Free Association press.

Long, M. (2003). Leadership and performance management. In T. Newburn (Ed.), *The Handbook of Policing*. Cullompton: Willan.

Lupton, R., Wilson, A., May, T., Warburton, H., & Turnbull, J. (2002). *Drug Markets in Deprived Neighbourhoods*. London: Home Office.

Luigio, A. J. (2000). Drug treatment availability and effectiveness: studies of the general and criminal justice populations. *Criminal Justice and Behaviour*, 27, 495–528.

MacDonald, D., & Mansfield, D. (2001). Drugs and Afghanistan. *Drugs: Education, Prevention and Policy*, 8, 1–6.

MacDonald, R. (2005). Social exclusion, youth transitions and criminal careers on Teesside: some critical reflections on risk, *Pathways into and out of crime: International research symposium*. Brisbane, Australia.

MacDonald, R., & Marsh, J. (2002). Crossing the Rubicon: youth transitions, poverty drugs and social exclusion. *International Journal of Drug Policy*, 13, 27–38.

MacDonald, R., & Marsh, J. (2005). *Disconnected Youth? Growing up in Britain's Poor Neighbourhoods*. Basingstoke: Palgrave.

MacDonald, R., & Shildrick, T. (2004). Street corner society: Youth culture, sub-culture and leisure careers amongst 'excluded' young people, *Leisure Studies Association Conference*. Leeds, United Kingdom.

MacGregor, S. (2000). The Drugs-Crime Nexus. *Drugs: Education, Prevention and Policy*, 7, 311–16.

MacLeod, J. (2003). *A Theory and Model of the Conviction Process in Modelling Crime and Offending: Recent Developments in England and Wales*. London: Home Office.

Macpherson, W. (1999). *The Stephen Lawrence Inquiry. Report of an Inquiry by Sir William Macpherson of Cluny (Cm 4262-1)*. London: HMSO.

Mailer, N. (1957). *The White Negro*. San Francisco: Light Books.

Malbon, B. (1999). *Clubbing: Dancing, Ecstasy and Vitality*. London: Routledge.

Marcuse, H. (1964). *One Dimensional Man*. London: Paladin.

Marks, A. (2004). "Think Tank: Sniffer dogs infringe our rights." *The Guardian* 24 March 2004.

Marmot, M. (2004). *Status Syndrome: How Our Position on the Social Gradient Affects Longevity and Health*. London: Bloomsbury.

Marsden, J., & Farrell, M. (2002). *Research on What Works to Reduce Illegal Drug Misuse in Changing habits: the Commissioning and Management of Community Drug Services for Adults.* London: Audit Commission.

Marsh, C. (1986). Medicine and the Media. *British Medical Journal*, 292, 895.

Matza, D. (1969). *Becoming Deviant.* Englewood Cliffs: Prentice Hall.

May, C. (1991). Research on alcohol education for young people: review of the literature *Health Education Journal*, 50, 195–99.

—— (1999). *Explaining Reconviction Following a Community Sentence: The Role of Social Factors.* London: Home Office.

May, T., Duffy, M., Few, B., & Hough, M. (2005). *Understanding Drug Selling in Local Communities: Insider or Outside Trading.* York: Joseph Rowntree Foundation.

May, T., Harocopos, A., Turnbull, P. J., & Hough, M. (2000). *Serving Up: The Impact of Low-level Police Enforcement on Drug Markets.* London: Home Office.

May, T., Warburton, H., Turnbull, P., & Hough, M. (2002). *Times They Are-A-Changing: Policing of Cannabis.* York: Joseph Rowntree Foundation.

McCoy, A. (1991). *The Politics of Heroin: CIA complicity in the Global Drug Trade.* New York: Lawrence Hill.

—— (2000). Coercion and its unintended consequences: a study of heroin trafficking in Southeast and Southwest Asia. *Crime, Law and Social Change*, 33, 191–224.

McGurk, H., & Hurry, J. (1995). *Project Charlie: An evaluation of a Life Skills Drug Education Programme for Primary Schools.* London: DPI.

McKay, G. (1996). *Senseless Acts of Beauty.* London: Verso.

McKeganey, N. (2005). *Random Drug Testing of School Children: A Shot in the Arm or Shot in the Foot for Drug Prevention?* York: Joseph Rowntree Foundation.

McWilliams, J. C. (1990). *The Protectors: Harry J. Anslinger and the Federal Bureau of Narcotics 1930–1962.* Newark: University of Delaware Press.

Measham, F. (2004). The decline of ecstasy, the rise of 'binge' drinking and the persistence of pleasure. *Probation Journal*, 51, 309–26.

Measham, F., Aldridge, J., & Parker, H. (2001). *Dancing on Drugs. Risk, Health and Hedonism in the British Club Scene.* London: Free Association Books.

Measham, F., Newcombe, R., & Parker, H. (1994). The normalisation of recreational drug use amongst young people in North West England. *British Journal of Sociology*, 45, 287–312.

Measham, F., Parker, H., & Aldridge, J. (1998). The teenage transition: from adolescent recreational drug use to the young adult dance culture in Britain in the mid-1990s *Journal of Drug Issues*, 28, 9–32.

Melechi, A. (1997). *Psychedelia Britannica.* London: Turnaround.

Melrose, M. (2004). Fractured transitions: disadvantaged young people, drug taking and risk. *Probation Journal*, 51, 327–41.

Meltzer, H., Gill, B., & Petticrew, M. (1994). *The Prevalence of Psychiatric Morbidity among Adults Aged 16–64, Living in Private Households, in Great Britain.* London: Office of Population Censuses & Surveys, Social Surveys Division.

Meltzer, H., Gill, B., Petticrew, M., & Hinds, K. (1995). *OPCS Surveys of Psychiatric Morbidity in Great Britain, Report 1: The Prevalence of Psychiatric Morbidity among Adults Living in Private Households.* London: HMSO.

Metropolitan Police Authority (MPA) (2002). *The Lambeth Cannabis Warning Pilot Scheme.* London: Metropolitan Police Authority.

Metropolitian Police Service (2000). *Clearing the Decks Metropolitan.* Police Service.

Mezzrow, M. (1946). *Really the Blues.* New York: Random House.

Millar, T., Craine, N., Carnwath, T., & Donmall, M. (2001). The dynamics of heroin use; implications for intervention. *Journal of Epidemiology & Community Health*, 55, 930–33.

Miller, P., & Plant, M. (1996). Drinking, smoking and illicit drug use among 15–16 year olds in the United Kingdom. *British Medical Journal*, 313, 394–97.

Ministry of Health (1926). *Report of the Departmental Committee on Morphine and Heroin Addiction. 'The Rolleston Report'.* London: Ministry of Health.

—— (1965). *Second Report of the Interdepartmental Committee on Drug Addiction. 'The Second Brain Report'.* London: HMSO.

Morris, S. (1998). *Clubs, Drugs and Doorman*. London: Home Office.

Mort, F. (1987). *Dangerous Sexualities*. London: Routledge and Kegan Paul.

Mott, J. (1985). Self-reported cannabis use in Great Britain in 1981. *British Journal of Addiction*, 80, 37–43.

Mott, J., & Mirlees-Black, C. (1993). *Self-Reported Drug Misuse in England & Wales: Main Findings from the 1992 British Crime Survey*. London: Home Office Research & Planning Unit.

Muncie, J. (2004). *Youth and Crime*, 2nd edition, London: Sage.

Muncie, J., & Hughes, G. (2002). *Youth Justice: Critical Readings*. London: Sage.

—— (2002). Modes of youth governance: political rationalities, criminalization and resistance. In J. Muncie, G. Hughes & J. McLaughlin (Eds), *Youth Justice: Critical Readings*. London: Sage.

NACRO (2003). *Drugs and Crime: From warfare to welfare*. London: NACRO.

Natarajan, M. (2000). Understanding the structure of a drug trafficking organisation: a conversational analysis. In M. Natarajan & M. Hough (Eds), *Illegal Drug Markets: From Research to Prevention Policy*. Monsey, New York: Criminal Justice Press.

Natarajan, M., Clarke, R., & Johnson, B. D. (1995). Telephones as Facilitators of Drug Dealing: A Research Agenda. *European Journal of Criminal Policy*, 3, 137–54.

National Audit Office (2004). *Drug Treatment and Testing Orders: Early Lessons*. London: National Audit Office.

National Centre for Social Research & National Foundation for Educational Research (2002). *Smoking, Drinking and Drug Use among Young People in England in 2002*. London: Department Of Health.

National Institute of Justice (NIJ) (2000). *1999 Annual Report on Drug Use Among Adult and Juvenile Arrestees. Arrestee Drug Abuse Monitoring Program (ADAM)*. Washington DC: National Institute of Justice.

National Treatment Agency (NTA) (2003). *Injectable Heroin (and Injectable Methadone): Potential Roles in Drug Treatment. Full Guidance Report*. London: National Treatment Agency.

—— (2004). *Key Statistics on Drug Misusers in Treatment, England 2003/04*. London: NTA.

—— (2005). *Statistical Release*. Manchester: NTA.

Neale, J., & Robertson, M. (2004). Recent cocaine and crack use among new drug treatment clients in Scotland. *Drugs: Education, Prevention and Policy*, 11, 79–90.

Neal, M. A. (1999). *What the Music said: Black Popular Music and Black Public Culture*. London: Routledge.

Negus, K. (1998). Cultural production and the corporation: musical genres and the strategic management of creativity in the US recording industry. *Media, Culture and Society*, 20, 359–79.

Nelson, E. (1989). *The British Counter-Culture 1966–1973*. London: Macmillan.

Newburn, T. (1998). Young offenders, drugs and prevention. *Drugs: Education, Prevention and Policy*, 5, 233–43.

—— (2002). Community safety and policing: some implications of the Crime and Disorder Act 1998. In G. Hughes, E. McLaughlin & J. Muncie (Eds), *Crime Prevention and Community Safety* (pp. 102–22). London: Open University Press/Sage.

Newburn, T., & Elliot, J. (1998). *Police Anti-Drugs Strategies: Tacking Drugs Together Three Years On*. London: Home Office.

Newburn, T., & Sparks, R. (2004). *Criminal Justice and Political Cultures: National and International Dimensions of Crime Control*. Cullompton: Willan.

Newcombe, R. (1990). *Drug use and drug policy in Merseyside. Report for Mersey Regional Health Authority to the First Conference of European Cities at the Centre of the Illegal Drug Trade*. Frankfurt, Germany.

—— (1992). The reduction of drug-related harm: a conceptual framework for theory, practice and research. In P. A. O'Hare, R. Newcombe, A. Matthews & E. Drucker (Eds), *The Reduction of Drug-Related Harm*. London: Routledge.

—— (1995). *Summary of UK drug prevalence surveys, 1964–94*. Liverpool: 3D Research Bureau (report).

—— (1997). The deviant majority: drug users in Britain in the late Nineties.

———— (1999). The people on drugs: British attitudes to drug laws and policy. *Druglink*, 14, 12–15.

———— (2005). Toward a theory of drug-related harm reduction. Paper presented at 16th International Conference on the Reduction of Drug Related Harm, Belfast, Northern Ireland.

Newcombe, R., Measham, F., & Parker, H. (1995). A survey of drinking and deviant behaviour among 14/15 year olds in North West England. *Addiction Research*, 2, 319–41.

Neyroud, P. (2003). Policing and ethics. In T. Newburn (Ed.), *Handbook of Policing*. Cullompton: Willan.

Northern Ireland Office (1999). *Drug Strategy for Northern Ireland*. Belfast: Health Promotion Branch.

Nurco, D. N., Kinlock, T. W., & Hanlon, T. E. (1995). The drugs-crime connection. In J. Inciardi & K. McElrath (Eds), *The American Drug Scene: An Anthology*. Los Angeles: Roxbury.

Observatoire Géopolitique des Drogues (1996). *The Geopolitics of Drugs*. Boston: Northeastern University Press.

O'Connor, L., O'Connor, D., & Best, R. (1998). *Drugs: Partnership for Policy, Prevention and Education*. London: Cassell.

Oerton, J., Hunter, G., Hickman, M., Morgan, D., Turnbull, P., Kothari, G., & Marsden, J. (2003). Arrest referral in London police stations: characteristics of the first year. A key point of intervention for drug users? *Drugs: Education, Prevention and Policy*, 10, 73–85.

Office for National Statistics (ONS) (1998). *Value of UK crime market*. London: Office for National Statistics.

———— (2001). *Survey of Psychological Morbidity in Britain 2000*. London: Office for National Statistics.

———— OFSTED (2002). *Drug Education in Schools:* www.ofsted.gov.uk.

O'Mahoney, B. (2000). *Essex Boys*. London: Mainstream Publishing.

O'Malley, P. (2004). Globalising risk? Distinguishing styles of "neoliberal" criminal justice in Australia and the USA. In T. Newburn & R. Sparks (Eds), *Criminal Justice and Political Cultures: National and International Dimensions of Crime Control*. Cullompton: Willan.

O'Shea, J., Jones, A., & Sondhi, A. (2003). *Arrest Referral Statistical Update: Statistics from the Arrest Referral Monitoring Programme from October 2000 to September 2002*. London: Home Office.

Oxford Dictionary of English (2000). *Oxford Dictionary of English*. Oxford: Oxford University Press.

Paoli, L. (2000). *Pilot Project to Describe and Analyse Local Drug Markets. First Phase Final Report: Illegal Drug Markets in Frankfurt and Milan*. Lisbon: European Monitoring Centre for Drugs and Drug Addiction.

Parker, H. (2000). How young Britons obtain their drugs: drugs transactions at the point of consumption. In M. Natarajan & M. Hough (Eds), *Illegal Drug Markets: From Research to Prevention Policy*. Monsey, NY: Criminal Justice Press.

———— (2001). Unbelievable? The UK's Drugs present. In H. Parker, J. Aldridge & R. Egginton (Eds), *UK Drugs Unlimited: New Research and Policy Lessons on Illicit Drugs*. Basingstoke: Palgrave.

———— (2003). Pathology or modernity? Rethinking risk factor analyses of young drug users. *Addiction Research and Theory*, 11, 141–44.

———— (2005). Normalisation as a barometer: recreational drug use and the consumption of leisure by younger Britain's. *Addiction, research and theory*, 13 (3), 205–15.

Parker, H., Aldridge, J., & Measham, F. (1998b). *Illegal Leisure: The Normalization of Adolescent Recreational Drug Use*. London: Routledge.

Parker, H., Aldridge, J., & Egginton, R. (Eds) (2001). 'UK Drugs Unlimited: New Research and Policy Lessons on Illicit Drugs' Basignstoke, Palgrave.

Parker, H., Bakx, K., & Newcombe, R. (1988). *Living with Heroin: The Impact of aDrugs "Epidemic" on an English Community*. Milton Keynes: Open University.

Parker, H., & Bottomley, T. (1996). *Crack Cocaine and Drugs-Crime Careers*. London: Home Office.

Parker, H., Bury, C., & Egginton, R. (1998a). *New Heroin Outbreaks Amongst Young People in England and Wales*. London: Home Office.

Parker, H., & Measham, F. (1994). Pick'n'mix: changing patterns of illicit drug use amongst 1990 adolescents. *Drugs: Education, Prevention & Policy*, 1, 5–13.

Parker, H., Measham, F., & Aldridge, J. (1995). *Drugs Futures: Changing Patterns of Drug Use Amongst English Youth*. London: ISDD.

Parker, H., & Newcombe, R. (1987). Heroin use and acquisitive crime in an English community. *British Journal of Sociology*, 38, 331–50.

Parker, H., Newcombe, R., & Bakx, K. (1987). The new heroin users: prevalence and characteristics in Wirral, Merseyside. *British Journal of Addiction*, 82, 147–57.

Parker, H., Williams, L., & Aldridge, J. (2002). The normalization of 'sensible' recreational drug use. *Sociology*, 36, 941–64.

Patel, K., & Wibberley, C. (2002). Young Asians and drug use. *Journal of Child Health Care*, 6, 51–59.

Pavis, S., & Cunnigham-Burley, S. (1999). Male street youth culture: understanding the context of health-related behaviour. *Health Education Research*, 14, 583–96.

Pawson, R., & Tilley, N. (1998). *Realistic Evaluation*. London: Sage.

Pearce, J. (2003). *'It's Someone Taking Part of You': A Study of Young Women and Sexual Exploitation*. London: National Children's Bureau/JRF.

Pearson, F. S., & Lipton, D. S. (1999). A meta-analytic view of the effectiveness of corrections-based treatments for drug abuse. *The Prison Journal*, 79, 384–410.

Pearson, G. (1984). *Hooligan: A History of Respectable Fears*. London: Macmillan.

Pearson, G. (1987a). *The New Heroin Users*. Oxford: Blackwell.

—— (1987b). Social deprivation, unemployment and patterns of heroin use. In N. Dorn & N. South (Eds), *A Land Fit for Heroin?* London: Macmillan.

—— (1991). Drug-control policies in Britain. In M. Tonry (Ed.), *Crime and Justice: A Review of Research*. Chicago: University of Chicago Press.

—— (1992). Drugs and criminal justice: a harm reduction perspective. In P. A. O'Hare, R. Newcombe, A. Matthews & E. Drucker (Eds), *The Reduction of Drug-Related Harm*. London: Routledge.

—— (2001a). Normal drug use: Ethnographic fieldwork among an adult network of recreational drug users in inner London. *Substance Use and Misuse*, 36, 167–200.

—— (2001b). Drugs and poverty. In S. Chen & E. Skidelsky (Eds), *High Time for Reform: Drug Policy for the 21st Century*. London: Social Market Foundation.

Pearson, G., & Gilman, M. (1994). Local and regional variations in drug misuse: the British heroin epidemic of the 1980s. In M. Gossop & J. Strang (Eds), *Responding to Drug Misuse: The British System*. Oxford: Oxford University Press.

Pearson, G., Gilman, M., & McIver, S. (1986). *Young People and Heroin: An Examination of heroin Use in the North of England*. London: Health Education Council.

Pearson, G., & Hobbs, D. (2001). *Middle Market Drug Distribution*. London: Home Office.

—— (2003). King Pin? A case study of a middle market drug broker. *Howard Journal of Criminal Justice*, 42, 335–47.

Pearson, G., & Hobbs, D. (2004). E is for enterprise: middle level drug markets in ecstasy and stimulants. *Addiction Research and Theory*, 12, 565–76.

Pearson, G., & Patel, K. (1998). Drugs, deprivation and ethnicity: outreach among Asian drug users in a Northern English city. *Journal of Drug Issues*, 28, 199–224.

Peck, D. F., & Plant, M. A. (1986). Unemployment and illegal drug use: concordant evidence from a prospective study and national trends. *British Medical Journal*, 293, 929–32.

Peele, S. (1985). *The Meaning of Addiction*. San Francisco: Jossey-Bass.

—— (2000). What addiction is and is not: The impact of mistaken notions of addiction. *Addiction Research*, 8, 599–607.

Pentz, M. A., Cormack, C., Flay, B. R., Hansen, W. B., & Johnson, C. A. (1986). Balancing program and research integrity in community drug abuse prevention: Project STAR approach. *Journal of School Health*, 56, 389–93.

Perri 6, Jupp, B., Perry, H., & Laskey, K. (1997). *The Substance of Youth*. York: Joseph Rowntree Foundation.

Peters, R. H., Greenbaum, P. E., Edens, J. F., Carter, C. R., & Ortiz, M. M. (1998). Prevalence of DSM-IV substance abuse and dependence disorders among prison inmates. *American Journal of Drug and Alcohol Abuse*, 24, 573–87.

Pilkington, H. (2003). Every day but not normal: understanding the recreational use of heroin among Russian youth, *European Sociological Association Conference*. Murcia, Spain.

Plant, M., & Miller, P. (2000). Drug use has declined among teenagers in United Kingdom (letter). *British Medical Journal*, 320, 1536.

Plant, M., Peck, D., & Samuel, E. (1985). *Alcohol, Drugs and School-leavers*. London: Tavistock.

Plant, M., & Plant, M. (1992). *Risk-Takers. Alcohol, Drugs, Sex and Youth*. London: Tavistock/Routledge.

Plant, M. A. (1987). *Drugs in Perspective*. London: Hodder and Stoughton.

Platzer, M. (2004). Illicit drug markets in the Caribbean: analysis of information on drug flows through the region. In A. Klein, M. Day & A. Harriott (Eds), *Caribbean Drugs: From Criminalization to Harm Reduction*. London: Zed Books and Kingston:Ian Randle.

Polhemus, T. (1994). *Street Style*. London: Thames and Hudson.

Polsky, N. (1961). The village beat scene: summer 1960. *Dissent*, No.8, 3, 339–59.

Power, M. (1997). *Audit Society: Rituals of Verification*. Oxford: Oxford University Press.

Power, R., Green, A., Foster, R., & Stimson, G. (1995). A qualitative study of the purchasing and distribution patterns of cocaine and crack users in England and Wales. *Addiction Research*, 2, 363–79.

Powis, B., Griffiths, P., Gossop, M., Lloyd, C., & Strang, J. (1998). Drug use and offending behaviour among young people excluded from school. *Drugs: Education, Prevention and Policy*, 5, 245–56.

Preble, E., & Casey, J. J. (1969). Taking care of business: the heroin user's life on the street. *International Journal of the Addictions*, 4, 1–24.

Prendergast, M. L., Podus, D., Chang, E., & Urada, D. (2002). The effectiveness of drug abuse treatment: a meta-analysis of comparison group studies. *Drug and Alcohol Dependence*, 67, 53–72.

Pryce, K. (1979). *Endless Pressure. A Study of West Indian Lifestyles in Bristol*. Harmondsworth: Penguin.

PSS Consultancy Group (2002). *Evaluation of Lambeth's Pilot of Warnings for Possession of Cannabis*. London: PSS Consultancy Group.

Pudney, S. (2002). *The Road to Ruin? Sequences of Initiation into Drug Use and Offending by Young People in Britain*. London: Home Office.

Ramsay, M., Baker, P., Goulden, C., Sharp, C., & Sondhi, A. (2001). *Drug Misuse Declared in 2000: Results from the British Crime Survey*. London: Home Office (research study 224).

Ramsay, M., & Partridge, S. (1999). *Drug Misuse Declared in 1998: Results from the British Crime Survey*. London: Home Office.

Ramsay, M., & Percy, A. (1995). *Drug Misuse Declared: Results of the 1994 British Crime Survey*. London: Home Office.

Ramsay, M., & Spiller, J. (1997). *Drug Misuse Declared in 1996: Latest Results from the British Crime Survey*. London: Home Office.

Ramsay, M., et al. (2001). Drug Misuse Declared in 2000: Results from the British Crime Survey. London: Home Office, Research Study 224.

Ramsey, M. (2003). *Prisoners' Drug Use and Treatment: Seven Research Studies*. London: Home Office.

Rawlings, T. (2000). *Mod: A Very British Phenomenon*. London: Omnibus Press.

Reiner, R. (1991). *Chief Constables*. Oxford: Oxford University Press.

——— (2000a). *The Politics of the Police (3rd edn)*. Oxford: Oxford University Press.

——— (2000b). Crime and control in Britain. *Sociology*, 34, 71–94.

Release (1997). *Drugs and Dance Survey: an insight into the culture*. London: Release research review.

Reuter, P. (1983). *Disorganised Crime*. Cambridge, Mass: MIT Press.

Reuter, P., & Haaga, J. (1989). *The Organisation of High-Level Drug Markets: An Exploratory Study Santa Monica*. Santa Monica, CA: RAND Corporation.

Reuter, P., MacCoun, R., & Murphy, P. (1990). *Money from Crime. A Study of the Economics of Drug Dealing in Washington, D.C.* Santa Monica, CA: RAND Corporation.

Reynolds, S. (1998). *Energy Flash.* London: Picador.

Richardson, A., & Budd, T. (2003). *Alcohol, Crime and Disorder: A Study of Young Adults.* London: Home Office.

Richardson, A., Budd, T., Engineer, R., Phillips, A., Thompson, J., & Nicholls, J. (2003). *Drinking, Crime and Disorder.* London: Home Office.

Roberts, B. (2002). *Biographical Research.* Milton Keynes: Open University Press.

Roberts, C., Kingdom, A., Firth, C., & Tudor-Smith, C. (1997). *Young People in Wales: Lifestyle Changes 1986–1996, Technical Report No.1.* Cardiff: Health Promotion Wales.

Roberts, K. (1995). *Youth Unemployment in Modern Britain.* Milton Keynes: Open University Press.

Roberts, R. (1971). *The Classic Slum.* Manchester: University of Manchester Press.

Robins, L. N., & Reiger, D. A. (1991). *Psychiatric Disorders in America: The Epidemiologic Catchment Area Study.* New York: Free Press.

Roe, S. (2005). *Drug Misuse Declared: Findings from the 2004/05 British Crime Survey.* London: Home Office.

Rogers, A., & McCarthy, M. (1999). Drugs and drugs education in the inner city: the views of 12 year olds and their parents. *Drugs: Education, Prevention and Policy*, 6, 51–59.

Rose, N. (1996). The death of the social? Refiguring the territory of government. *Economy and Society*, 25, 327–56.

Rosenbaum, M. (1997). The de-medicalization of methadone maintenance. In P. G. Erickson, D. M. Riley, Y. W. Cheung & P. A. O'Hare (Eds), *Harm Reduction: A New Direction for Drug Policies and Programs.* Toronto: University of Toronto Press.

Roszak, T. (1970). *The Making of a Counter Culture.* London: Faber and Faber.

Rowe (2004). *Policing, Race and Racism.* Cullumpton: Willian.

Royal College of Physicians (1986). *Health or Smoking?* London: Pitman.

Royal College of Physicians (2001). *Alcohol – can the NHS afford it?* London: Royal College of Physicians.

Ruggerio, V., & South, N. (1995). *Eurodrugs: Drug Use, Marketing and Trafficking in Europe.* London: UCL.

Rumgay, J. (2003). Drug treatment and offender rehabilitation: Reflections on evidence, effectiveness and exclusion. *Probation Journal: The Journal of Community and Criminal Justice*, 50, 41–51.

Rutherford, A. (1992). *Growing Out of Crime: The New Era.* London: Waterside Press.

Salzman, P. (2000). *The Beatles in Risikesh.* New York: Viking.

Sanders, B. (2005). In the club: ecstasy use and supply in a London nightclub. *Sociology*, 39, 247–58.

Saunders, B. (2005). In the club: ecstasy use and supply in a London nightclub. *Sociology*, 39 (2), 241–58.

Saunders, N. (1993). *E for Ecstasy.* London: Neal's Yard Desk Top Publishing.

Saunders, W., & Marsh, A. (1999). Harm reduction and the use of current illegal drugs: some assumptions and dilemmas. *Journal of Substance Use*, 4, 3–9.

Scarman, L. (1981). *The Brixton Disorders 10–12 April.* London: HMSO.

SCODA (1999). *The Right Approach: Quality Standards in Drug Education.* London: SCODA.

Scott, I. (1998). A hundred-year habit (centenary of Bayer's chemical medicinal – heroin). *History Today*, 48, 6–8.

Scott, P. D. (2003). The CIA's secret powers: Afghanistan, 9/11, and America's most dangerous enemy. *Critical Asian Studies*, 35, 233–58.

Scottish Executive (2000). *National Evaluation of Drug Education in Scotland: Final report.* Edinburgh: Scottish Education Department.

Seddon, T. (2000). Explaining the drug-crime link: theoretical, policy and research issues. *Journal of Social Policy*, 29, 95–107.

Seivewright, N. (2000). *Community Treatment of Drug Misuse: More than Methadone.* Cambridge: Cambridge University Press.

Shapiro, H. (1988/1999). *Waiting for the Man.* London: Helter Skelter.

—— (1999). Dances with drugs: pop music, drugs and youth culture. In N. South (Ed.), *Drugs: Cultures, Controls and Everyday Life*. London: Sage.

—— (2003). *Shooting Stars: Drugs, Hollywood and the Movies*. London: Serpent's Tail.

Sharpley, A. (1964). "Purple Hearts dearer, but still plentiful." *Evening Standard*. 1 May 1964.

Shewan, D., & Dalgarno, P. (2005). Low levels of negative health and social outcomes among non-treatment heroin users in Glasgow (Scotland): Evidence for controlled heroin use? *British Journal of Health Psychology*, 10, 33–48.

Shewan, D., Dalgarno, P., Marshall, A., & Lowe, E. (1998). Patterns of heroin use among a non-treatment sample in Glasgow, Scotland. *Addiction Research*, 6, 215–34.

Shildrick, T. (2002). Young people, illicit drugs and the question of normalisation. *Journal of Youth Studies*, 5, 35–48.

—— (2003). 'Trackers,' 'Spectaculars' and 'Ordinary Youth': Youth Culture, Illicit Drug Use and Social Class. Unpublished PhD thesis, University of Teesside.

Shiner, M., & Newburn, T. (1997). Definitely, maybe not? The normalisation of recreational drug use amongst young people. *Sociology*, 31, 511–29.

—— (1999). Taking tea with Noel: the place and meaning of drug use in everyday life. In N. South (Ed.), *Drugs: Cultures, Controls and Everyday Life*. London: Sage.

Silverman, D. (1975). *Reading Castaneda: A Prologue to the Social Sciences*. London: Routledge.

Silverstone, D. (2003). *The Ecstasy of Consumption. The Drug Ecstasy as a Mass Commodity in a Global Market*, London: University of London.

Simon, R. (1997). Estimating prevalence using the case-finding method: an overview. In C. Taylor, G. Stimson, M. Hickman, A. Quirk & M. Frischer (Eds), *Estimating the Prevalence of Drug Use In Europe*. Luxembourg: Council of Europe/EMCDDA.

Simpson, D. D., Joe, G. W., & Bracy, S. A. (2002). A national 5-year follow-up of treatment outcomes for cocaine dependence. *Archives of General Psychiatry*, 59, 538–44.

Simpson, D. D., Joe, G. W., & Brown, B. S. (1997). Treatment retention and follow-up outcomes in the Drug Abuse Treatment Outcome Study (DATOS). *Psychology of Addictive Behaviours*, 11, 294–307.

Simpson, M. (2003). The relationship between drug use and crime: a puzzle inside an enigma. *International Journal of Drug Policy*, 14, 307–19.

—— (2004). *An ethnographic study exploring the relationship between drug use and crime amongst a sample of young people from a town in the Northeast of England*. Unpublished PhD thesis, University of Teesside.

Singleton, N., Farrel, M., & Meltzer, H. (1999). *Substance Misuse Among Prisoners in England and Wales*. London: ONS.

Singleton, N., Meltzer, H., Gatward, R., Coid, J., & Deasy, D. (1998). *Psychiatric Morbidity among Prisoners in England and Wales*. London: Office of National Statistics.

Smit, F., Toet, J., Van Oers, H., & Wiessing, L. (2003). Estimating local and national problem drug use prevalence from demographics. *Addiction Research & Theory*, 11, 401–13.

Sneader, W. (1998). The discovery of heroin. *The Lancet*, 352, 1697–699.

Social Exclusion Unit (2002). *Reducing Re-Offending byEx-Prisoners*. London: Social Exclusion Unit.

Sondhi, A., O'Shea, J., & Williams, T. (2002). *Arrest Referral: Emerging Findings from the National Monitoring and Evaluation Programme*. London: Home Office.

South, N. (1999). Debating drugs and everyday life: normalisation, prohibition and 'otherness'. In N. South (Ed.), *Drugs: Cultures, Controls and Everyday Life*. London: Sage.

—— (2002). Drugs, alcohol, and crime. In M. Maguire, R. Morgan & R. Reiner (Eds), *The Oxford Handbook of Criminology*. Oxford: Oxford University Press.

Spear, H. B. (1969). The growth of heroin addiction in the United Kingdom. *British Journal of Addiction*, 64, 245–55.

—— (2002). *Heroin Addiction Care and Control: the British System 1916–1984*. London: Drug-Scope.

Springhall, J. (1998). *Youth, Popular Culture and Moral Panics: Penny Gaffs to Gangsta Rap 1830–1996*. London: Macmillan.

Starks, M. (1982). *Cocaine Fiends and Reefer Madness*. New York: Cornwall Books.

Statistics, Bureau of Justice Statistics (1998). *Substance Abuse and Treatment of Adults on Probation, 1995.*: NCJ 166611.

Stead, M., MacKintosh, A. M., Eadie, D., & Hastings, G. (2000). *NE Choices: The Results of a multi-component drug prevention programme for adolescents*. London: Home Office.

Stephen, D., & Squires, P. (2003). 'Adults don't realise how sheltered they are.' A contribution to the debate on youth transitions from some voices on the margin. *Journal of Youth Studies*, 6, 145–64.

Stevens, A., Berto, D., Kerschl, V., Oeuvray, K., Van Ooyen, M., Steffan, E., Heckmann, W., & Uchtenhagen, A. (2003). Summary literature review: the international literature on drugs, crime and treatment, *ook*. Kent: University of Kent.

Stevenson, J. (2000). *Addicted UK: The Myth and Menace of Drugs in Film*. Los Angeles: Creation.

Stewart, D., Gossop, M., Marsden, J., & Rolfe, A. (2000). Drug misuse and acquisitive crime among clients recruited to the National Treatment Outcome Research Study. *Criminal Behaviour and Mental Health*, 10, 13–24.

Stimson, G. (1987). The war on heroin: British policy and the international trade in illicit drugs. In N. Dorn & N. South (Eds), *A Land Fit for Heroin?* London: Macmillan.

Stimson, G., & Des Jarlais, D. C. (1998). *Drug Injecting and HIV Infection: Global Dimensions and Local Responses*. London: UCL.

Stimson, G., Hickman, M., Quirk, A., & Frischer, M. (1997). *Estimating the Prevalence of Drug Misuse in Europe*. Strasbourg: Council of Europe.

Stimson, G., & Oppenheimer, E. (1982). *Heroin Addiction: Treatment and Control in Britain*. London: Tavistock.

Stimson, G. V., & Metrebian, N. (2003). *Prescribing Heroin: What Is the Evidence?* York: Joseph Rowntree Foundation.

Stover, H., Von Ossietzky, C., & Merino, P. P. (2001). *An Overview Study: Assistance to Drug Users in European Union prisons. EMCDDA Scientific Report*. Lisbon: European Monitoring Centre for Drugs and Drug Addiction.

Strang, J. (1993). Drug use and harm reduction: responding to the challenge. In N. Heather, A. Wodak, E. Nadelmann & P. O'Hare (Eds), *Psychoactive Drugs And Harm Reduction: From Faith To Science*. London: Whurr Publishers.

Strang, J., Griffiths, P., & Gossop, M. (1997). Heroin smoking by 'chasing the dragon': origins and history. *Addiction*, 92, 673–83.

Strang, J., Heuston, J., Gossop, M., Green, J., & Maden, T. (1998). *HIV/AIDS Risk Behaviour Among Adult Male Prisoners*. London: Home Office.

Stratford, N., Gould, A., Hinds, K., & McKeganey, N. (2003). *The Measurement of Changing Public Attitudes Towards Illegal Drugs in Britain*. Swindon: Economic and Social Research Council.

Sutherland, I., & Miller, P. (2000). Drug use has declined among teenagers in United Kingdom (letter). *British Medical Journal*, 321, 1161.

Swadi, H., & Zeitlin, H. (1987). Drug education to school children: does it really work? *British Journal of Addiction*, 82, 741–46.

Tasker, T., Raw, M., McNeil, A., O'Muirecheartaigh, C., Bowden, C., & Heuston, J. (1999). *Drug use in England: results of the 1996 National Drugs Campaign Survey*. London: Health Education Authority.

Taylor, B., & Bennett, T. (1999). *Comparing Drug Use Rates of Detained Arrestees in the United States and England*. Washington: National Institute of Justice.

Taylor, C., Stimson, G., Hickman, M., Quirk, A., & Frischer, M. (1997). Estimating the prevalence of drug misuse in Europe. Strasbourg: Council of Europe.

Taylor, D. (2000). The Word on the street: advertising, youth culture and legitimate speech in drug education. *Journal of Youth Studies*, 3, 333–53.

TDPF (2004). *After the War on Drugs: Options for Control (A Report by Transform Drug Policy Foundation)*. Bristol: Transform Drug Policy Foundation.

The Guardian (2005). Revealed: how drugs war failed. *The Guardian*, 5th July 2006

——— (2006a). Expert advisers threaten revolt against Clarke. *The Guardian*, 14th January 2006

——— (2006b). Clarke likely to rule out shift in legal status of cannabis. *The Guardian*, 15th January 2006

The Prime Minister's Strategy Unit (2005). *Strategy Unit Drugs Project Phase One Report: Understanding the Issues*.

Thompson, E. P. (1991). *Customs in Common*. London: Penguin.

Thompson, T. (2000). *Blogs 19. The Story of the Essex Range Rover Triple Murders*. London: Warner Books.

Thornton, S. (1995). *Club Cultures: Music, Media and Subcultural Capital*. Cambridge: Polity.

Tonry, M. (1995). *Malign Neglect: Race, Crime, and Punishment in America*. Oxford: Oxford University Press.

Townsend, P. (2000). *Jazz in American Culture*. Edinburgh: Edinburgh University Press.

Toynbee, J. (2000). *Making Popular Music*. London: Arnold.

Turnbull, P. J., & McSweeney, T. (2000). *Drug Treatment in Prison and Aftercare: a literature review and results of a survey of European countries*. Pompidou Group: Council of Europe.

Turnbull, P. J., McSweeney, T., Hough, M., Webster, R., & Edmunds, M. (2000). *Drug Treatment and Testing Orders: Final evaluation report*. London: Home Office.

Turner, B. (1999). *Ibiza*. London: Ebury.

Unell, I. (1987). Drugs and deprivation. *Druglink*, 2, 14–15.

United Nations (2003). *Global illicit drug trends*. New York: United Nations Office on Drugs & Crime.

United Nations International Drug Control Programme (1998). *Economic and Social Consequences of Drug Abuse and Illicit Trafficking*. Vienna: UNDCP.

——— (2001). *World Drug Report 2000*. Oxford: Oxford University Press.

United Nations Office on Drugs & Crime (2003). *Report on Ecstasy*. Vienna: UNODC.

United Nations Office on Drugs and Crime (2004). *World Drug Report 2004*. Geneva: United Nations Publications.

US Department of Health & Human Services (2003). *Results from the 2002 National Survey on Drug Use and Health: National Findings*. USA: DHHS.

Waldorf, D. (1993). Don't be your own best customer: drug use and San Francisco gang drug sellers. *Crime, Law, and Social Change*, 19, 1–15.

Walters, G. (1998). *Changing Lives of Drugs and Crime*. Chichester: Wiley and Sons.

Wanigaratne, S., Dar, K., Abdulrahim, D., & Strang, J. (2003). Ethnicity and drug use: exploring the nature of particular relationships among diverse populations in the United Kingdom. *Drugs: Education, Prevention and Policy*, 10, 39–55.

Warburton, H., Turnbull, P. J., & Hough, M. (2005). *Occasional and Controlled Heroin Use: Not a Problem?* York: Joseph Rowntree Foundation.

Ward, J. (1998). Substance use among young people 'looked after' by social services. *Drugs: Education, Prevention and Policy*, 5, 257–67.

Ward, J., & Fitch, C. (1998). Dance culture and drug use in London. In G. V. Stimson, C. Fitch & A. Judd (Eds), *Drug Use in London*. London: The Centre for Research on Drugs and Health Behaviour, University of London.

Ward, J., Henderson, Z., & Pearson, G. (2003). *One Problem Among Many: Drug Use Among Care Leavers in Transition to Independent Living*. London: Home Office.

Ward, J., & Pearson, G. (1997). Recreational drug use and drug dealing in London. In D. Korf & H. Riper (Eds), *Illicit Drugs in Europe*. Amsterdam: University of Amsterdam.

Webb, E., Ashton, C. H., Kelly, P., & Kamali, F. (1996). Alcohol and drug use in UK university students. *Lancet*, 348, 922–25.

Webster, C., MacDonald, R., & Simpson, M. (2006). Predicting Criminality? Risk Factors, neighbourhood influence and desistance. *Youth Justice*, 6, 7–22

Webster, C., & Robson, J. (2001). *Needs Assessment of Substance Misusers and Drug Services in Stockton*. Stockton: DAT and DPAS.

Webster, C., Simpson, D., MacDonald, R., Abbas, A., Cieslik, M., Shildrick, T., & Simpson, M. (2004). *Poor Transitions: Young Adults and Social Exclusion*. Bristol: Policy Press.

Welte, J. W., Zhang, L., & Wieczorek, W. F. (2001). The effects of substance use on specific types of criminal offending in young men. *Journal of Research in Crime and Delinquency*, 38, 416–38.

Whelan, S., & Moody, M. (1994). *DARE Mansfield*. Nottingham: North Nottinghamshire Health Promotion.

White, R. (2001). Heroin use, ethnicity and the environment: the case of the London Bangladeshi community. *Addiction*, 96, 1815–24.

Whiteley, S. (1997). Altered sounds. In A. Melechi (Ed.).*Psychedelia Britannica*. London: Turnaround.

Wibberley, C. and Price, J., F. (2000) Young People's Drug Use: facts and feelings – implications for the normalisation debate. *Drugs: Education, Prevention and Policy*, 7(2), 147–162.

Williams, L., & Parker, H. (2001). Alcohol, cannabis, ecstasy and cocaine: drugs of reasoned choice amongst young adult recreational drug users in England. *International Journal of Drug Policy*, 12, 397–413.

Wilson, S., & Zambrano, M. (1994). Cocaine, commodity chains and drug politics: a transnational approach. In G. Gereffi & M. Korzeniewicz (Eds), *Commodity Chains and Global Capitalism*. London: Greenwood Press.

Wincup, E., Buckland, G., & Bayliss, R. (2003). *Youth Homelessness and Substance Use: Report to the Drugs and Alcohol Research Unit*. London: Home Office.

Winlow, S. (2002). *Badfellas*. Oxford: Berg.

Wright, J., & Pearl, L. (2000). Experience and knowledge of young people regarding drug use, 1969–1999. *Addiction*, 95, 1225–35.

Young, D. (2002). Impacts of perceived legal pressure on retention in drug treatment. *Criminal Justice and Behaviour*, 29, 27–59.

Young, J. (1971). *The Drugtakers*. London: Paladin.

Young, R. (2002). *From War to Work: Drug Treatment, Social Inclusion and Enterprise*. London: The Foreign Policy Centre.

Zaitch, D. (2002). *Trafficking Cocaine: Colombian Drug Entrepreneurs in the Netherlands*. The Hague: Kluwer.

Zhang, S., & Chin, K. L. (2003). The declining significance of triad societies in transnational illegal activities: a structural deficiency perspective. *British Journal of Criminology*, 43, 469–88.

Zinberg, N. (1984). *Drug, Set and Setting: The Basis for Controlled Intoxicant Use*. New Haven: Yale University Press.

Index

203